W9-AYN-848

PRAISE FOR ERIC IDLE AND
The Greedy Bastard Diary

"A paean to fun. . . . A perfect beach book. . . . The anecdotes are antidotes
for a world in turmoil." —*Washington Times*

"[Idle] is a very funny man, and this is a very funny book."
—*San Jose Mercury News*

"Do yourself a favor and grab a copy of *The Greedy Bastard Diary* . . . bits
and pieces, missives from the road, the best stuff saucy enough that they
can't be printed here." —*San Diego Union-Tribune*

"Charming, witty, and very funny." —*Milwaukee Journal Sentinel*

"Idle's inventively loo-mouthed journal includes a witty Brit's impressions
of the United States, onstage and backstage views of his show, and un-
Pythonlike affectionate memories of George Harrison. He suffers many
of the woes we all encounter on the road (although somehow, his woes
are funnier)." —*Washington Post*

"A road trip through Idle's strange, irreverent, and witty mind as he offers
reflections on Monty Python, on comedy, and on an unhappy childhood.
. . . It's a given that Idle's book would be funny, but most compelling are
his thoughts on the process of comedy and on his peers. . . . Witty gems
abound. . . . Idle proves himself a wry, adroit observer of American life—
not unlike the great Bill Bryson, only more twisted in his sensibility, and
even more hilarious." —*Los Angeles Times Book Review*

About the Author

Eric Idle has appeared in a variety of guises and disguises—from a writer and actor in the legendary *Monty Python* TV series and movies to the creator and director of *The Rutles*, the pre–Fab Four, whose legend will last a lunchtime. He has multihyphenated his way through life assiduously avoiding a proper job. He has written movies, books, novels, plays, and songs popular, political, and scurrilous. Idle has appeared in many movies, on TV, on stage as a comedian, and even as an opera singer (well, Gilbert and Sullivan). Educated at Cambridge University, where he met the other Pythons (some of whom were hiding at Oxford), he has gone on to prove that wasting a decent education can prove highly rewarding. He and his wife, Tania, have a daughter, Lily. Idle has a son, Carey, from a former wifetime. Recently he has cowritten the Tony Award–winning Broadway musical *Spamalot!* with musical partner John Du Prez, and has directed and starred in *Can't Buy Me Lunch*, a further look at the Rutles.

THE GREEDY BASTARD DIARY

A COMIC TOUR OF AMERICA

ERIC IDLE

Harper

An Imprint of HarperCollins*Publishers*

Photograph of John Du Prez on page vii by Larry Mah.

"Sit on My Face," "Bruces' Philosophers Song," "The Penis Song," "I Bet You They Won't Play This Song on the Radio," "Always Look on the Bright Side of Life," "Do What John," and "Henry Kissinger," words and music by Eric Idle. Reprinted with permission of Python (Monty) Pictures Ltd. "The Galaxy Song," words and music by Eric Idle and John Du Prez. Used by permission. "Finland," words and music by Michael Palin. Reprinted with permission of Python (Monty) Pictures Ltd. "Bing Tiddle Tiddle Bong," words and music by Graham Chapman and Fred Tomlinson. Reprinted with permission of Python (Monty) Pictures Ltd. Jailor scene dialogue from Monty Python's Life of Brian, reprinted by permission of Python (Monty) Pictures Ltd. "The Meaning of Life," words and music by Eric Idle and John Du Prez. Reprinted by permission of Python (Monty) Pictures Ltd. "The Gay Animal Song," words and music by Eric Idle and John Du Prez. Used by permission. "Madrigal," words and music by Eric Idle and John Cameron. Used by permission. "The Pirate Song," words and music by Eric Idle and George Harrison. Used by permission. "The Getty Song," words and music by Eric Idle. Used by permission. "Killing for God," words and music by Eric Idle and John Du Prez. Used by permission. "Torturer's Apprentice," words and music by Eric Idle and Michael Kamen. Used by permission. "Fuck Christmas," words and music by Eric Idle and John Du Prez. Used by permission.

A hardcover edition of this book was published in 2005 by HarperEntertainment, an imprint of HarperCollins Publishers.

HarperCollins books may be purchased for educational, business, or sales promotional use. For information please write: Special Markets Department, HarperCollins Publishers, 10 East 53rd Street, New York, NY 10022.

First Harper paperback published 2006.

Designed by Jeffrey Pennington

The Library of Congress has catalogued the hardcover edition as follows:

Idle, Eric.
    The greedy bastard diary: a comic tour of America / Eric Idle.—1st ed.
        p. cm.
    ISBN 0-06-075864-3
    1. United States—Description and travel. 2. United States—Social life and customs—1971– 3. United States—Social life and customs—1971– —Humor.
    4. Canada—Description and travel. 5. Canada—Social life and customs—1945–
    6. Canada—Social life and customs—1945– —Humor. 7. Idle, Eric—Travel—United States.
    8. Idle, Eric—Travel—Canada. 9. Bus travel—United States. 10. Bus travel—Canada.
    I. Title.
    E169.04134 2005
    792.702'8'092—dc22
    [B]
                                                                            2004059797

ISBN-10: 0-06-075865-1 (pbk.)
ISBN-13: 978-0-06-075865-3 (pbk.)
06 07 08 09 10 ❖/RRD 10 9 8 7 6 5 4 3 2 1

For John Du Prez

My extraordinary musical partner

*History will be kind to me
for I intend to write it.*

—Winston Churchill

A GREEDY BASTARD TOUR

I'm eating dim sum with my friend Danny the guitar maker.

"I'm thinking of going on the road again," I say, "but the trouble is it costs so much to take a whole cast out on the road, you can't make any money."

"You should do a greedy bastard tour," says Danny.

"A what?"

"A greedy bastard tour. It's a rock-and-roll term."

"Really?"

"Yeah, that's like when you go out first time, you take a full band with a big crew and tons of buses and lots of lighting and fireworks, and it costs a bundle, and you lose a ton. So the next time you go, you do a greedy bastard tour, and it's just you and a geetar."

"I love it, that's it," I said. "That's the title: The Greedy Bastard Tour."

"But what if they don't get the irony . . . ?"

Good evening, ladies and gentlemen, and welcome to the Greedy Bastard Tour. I am your Greedy Bastard for tonight . . .

DAY 1

TO CANADA AND BEYOND!

AS I LEAVE HOME, THE TEARS IN MY DAUGHTER'S EYES REMIND ME THAT THIS ADVENTURE COMES WITH SOME REAL COSTS, AND THAT I STAYED HOME FOR THE FIRST THIRTEEN YEARS OF HER LIFE FOR A VERY GOOD REASON.

I try to reassure her that Thanksgiving isn't such a long time away, and I have a sudden flashback of my mother sending me off to boarding school with the same bullshit. Even my wife looks sad, which after twenty-seven years with the Greedy Bastard is certainly impressive.

I think of Michael Palin setting out on his great journeys. Mine won't be quite so bold: just to Canada, which is no longer terribly dangerous. Palin is probably in Pakistan at this very moment, eating dog with an Oxford-educated goatherd, interviewing yaks, and having his picture taken in front of a yurst, which is a kind of straw hut used for storing squirrels [*Bollocks.* —Ed.] while I am headed for an executive-class seat on Air Canada, but *chacun à son goût*, as the French say when looking at English food. I feel a bit

ERIC IDLE

nervous encroaching on Palin territory by writing a travel diary. I want to avoid any unpleasant sense of stealing Michael's thunder, but most of the Pythons have been involved in documentaries recently: Jonesy walked halfway to Jerusalem in Crusader armor, holding a spear; Gilliam is the tragic hero of a classic documentary about the nonmaking of a movie; and even Cleesy went to Madagascar to invade the privacy of the lemurs. Only Graham has remained quiet. Death will do that to you. That's one of the reasons I am so against it. So, what is this urge by ex-comedians to get out there and examine the world? Are they tired of dressing up as women? Surely not. This tour will be almost *my* first time onstage drag-free.

For my diary, instead of a coffee-table book, I am planning to publish a dining-table book: a book so large that eight people can comfortably have dinner on it. Maybe it could even be a bedside-table book, or better yet a bathroom-table book with lots of photographs of nude women, but then I don't suppose there will be all that many nude women at my shows.

▽

I am going on a bus tour of North America. Three months, and almost fifty gigs across the entire continent. It may seem a little odd at my age to be heading out on the road, but I have never done this and it seems to have a romantic gypsy feel to it. I like the idea of slipping offstage into a bed that takes me to the next gig, rather than having to line up to show strangers my socks at airports. As Kevin Nealon so brilliantly observed: How selfish and unthinking of the shoe bomber. *Why couldn't he have been the bra bomber? Or the panty bomber?* Kevin is a spectacularly funny man. Will I still be funny? Was I ever? These are the sort of anxious thoughts that fill my mind as I head for Canada.

I am flying into Toronto because my promoters are also greedy bastards, and it is cheaper to have me flogging my show on TV and pimping my ass to the newspapers than buying expensive ads. In my experience there is nothing you can't do for promoters. It is only with the greatest reluctance that they allow you to spend a couple of hours onstage, away from the relentless interviews.

▽

My Greedy Bastard Tour is kicking off in Rutland, Vermont, in four days' time, a starting point suggested by the Greedy Bastard's agent, who was formerly the head of the Greedy Bastard's record label. Having sold precisely three copies of *Eric Idle Presents Nigel Spasm's Journey to the Rutland Isles* (a pithy enough title), he has been trying to lure me out on the road in a blatant attempt to flog off the remaining twelve copies that lie unsold in the Artist Direct storeroom (a small closet near Wilshire Boulevard).

▽

As the car searches for fast back routes through L.A.'s increasingly bad traffic, I congratulate myself on *not* bringing a camera crew. The observer alters the experiment as we all know from our readings of Heisenberg (actually, none), and the thought of having to appear cheery to a documentary crew first thing in the morning makes me sleepy, so I settle down for the first of many naps, unencumbered by the effort of having to make smart one-liners to a lens.

▽

The flight to Toronto is on time and half empty or half full, depending on your point of view. The stewardess offers me a can of Spam to sign for her

If you really want to attract attention, release a comedy CD just as America goes to war. I won't say my CD did badly, but weapons of mass destruction were easier to find....

3

ERIC IDLE

brother while the West slips by beneath a huge, round jet engine, and I am struck by how colorful it is: reds and oranges and blues and tortuous canyons of rivers winding between towering cathedral bluffs. There is nothing at all down there, and I ponder a short fantasy about a tribe of Indians offering a new promised land to the Israelis. In no time they would have it blooming, if not Bloomingdale's, but would they really relocate here if lured by the prospect of easy gaming facilities? And who would the Indian tribe be: the Schmioux, the Dakoshers, or the Moe Hawks, perhaps?

Soon the land below is covered by a rust color, which looks like lichen from the air, before I realize that it is fall. The Rockies have an early sprinkling of snow, which outlines the winding paths of their peaks; an improbable pure blinding white line, snaking among the amber and russet of the forests. The stewardess is in a chatty mood and claims she saw us on our first visit to Toronto—good God, thirty years ago—on Monty Python's First Farewell Tour. We staggered off the plane jet-lagged, and as we came through customs there was a tremendous screaming, and we all looked behind us to see which rock-and-roll stars were arriving, only to be amazed by the realization that this yelling crowd was there to greet us: our first experience of the hype that occasionally surrounded Python. It all seemed rather agreeable, and we were placed on top of an open bus and led into Toronto by car horn–tooting fans. Welcome to North America. Not quite the Beatles, but not bad for comedians.

Incidentally, did you know that the first draft of the Canadian national anthem, "O Canada," was originally "Oh Sorry"?

DAY 2

I AWAKE REFRESHED AT 4:00 A.M. AFTER A NAP. THIS MORNING I HAVE TO FACE THE PRESS. I AM ON *GOOD MORNING CANADA*, BUT FIRST I HAVE A FEW HOURS TO MYSELF. I LOVE EARLY MORNINGS. I LIKE NOTHING more than a little laptop and a nice cup of tea. Oh, and a decent pair of pants, of course. *And* a good book, comfortable shoes, cashmere close to the skin, and a decent bed—that goes without saying. A warm bath, naturally, Egyptian cotton sheets, a plumpy duvet, and a Taylor guitar—mustn't forget that—as well as a fabulous sound system, a portable CD player, and a nice invigorating massage from a scantily clad . . . Come to think of it there's quite a lot more I like than just a bloody computer and a mug of tea.

▽

This is supposed to be a greedy bastard tour but sadly I have already strayed miserably from the concept and brought along a large cast to help me onstage and off. Point man is my partner, the semilegendary John

ERIC IDLE

Du Prez, who has spent twenty-five years writing and producing songs with me, from the Python days and now to Broadway with *Spamalot,* a musical we have adapted from *Monty Python and the Holy Grail.*

My foil onstage is Peter Crabbe, a huge, terrifying, shaven-headed hunk of a man who is not averse to leaping into women's clothing at the drop of a chapeau. Peter will do duets with me, such as Nudge Nudge and the Bruces, and will also abuse the audience as a member of Homeland Security, a role he will rewrite every night as he panders shamelessly to local prejudices. On Friday in Rutland he will be ranting about New Yorkers coming out to watch the trees turning.

Onstage also is the lovely Jennifer Julian, who I exploited on my previous tour of North America. She is a very funny blond comedienne whom I have stolen from her radio station in Montana. Jennifer has a friend who made us a Penis Fish for the Bill Maher show and is currently making some kind of aquatic muff diving creature and a trouser snake. All these beasts, as well as Jennifer, will be along on the tour.

I seem to have developed a silly walk. I have been limping for the past three months and have been undergoing thrice-weekly physio for tendonitis, but my doctor, the legendary Kipper, announced just as I was leaving that it might be gout (what?) and gave me a couple of pain pills. They worked, too, but had worn off by the time I reached Canada, so I came into Toronto Airport in a peculiarly silly crab walk, with a bit of a sideways twist. Serves me right for my joke about John.

It was at Cambridge that I met the incomparable John Cleese. That was forty years ago. Nowadays John is using a silly walker . . .

It'll be me who needs the walker on this tour. Will I ever again dance naked in front of the Taj Mahal by moonlight? [*No. And he never has. The Greedy Bastard is clearly using too much tea again.*—Ed.]

The Canadian immigration official, softened by my oblique and obviously insane sideways approach to his desk, politely claimed to have seen my TV ads, so that's a good sign, although he didn't say whether he had bought any tickets. There is a hilarious moment in the arrival hall as baggage claim plays their own version of musical chairs, constantly switching the numbers on the luggage carousels so that just as seventy passengers have settled expectantly with their trolleys, they flash a new number, which sends the whole lot scuttling off down the far end of the hall. Then they change the number again. This is a good gag and clearly amuses the baggage handlers, since they try it a few more times. Eventually the baffled passengers give up and hover about in the center of the hall, muttering, defeated. This must be some kind of Canadian indoor sport.

▽

My greedy bastard agent calls as I reach the room. He announces there is a beautiful woman on the phone with him. He seems to employ only beautiful young women. I must watch him rather carefully on this tour. He spells his name "Marc," with a *c*, and that is a little too hairdressery, don't you think? I bet he's a secret Mark who upgraded. He is sending me T-shirts for approval. This is what the Greedy Bastard Tour is all about: shifting merchandise. They refused to make the shirt

ERIC IDLE

I wanted. They said there would be no market for a shirt with the Penis Fish on it. Well, little do they know about the bastards who come to these shows . . .

The second day of the Greedy Bastard Tour passes in a whirlwind of interviews interspersed with sitting in traffic jams in the Don Valley Parking Lot, which is what they call their freeway. Everyone seems to like the Greedy Bastard Tour title, though *Good Morning Canada* will not say it on air, and when I mention it, they look shocked. Mild irreverence passes for wit at this time in the morning, and they all look very happy as I leave. Unless it's *because* I'm leaving. Only John Gibson on a Fox remote seems alive to the satirical possibilities of the title. "It's the greedy bastard era," I hear myself say, and I add, "I always liked your hair." He tells me he has ten wigs in it if I'd like one.

I am so brain-dead by the end of the day, after being endlessly questioned as to my motives for the Greedy Bastard Tour (duh, to make money) that I inadvertently say the "F" word on CBC Radio. Ooops. There is a shocked reaction from the control booth, and some people hold their hands over their mouths while others sneakily put their thumbs up in glee. Avril Benoit takes it in her stride and skips straight along. On CFRB (no, I don't know what it means, either) John Moore permits only one question from a listener, a man who goes on and on about how much he loves Monty Python, and how much Python merchandise he has bought. He has spent hours watching Monty Python, he says, *"while spanking the*

monkey!" I don't even have the good taste to let it go. "Spanking the monkey?" I say. "What kind of freak watches Monty Python while beating a chimp?" The host cuts quickly to the news and the newsreader says—honestly, I swear—"Welcome to the spanking news!"

DAY 3

TORONTO TO BOSTON

 WAKE UP THIS MORNING EXCITED. NO DOUBT ABOUT IT, THERE IS THAT ICY, ALERT, ANTICIPATORY FEELING OF EXPECTATION. SOMETHING DEFINITELY BEGINS TODAY. BEYOND THE FULL DAY SPENT FIELDING ENDLESS MONTY Python questions, the adventure will really begin this evening, when I fly into Logan and meet the buses. They will be our home for three and a half months. There is something essentially North American in attempting to cross the continent in these covered wagons. I feel like an early settler. [*Hang on I'll get you one.*—Ed.] Opinions are divided as to how mad this is. Richard of York, my temporary PR man, who has long, flowing white hair and battles along like a cross between Max Wall and Shakespeare's cheerful Richard the Third, looks at me as though I am mad. To him, the very thought of being stuck on a tour bus is insane. My friend Dave Mirkin, who is the number one James Taylor fan in the world, says that James likes the tour bus, and even, in his own egalitarian way, sleeps in one of the bunks and not in the huge Big Bastard Bedroom at the back. My own egalitarianism does not stretch quite that far. I can't wait to see how being in that lit-

tle moving cabin will feel. We have a four-hour journey from Boston to Rutland this evening, so there's a great chance to try it out. Also I have asked our tour manager to shove some grub aboard for everyone. Skip Rickert is our tour manager, a handsome chap, onetime actor, and current Pat Boone impersonator. He has flown in from Tucson and has prepared for his role on the Greedy Bastard Tour by taking the Sex Pistols around America. Surely after that we should be a doddle.[1]

The challenge of the incessant interviews—really a form of verbal swordplay—has driven from my mind last week's rehearsal anxiety of trying to remember my lines. For the first time in my life I intend to do some stand-up material, and as I have never done this before, I am anxious about remembering the sequences. Of my comic friends both Eddie Izzard and Billy Connolly claim not to learn their stuff. Billy says he just walks onto the stage and starts talking. I believe him. He always talks the same, whether his audience is one or one thousand. It's a form of exterior monologue. He's like a man constantly querying reality, endlessly reflecting on what is unfurling in front of him.

Eddie is different but claims to use the same technique. He talks in paragraphs of subject, and these can extend or shrink or swap position depending on his mood. He does leap into total improv at times and says these are the times he loves best. He can even make himself laugh at these moments. Kevin Nealon usually works from a tight script. He has his material

> No day of my life passes without someone saying the words "Monty Python" to me. It's not bad. People stop me on the street and say, "Hello, Mike." They congratulate me on the travel show and they say how much they enjoyed A Fish Called Wanda ... and whenever I'm mistaken for Michael Palin, I always say "Yes I am him. Now fuck off you ugly old bastard!" Because I want to help destroy his reputation for niceness.

---

[1] A stroll in the park.

ERIC IDLE

My name is Eric Idle. If you think you're here to see Billy Idol you can fuck off now....

prepared and will occasionally glance at his notes or openly pretend to distract the audience, pointing to the back of the room ("Will you look at that?") while he produces his notes from his pants. It's tough to tell with Robin Williams. He is so fast you never really know when he has slipped into pure inspiration and when he is recalling some previously explored thought pattern. In a sense he is always rehearsing and will stop anywhere and grab a little crowd whom he delights with a swift verbal workout. I have seen him do this from Paris to St. Petersburg, and there have been times when I have been certain he is utterly improvising. It still flies out in finished sentences, making broad plain sense. No one is faster than him. He is faster than the speed of thought. He can take a concept from my lips and before I can get a second thought out he will have turned it upside down, inverted it, examined the flip side, stood it on its head, agreed with it, destroyed it, and handed it back x-rayed, stamped, and marked "thoroughly examined." Of course it is genius, and I don't like using that word in showbiz, since it so often means a guitarist of merely moderate ability. But trying to do comedy alongside Robin is like trying to solve a math problem alongside Einstein: you're lucky to be in the same room. My own humble experience with direct communication with an audience lies not in stand-up but in speeches. Once or twice I have been cornered into delivering public addresses at rubber-chicken events and have managed to garner a few laughs. I am hoping that stand-up won't be all that different, but, no question, it gives this tour an extra nervous edge for me. On my last tour, Eric Idle Exploits Monty Python, I used to open act two by talking di-

rectly to the audience. Now I am preparing to open act one in this way. We shall see.

I begin the day's promo activities with a quick cab ride to The Edge, an edgy radio station named unaccountably after an Irish guitarist. A twenty-four-hour game of Twister is in progress in the middle of the studio and three young women are in obscene positions on the floor as I enter. On the air, live, I say how enjoyable it is to watch *nude* Twister on the radio. I am fairly rude throughout—hello, what else is new? I even sing the whole of "Sit on My Face" in my adrenaline-driven panic.

> *Sit on my face and tell me that you love me.*
> *I'll sit on your face and tell you I love you, too.*
> *I love to hear you oralize,*
> *When I'm between your thighs;*
> *You blow me away!*
> *Sit on my face and let my lips embrace you.*
> *I'll sit on your face and then I'll love you truly.*
> *Life can be fine if we both sixty-nine,*
> *If we sit on our faces in all sorts of places and play,*
> *Till we're blown away!*

The deejays mercifully guffaw and seem not to have heard it before. Thank God for Monty Python! As we begin broadcasting, a news TV station on a monitor in the studio scrolls my name as a forthcoming attraction at Massey Hall. It is spelled Eric Idol. I rant about this on air, insisting I am a lazy bastard not a fucking goddess. You would think the promoters might get my name right, wouldn't you?

On *Inside Entertainment* with David J. Roberts I get carried away and start improvising a new reality show called *The*

ERIC IDLE

Binnie Laden Show, live from a cave in Afghanistan, where Binnie, the little-known brother of the world's most famous terrorist, shows people around his new cave. "We have knocked through here to scrape out a kitchen/dining area." I feel it could be some kind of reality show like *The Osbournes;* a sort of BBC *Changing Caves* show. Then I get a sudden flash of trying to pitch this to network executives and start giggling hysterically. Network executives are the pits. The word "executive" is pretty much of a warning signal. "Executive producer" tends to mean the brother-in-law of the man who does nothing. When I worked with network executives I found them comfortably the least funny people in the world, and I always wondered how they managed to achieve their domination over the funny people and the funny process. The record industry was ruined by executives, and so was the video industry; and now the DVD industry is busy bullshitting itself into thinking it creates the product that it merely sells. It's as if greengrocers suddenly claimed credit for creating strawberries. I once did a sitcom with John Rich, a man who directed *All in the Family* and *The Dick Van Dyke Show* and knows a thing or two about where the laughs are. A young female executive rushed in and gave us a note.

"Wear more green," she said.

"What?" we said. "What did you just say?"

"Wear more green," she said. "Tests have proven people feel more comfortable watching people who wear more green."

We were too stunned to ask if we should employ leprechauns.

What could be finer than a decent meal and a chance to talk about oneself to a polite Canadian jour-

Sadly, this is still the Bush era. If you're going to try to impose democracy on somewhere weird, filled with lots of foreigners, why not start with Florida?

nalist? Richard Ouzounian tells me his daughter is at college in Halifax, and her friends are without power after a hurricane. They save up their batteries so they can watch a Python movie every night on someone's laptop. To keep up their spirits they are singing "Bruces' Philosophers Song"! Too bad I won't be going near Halifax, though we are singing the "Philosophers Song" and have brought along a huge flat with the words on.

Immanuel Kant was a real pissant who was very
*   rarely stable.*
Heidegger, Heidegger was a boozy beggar who could
*   think you under the table.*
David Hume could out-consume Schopenhauer and
*   Hegel,*
And Wittgenstein was a beery swine who was just as
*   sloshed as Schlegel.*
There's nothing Nietzsche couldn't teach ya 'bout the
*   raising of the wrist.*
Socrates, himself, was permanently pissed.
John Stuart Mill, of his own free will, on half a pint of
*   shanty was particularly ill.*
Plato, they say, could stick it away, half a crate of
*   whiskey every day!*
Aristotle, Aristotle was a bugger for the bottle,
Hobbes was fond of his dram.
And René Descartes was a drunken fart: "I drink,
*   therefore I am."*
Yes, Socrates himself is particularly missed;
A lovely little thinker, but a bugger when he's pissed.

DAY 4

BOSTON TO RUTLAND, VERMONT

I PASSED THROUGH TORONTO AIRPORT, QUALIFYING NICELY FOR ALL THE EXTRA SEARCHES AVAILABLE. STOPPED FOR THE THIRD TIME IN TEN YARDS BY AN INDIAN GENTLEMAN, I ASK HIM POLITELY IF I AM irresistible to all Asian men. He laughs and assures me that it is purely numerical, but I suspect some deep Raj rage. The only compensation is that my hand baggage is then searched by three of the most beautiful security women I have ever seen, each one a gem for Shiva. I cannot resist telling them this, and they smile in that way women have when you compliment them on what they know already. Having passed through more steps than a recovering alcoholic, I am, finally, safe to travel. It has become so complicated to fly these days that sometimes I believe only a terrorist could get through an airport without a search.

▽

Skip is waiting for me at Logan Airport in Boston, a quietly efficient man who is relieved to be out of three-figure temperatures in Arizona. He

guides me to a shuttle, which drops us in a car park where our two tour buses are waiting. This is the moment of truth. Right on cue it begins to rain. A large gentleman of Dickensian proportions emerges holding aloft a tiny umbrella. He looks like an etching by Edward Lear, which impression is reinforced when a sudden gust of wind snaps the umbrella inside out and he is left holding a collapsed metal frame attached to a useless flapping rag: a nice comic touch.

This is English, our driver. He is from the Wirral, just by Liverpool. He gives me a quick tour of the bus, including my little stateroom, pointing out the Game Boy. He seems very fond of the Game Boy. He shows me the Game Boy controls and the Game Boy box. I don't like to disabuse him that I never touch Game Boys. Fox TV is showing English football, which is good news for me. Glynn assures me we get two hundred channels of satellite. "Everything," he says, "but the Playboy Channel." I'm not quite sure what I am supposed to understand from this, so I look inscrutably at Manchester City failing to score. The girls on the Playboy Channel would surely do better.

▽

Within minutes the rest of our party are clambering aboard. There are nine of them: John Du Prez, our musical director; Peter Crabbe, actor/singer; Jennifer Julian, actress/singer; Skip Rickert, tour manager; Gilli Moon, stage manager; Scott Keeton, guitar tech; Larry Mah, sound engineer; Tom Husman, merchandising; and Ann Foley, wardrobe. Everyone looks fit and well after their flight from L.A. John particularly. Peter has had a special bunk adapted to fit his six-foot-seven frame. He is looking very handsome and well groomed. Hoping for a little action on the road no doubt.

▽

ERIC IDLE

There is a little mutinous muttering from the men when they discover both girls are assigned to my tour bus, but I am responsible for the moral welfare of my crew, and I can hardly leave two attractive blondes with these sweaty jocks. They'll be safer on my bus, and if not, well, I can always lock my door. Skip elects to share my quarters with the girls: the lovely Jennifer and the compact dynamo Gilli Moon, a hardworking sheila from Down-unda.[2] Ann Foley, my foxy red-haired costume designer, is along just for the opening in Rutland, and announces she is thrilled that Eddie Izzard is giving her a credit on *his* tour. I *always* give her a credit, as she is fantastic, though she has a homing device that heads straight for Barneys. She said it was fun shopping with Eddie, though he still shops too much like a man. He needs to learn to shop like a girl.

"How's that?" I ask.

"Don't look at the prices."

⟁

D ay three," I say, "and we are still in the car park."

The girls laugh politely, but the gag turns out to be surprisingly prescient when, thirty minutes later, English, our driver, announces sheepishly that we can't find our way out of the airport and are returning to the car park to start over. Oops. Perhaps it is a new Homeland Security thing, so terrorists can't find their way out of Logan. Even the police can't help and shrug politely. Eventually, a sympathetic limo driver shows us a way through the maze of reconstruction and we are on the road at last. Ah, the open road! I feel like Mr. Toad, filled with enthusiasm. The adventure, the romance, peep, peep! We are setting off to cross America; fifteen thousand miles ahead of us, from Boston to L.A.; unforgettable sights, unforgettable views . . . wait up, we'll be traveling largely by

---

[2] A woman from Australia.

night. Never mind; we shall see unforgettable views *by night.* We shall visit interesting places—oh, all right we'll only be backstage at another theater, but goddammit we *are* traveling. I decide to try out the bed.

▽

At 2:00 A.M. I am still wide awake. As we rattle through Woodstock, I raise the swaying blind to find myself looking into brightly lit Queen Anne shop windows. We roar past white painted houses, broad wide greens, a perfect, sleepy church. I can't sleep as we bounce along the country roads. It's like being on a boat on a slightly rough sea. Despite ear plugs, I can hear the grinding of the gears shifting below me and the gruff growl of the engine as we race up hills. Will this thing really make it the fifteen thousand miles to L.A.?

We pull into the car park of the Red Roof Inn, Rutland, at three in the morning.

"Oh no," says Peter. "In my contract I demanded a *blue*-roof inn."

I stagger up at dawn to find a message waiting from another of the greedy bastard agent's beautiful women. This one is a sultry beauty called Tiarra, another gift from Shiva, who looks about nineteen and has been appointed for a paltry sum by Marc the hairdresser as my own special PR person. She informs me, via fax, that I have just the eight interviews in a row this morning. Manfully I stick my face into a muffin (muffin diving?), pop my tea bag into the coffeemaker (that is *not* a double entendre), swallow some hot Lapsang souchong (a smoky blend that is like tea *and* a cigarette), and hit the phone lines. An annoying sequence of unanswered calls from radio stations leaves me a little testy with the sultry Tiarra, but soon the jocks begin answering and I pick

I am the nicest of the six old Monty Python boys....Well, Mike is probably the nicest, but I'm certainly the second nicest. Actually, Terry Jones is pretty nice come to think of it, but I am definitely the third nicest. You know, Terry Gilliam can be very nice, especially at parties. Perhaps too nice at parties. So I'm the ... Graham Chapman was a very nice man and even John Cleese is a lot nicer than he used to be. So I guess I am the sixth nicest of the old Python group.

What's so fucking great about being nice, anyway?

ERIC IDLE

Welcome to the Senior Comedy Tour. I was going to call this evening The Angina Monologues—but greed prevailed.

up on their coffee-driven energy. Everyone wonders why I am doing this tour. After about seven of these calls even *I* wonder why I am doing this tour. Maybe I should give up the whole show thing and just do interviews for a living?

I have a joke in my show that this is a senior tour, but the local Denny's is not joking. They have a senior menu, serving "senior food." (I thought Senior Food was a Spanish chef.)[3] There is a choice between the senior French toast, the senior Belgian waffles, and some senior omelets, which are probably made with old eggs. I settle for some senior poached eggs and a plate of middle-aged hash browns. The waitress, who is seventy, flirts with me. I resist her advances, since I believe in safe sex and will do it only with my lawyer present. After settling the senior bill I am ready to face "the get in." This is a technical theatrical term, that, roughly translated, means you *get in* to the theater. I have asked the cast to be DLP (another very useful theater term that means "dead letter perfect"). One or two other very useful theater terms you may need: "stage left" means the right side of the stage; "stage right" means the left; the "wings" are the side bits where the union stagehands sleep; and the "flies" are the things on their pants they leave open. The "prompt side" of the stage is opposite the "OP side," and "OP" means the side opposite the prompt side, which is where it is found, either on the right or left of the stage. In some houses the prompter, who is invariably late, sits not on the prompt side but on the opposite prompt or OP side. "Front of house" means

---

[3] This joke is so bad it has been entered in the Eurovision Joke Contest.

the *back* of the auditorium. The "greenroom" is a room that is never green but is where the actors hang out when the bathrooms are full, and the "flaps" are uhm . . . Look, I don't want to overburden you with too many theatrical slang terms at this point. Just stick with me, and I'll guide you through it all.

DAY 5

THE PARAMOUNT THEATRE, RUTLAND

RUTLAND IS A TOTAL TRIP. BEING HERE FEELS SO GREAT FOR ME. I HAVE SPENT SO MANY YEARS WRITING THINGS ABOUT RUTLAND THAT IT SEEMS IMPOSSIBLE THAT IT IS A REAL PLACE. EVERYTHING SAYS RUTLAND: THE Rutland Bank, the Rutland fire station, the Rutland chapter of the Shriners, and the Rutland Order of Mooses (surely that should be Meese?). It all looks like something I wrote.

▽

We climb onto the bus to go to our first theater. It's only a short journey by Palin standards, about five minutes, but as we pass the neat Palladian front of the Paramount Theatre I get what the French call a *frisson*, which, I believe, is a small ice cream. [*Bollocks.*—Ed.] Peter Crabbe regales us with a history of the theater.

"Houdini performed here," he says, "and Mark Twain and Sarah Bernhardt."

"What did they do?" someone asks.

"Monty Python skits, I think."

"And Houdini escaped," says Peter.

"From Sarah Bernhardt's acting," I add cynically.

▽

Our English driver manages to drive past the theater, so we circumnavigate the center of town for a second time.

"Couldn't we afford a Yank?" someone asks.

The Paramount is an old and very beautiful theater that has been lovingly restored. Inside it is bright, shining clean, and, amazingly, everything works. It has the feel of the Pump Room in Bath, with creamy paint and gold leaf everywhere. It looks as though Jane Austen just left the building.

"It's older than some of your material," says Peter.

▽

Our tech run is delayed while we sort through everything that has been shipped across America from my basement rehearsal room. Larry Mah and Scott Keeton quietly and efficiently go about getting the sound ready, sticking tiny face mikes on us. Neither of them has seen the show yet but I feel very confident with them. Both were along on the last tour, and Larry records everything for John and me in his tiny Sylmar garage studio. He has just finished mixing the third *Matrix* movie.

▽

We stop/start the show for our technical people. It's slow going, but it's the first most have seen of what we are trying to do. We take a dinner break, and the second half goes much quicker, so we are in position for a full dress rehearsal at nine. We may not be here all night as I had at first feared.

▽

ERIC IDLE

The T-shirts have arrived from the Greedy Bastard's agent and they are somewhat disappointing. The poster T-shirt is fine, and the picture of Nigel Spasm in a pith helmet standing on top of a mountain of money should do well, but I am disappointed by the animals of the Rutland Isles: the bipolar bears are too small and the surfing ape doesn't work. I long once again for the Penis Fish, though I do like the Tree Farter Squirrel.

Jennifer Julian turns up in a smart black T-shirt that boldly proclaims I LOVE MY PENIS, which draws ironic comments. She claims she got it in a gay shop in New York. Didn't I write this anthem already?

> *Isn't it awfully nice to have a penis?*
> *Isn't it frightfully good to have a dong?*
> *It's swell to have a stiffy.*
> *It's divine to own a dick,*
> *From the tiniest little tadger*
> *To the world's biggest prick.*
> *So, three cheers for your willy or John*
> *   Thomas.*
> *Hooray for your one-eyed trouser snake,*
> *Your piece of pork, your wife's best friend,*
> *Your Percy, or your cock.*
> *You can wrap it up in ribbons.*
> *You can slip it in your sock,*
> *But don't take it out in public,*
> *Or they will stick you in the dock,*
> *And you won't come back.*

Our dress rehearsal goes surprisingly smoothly and we are out of the theater shortly after midnight. I make one further cut in act one, excising the "Gay Animal Song," which I felt was one too many gay gags; and after Peter's glorious Homeland Security rant it's important to head swiftly to the intermission.

Noël Coward

Good evening, ladies and gentlemen, you look
   and smell divine.
In the Origin of Species
Charles Darwin liked to say
That dressing up and showing off
Was purely male display
But sadly scientifically
He led us all astray
For what he failed to notice
Was these creatures are all gay.

There's a little bird in Kent
Who's ridiculously bent
And a rutting stag who is a total deer
There are naughty big blue whales
And the sperm whale prefers males
And the dolphin is of course completely
   queer
There's a very brazen chimp
Who is very rarely limp
And a shrimp who's pink and utterly
   obscene
While the small transvestite prawn is
   completely into porn
And the king crab is of course an utter queen.

Gay gay gay
They all are madly gay
But in Victorian times
That was not the thing to say.

I sometimes wonder why my songs are so filthy and then I look at you lot.

THE GREEDY BASTARD DIARY

ERIC IDLE

In the Rutland Isles' warm waters
There's a young cross-dressing tortoise
And an ass who makes a pass at everyone
There's a masturbating monkey
And a terribly rude donkey
And a very very famous lesbian swan
There's a big bisexual elk
And a tiny gay young whelk
And a snake who is a rake all night and day
And a sorry little sheep
Who is into Meryl Streep
And don't tell me that the anteater's not gay.

Gay gay gay
They all are madly gay
Ten percent of nature's bent
At least that's what they say.

We now run fifty-five minutes for act one and forty-six for act two. This will spread with laughs (hopefully) but we are right in the ballpark and can make further tightens when we see how the audience reacts. The good news for me is that I was not wiped out by the show. I had plenty of stamina on-stage and my new weight-training regime is paying off, although I still limp like a latter-day Sarah Bernhardt. Where's Houdini to make this disappear? This is all now very exciting. I have got past my first alarm that no one will find any of it funny and feel confident that at least we can get through the show and they *will* find it amusing. But as always with comedy, it is only a theory. Tonight comes the test.

DAY 6

RUTLAND TO TORONTO

L AST NIGHT IN RUTLAND THERE WAS A FANTASTIC AND WILDLY NOISY RECEPTION FOR THE START OF THE GREEDY BASTARD TOUR. WE HAD STANDING OVATIONS AND CHEERS AND LOUD HAND CLAPPING AND FOOT-stomping demands for encores. The house was packed long before the curtain rose and the atmosphere in the auditorium was electric. They came for a good time and there was almost nothing we could do to stop them. Right from the off they cheered and laughed and applauded. I know Eddie Izzard has got rather fed up with that big, warm, whooping American reception when he walks on ("I haven't *said* anything yet," he says reprovingly), but I can tell you on the first night of a three-month tour, that big warm, noisy hello as you walk onstage is a very heartwarming and encouraging welcome.

Rutland is a small place and almost everyone was there. They laughed at my jokes and sang along lustily in all the right places, and almost all the sketches went really well. It is still an odd thing to me that the best-known material goes over the best, but we had some good new zingers for them,

Tonight for the very first time on any stage anywhere we are introducing a brand-new concept in show business: Will you welcome please the encore bucket!

Let me explain the concept. In most other shows, at the end you applaud the performers who go off, hide in the wings and then come back on and do an encore. For nothing.

Not on this show, baby. This is the encore bucket. If you'd like an encore, then just feel free to come up and put some money in the bucket, and at the end of the show—we'll talk about it.

and Peter's rant about tourists watching the trees die went over especially well. John was unusually nervous and missed the first sound effect on "I bet you they won't play this song on the radio," which left me with a bit of egg on my face. I have never known him to miss a cue ever. He spent all day rehearsing it, which may be the problem. Sometimes you can get too anxious about stuff like this. Later he wandered off into a different version of the madrigal, but we recovered and still got our big laugh at the end. Ah well, that is what a first performance is all about, and the good people of Rutland were highly supportive and warmly encouraging. At the intermission the audience wouldn't leave to go to the lobby, they just stood and cheered. I had to go out and tell them to take a break and buy some merchandise.

The encore bucket surprised us all. At the start of the show I introduced this brand-new showbiz concept, explaining how, if they want an encore, they can pay for it. There was a big laugh as I produced a huge, shiny, silver trash can that remained prominently onstage throughout the show. What I hadn't bargained for was people taking it seriously. Just before the final curtain Jen was supposed to discover that there was nothing in there, and I had written a few gags about what she found instead, but by the end the Rutland audience were already on their feet and making so much noise that we all took our bows and simply left the stage. When I came back on after a few minutes of stamping and yelling and screaming for more, I ignored the audience completely and walked straight over to the encore bucket. That got a big laugh. Imagine my surprise when I found it contained several dollar notes and loads of change! People were walking up

and putting in bills and they were throwing down change from the balcony, chucking cash and screaming for more. One young boy came up and put a buck in the bucket and indicated he wanted the parrot that sits in a cage on one of the speakers.

"You can't have that," I said. "It's dead."

Big laugh.

They settled for "The Lumberjack Song," with Peter Crabbe in a hat as an entire troop of Mounties. The final score for the encore bucket was twenty bucks, a love note, and a rubber ducky. Which raises the question, what to do with it? Peter Crabbe, the greedy bastard, suggests it should be donated to him as a tour bonus, but I decide unanimously that we'll save it up and donate it to charity.

▽

By eight thirty the next morning we're already into Canada, rolling through the wide, flat, woodlands around Fort Erie en route to Toronto. Canadian Immigration insist we tumble out of our warm bunks to show our bleary morning faces to a foxy minx in a snappy uniform, and now I'm awake, sitting up in my queen-size bed with my lap dancer on my knee as we head up the highway. [*I'm sure he means laptop.*—Ed.] It's a Saturday morning and in all reasonable worlds I should be watching Arsenal play Liverpool but I have the inevitable interviews awaiting me. We are sliding alongside a gray-blue Lake Superior. The morning sunlight glints on the water and the tall chimneys on the far shore look like graphs. Soggy rolls of hay lie like Weetabix in the damp green fields. Somewhere over to our right Niagara Falls is busy falling but, since I can't actually see it, perhaps I should admit the philosophical possibility that it is *not* falling. (Somewhere in a forest a tree falls on a philosopher, killing him and his silly theory.) It seems incredible but post-9/11 it's almost as quick to return to Toronto by road as it was for me to fly. The other day, as I was passing through U.S. Immigration, a large

ERIC IDLE

uniformed man came toward me snapping on a pair of blue rubber gloves. *Oh no, not the anal probe!* But he walked straight past me and my sphincter relaxed a little. What kind of a job *is* that? And what sort of man applies for it?

"We need someone to look up the butts of strangers passing through the airport."

"Do you get a uniform?"

"Yes."

"I'll do it."

It's not romantic work, is it? I doubt there are anal probe work songs.

"O Lordy I bin probin' de anuses all de lib long day . . ."

I know *someone* has to do it, but what does he tell his wife at the end of the day?

"And then I found a rabbit, and some flags of all nations . . ."

EMPIRE THEATRE, BELLEVILLE, ONTARIO

AST NIGHT I TOOK THE CAST AND SOME OF THE SCURVY CREW OUT TO DINNER. YOU HAVE TO FEED THE GREEDY BASTARDS, AND BOY CAN THEY EAT. THEY CONSUMED VAST QUANTITIES OF EXPENSIVE CHINESE FOOD AT DYNASTY, on Bloor, a favorite of mine in Toronto. I have decided to make some cuts in the running order. I outlined the changes while they muttered darkly about not having been paid. You'd think they'd pay *me* for a chance to be out on the open road with such an agreeable and pleasant leader, but no, here I am feeding them at expensive watering holes, putting them up in fancy hotels, and they expect to be paid as well! We were never paid in the old Python days. We'd be lucky to have a bag of dry oats and a good slap about the head. Some days we never ate for twelve weeks. *Paid?* We would have to cry ourselves to sleep in the damp seedy costumes we'd stood up in, while that John Cleese thrashed us to sleep wi' his belt. PAID?? I promise them meekly I'll see what I can do.

ERIC IDLE

We are "hubbing" from Toronto, making little darts up and down the same stretch of freeway, returning to sleep in the same hotel.

"It's a dartboard tour," says English.

"What?"

"The agent threw darts at a dartboard to determine the route."

We are cocooned in our own world now: bus, theater, bus, theater, hotel, bus theater, strip club. *Mall!* Sorry. Strip mall. Major issues of the day mean nothing to us. Will Arnold Schwarzenegger become governor of California on a minority vote? Everyone in the media seems to think I have the answer. The answer is, of course he will, the media have already seen to that, but it will serve him right. He will have to go and live in Sacramento. That'll teach him. (Be careful what you ask for.) Actually he'll probably just commute by private jet. Private jet lag is so much more acceptable, don't you think? I love the delicious irony of someone whose movies go spectacularly over budget campaigning to solve a budget crisis in California, but then *Pumping Irony* is the story of Arnold's life; he is the man who single-handedly popularized the sport of waitress lifting.

Tell people you are playing Belleville and they look at you strangely. Actually these small places are invaluable and have been hand-picked by the Greedy Bastard's agent so that we can iron out the kinks from the show. (No, Ray Davies is not in it.) The capacity of the Empire Theatre is only 700, but Kitchener, on Tuesday, holds 1,800 and Massey Hall, on Wednesday and Thursday in Toronto, holds 2,545. Even the Théâtre St-Denis in Montreal next Monday holds more than 2,000 so tonight is our last chance to feel

I love the fact that "spam" has come to mean unwanted garbage on the Internet. Every day I receive four or five offers to add three or four inches to my penis. All of which I accept. And now I have a nine-foot penis.

close to a smallish audience and experiment a little with the running order. The pitfall of comedy is going on too long and tonight I want to try and get to the intermission quicker. I'm looking to take out about ten minutes from act one. The main victim is Jen, and I know these cuts are hard for her to take. I'm cutting my own Nigel Spasm piece as well, but I can see that's not much consolation for Jennifer. It's not her fault. The main problem is that Peter's Homeland Security rant lifts the audience to such a high pitch that it's hard to follow it with gentle stuff about the Rutland Isles. So tonight I'm going to try removing all of that and simply come in with the Bruces after John's Bad Beethoven. This should help to move the show along.

I was very sorry to see Roy of Siegfried and Roy was savaged by one of his performers. At least I don't risk getting bitten on the neck and dragged offstage, though I'll have to watch it by the look in Jennifer's eyes.

We leave our hotel by camel at dawn in a swarm of flies after beating off some local beggars with a brolly. . . . [*Stop that. This is not Michael Palin's diary.*—Ed.] Sorry. We climb into our luxury coach for the short journey to tonight's gig. As if perfectly timed Chelsea v. Middlesborough kicks off on Fox Sports World. Thank you, thank you, Soccer God, the satellite works! It will not be a football-free three months. Sex I can do without [*Yeah, right.*—Ed.] but to do without soccer is asking too much. Reminds me of the old English gag "Football's better than sex. Where else can you get forty-five minutes each way and a brass band in the middle?"

33

ERIC IDLE

I'm a happily married man—if that's not an oxymoron.

My favorite sexual position is the Male Marital Position: flat on your back with your wallet wide open.

Talking of sex, who are these kind ladies who leave their phone numbers in the encore bucket for an ancient British comedian? I mean, it impresses the crew and it's very flattering to the ego, and I don't wish to seem rude, but I am now over thirty. [*Double thirty, you lying bastard.*—Ed.] My wife has always said I can sleep with as many women as I want: but if I do, she'll kill me. So I choose life. Also she is a cutie. And I do miss her. And so would you if you'd spent twenty-seven years with her.

Belleville is a quaint little place on a picturesque river with several beautiful churches about ninety-five miles northeast of Toronto. As we drive into town on a Sunday afternoon there is no one to be seen. All the shops are shut, and the streets deserted. It looks like a ghost town where all the people have been carried away by aliens. It has obviously been hit hard economically with several shut-down shops and businesses and we are given dinner in a very nice little French restaurant, which has a notice up that it is closing this week. So it is very impressive that at the end of the show the audience line up in the foyer for me to sign tons of merchandise.

▽

They're a much quieter audience, and we have to work harder to win them, but we do. I am very proud of my cast and crew. Where do I begin? Obviously with me. I am the greedy bastard, after all. As you know most people in showbiz are out there performing just for the benefit of their audiences, purely from the goodness of their hearts. [*Irony detector just went off again. Now stop it.*—Ed.] But not me, oh no. I am in it just for the encore bucket, and tonight they are out of their seats dropping in Canadian dollars (called "loonies," appropriately) and hundreds of *tire dollars* (fairly useless vouchers from a hardware chain). I realized quite early that they were a listening audience. They weren't whooping and yelling; indeed they were an older crowd, very polite, the first act passed swiftly at fifty minutes. The cuts worked, and Jen was great, and Peter was great, and John was brimming with confidence and picked up many extra laughs in The Four Yorkshiremen, so that even when Peter had a brain fart and didn't show up for Nudge Nudge it didn't bother me one bit. In fact several of the people said they *liked* the mistakes! Maybe we should keep them in. Act two is much more reflective and far less filthy, and I talk about myself more, and I felt very relaxed and easy with them, plus we really made them laugh and won them over so that by the end they were as noisy as Rutland and gave us several standing ovations.

When I was born in England in World War Two, Adolf Hitler was trying to kill me. I don't think it was personal.

A DAY OFF IN TORONTO

THIS IS A DAY OFF? TIARRA THE TEENAGE PR GODDESS IS GOING TO HAVE TO BE PUNISHED. SHE HAS SCHEDULED FIVE INTERVIEWS TODAY, BUT WHAT BUGS ME IS SHE PUT ONE IN AT NINE-THIRTY. IT'S BAD ENOUGH STAGGERING up early after a late night and a hard show but to have to talk enthusiastically about myself at that hour is cruel and unusual punishment. No gentleman talks to anyone before noon. (See *Go Fuck Yourself: The Idle Book of Etiquette*.) One of the reasons I write alone is that I can't bear speaking to anyone first thing in the morning. I'd much rather get up at dawn with a pencil and a sheet of paper and see what happens. Writing is like fishing: You have to go to the river every morning, or you won't catch anything. You can't predict what sort of fish you'll catch, but if you're not *there* you'll get nothing. Keith Richards said that he couldn't claim credit for writing his songs, only for being awake when they came in. So I resent having to waste time talking enthusiastically about how great my show is to adrenaline-driven deejays. I curse Tiarra roundly in Hindi, but only in my imagination. I threaten her instead that she is going to be punished by being lightly rubbed in oil and spanked with feathers. She says that doesn't seem so bad. She adds she has been sick, and isn't that punishment enough? I agree that perhaps it is, but I'd still like to go ahead with the oil thing. She thanks me for making her laugh, which means that laughter is the best medicine and I can probably charge her insurance for medical expenses. Maybe I can even get the oil discounted.

▽

It turns out that the interviews are actually fun and, speedy on tea, I natter away happily to several reporters from Pittsburgh to Poughkeepsie. I am asked about the new Bill Murray film *(Lost in Translation)*, which I say I loved. I am predisposed to enjoy a story about an elderly fame victim suffering from accidie *(Boredom with life.—Ed.)* drawn toward the freshness and vitality of a young married woman in a foreign hotel. It's *Brief Encounter*, of course, but I thought it was very finely acted by Bill, and the lovely Scarlett Johansson is an utter doll. In fact she is *so* lovely I checked whether she was downstairs in the hotel lobby, but sadly Bill has better luck in foreign hotels. . . . I remember him well from the early days of *Saturday Night Live,* when he came in to replace Chevy Chase. He improvised wonderfully for me as Bill Murray the K. in my 1977 mocumentary *All You Need Is Cash*, the story of the Prefab Four, the semi-legendary Rutles, which I made for NBC. When I was making the sequel *(Can't Buy Me Lunch)* a couple of years ago, I found some of the original unused footage in an old warehouse in New Jersey and promptly used it. As an actor Bill was very fond of Richard Burton, but now he seems to have matured into Trevor Howard. A good choice. He has

I'm just trying to earn enough to get my daughter through college and my wife through collagen.

37

ERIC IDLE

such a lived-in face, and how rare it is to see a decent wrinkle on the screen. Hollywood is into facial prejudice in a big way. Age denial is the national sport.

Someone once said of Americans that they think death is optional. Here in Canada it's very refreshing to see older faces on television. Some of them are even allowed to read the news. I think you should never trust newsreaders who are wearing makeup and wigs. If they're lying about their appearance, why would you trust what they say?

CENTRE IN THE SQUARE, KITCHENER, ONTARIO

TORONTO. DAWN. I AM WOKEN EARLY BY THE RUSH OF WARM AIR THROUGH THE NOISY AIR-CONDITIONING. IT REMINDS ME THAT WINTER IS ON ITS WAY. THE SLOW EARLY BUILD TO THE TOUR IS ALMOST OVER AND NOW the real work begins. We will be performing nightly and sleeping in the bus for days on end. After next weekend in Ottawa no more luxury hotels for a while. And it's going to get colder. Right now, though, it's beautiful and sunny and it's the publication day of a new autobiography of the Pythons called *The Pythons*, a huge coffee-table tome. It is so heavy Michael Palin has described it as un-putdownable and un-pickupable.

We have picked up a stowaway: Jennifer, a wardrobe person from Rutland, has come along for the ride, perhaps lured by the proximity of so many rutting males, so our touring party is now temporarily swollen to ten. I don't think she has come on the road *just* to help me change into my shorts for the Bruces. . . .

Tonight's show is in Kitchener, which was called Berlin until World War

Well, it's sing-along time, so let's have the lights up and let's have a bit of karaoke, which is Japanese for "drunken bastards singing out of tune." This is your chance to get off your butts and join in, including all of you up there in the liposection. Blimey, they've been lifted more than Cher!

O Death, O Death
Thou art so
      unfair!
To take away
      Sonny
And still leave us
      Cher.

One, when they renamed it after a British general who was busy helping wipe out Canadians. We drive south through pleasant, wooded countryside with hillsides lined with maples, broken by wide, placid brown rivers. Except for the occasional shock of rust, the leaves haven't yet turned, and it's still remarkably green for October. The sun is shining, and all is well with the world. Ah, how agreeable to be a greedy bastard, carried in comfortable carriages from gig to gig.

▽

Canadians are a quieter and politer people than the Americans, and act one is something of a struggle. We win them by the end, though, and they stand and yell and shout for more; but at times it was distinctly hard work. Part of the problem is the sheer size of the auditorium. Centre in the Square is a very large house and seats eighteen hundred. It is also very wide and very deep. You could play baseball in here. The balconies are a long way off and the whole thing is a vast empty horseshoe. Even during the performance I am worrying that there is something wrong with the beginning of the show. Act one is just not taking off as it should, and though we get there by the time the Bruces come on, there is still something seriously adrift at the start. I didn't get time to eat before the show, and by halftime I am really dragging. I wolf down some food and swallow a hot tea, and act two goes much better. After the show I pounce on Scott Sansom, our stage manager from the 2000 tour, and demand he gives me his harshest notes. It's no good pissing about with politeness; we have a couple of nights of big shows in Toronto coming up, and I don't want to blow it. Scott's thoughts reinforce my own feelings about act one. It's time to take drastic action.

▽

I call a cast meeting on the bus while we drive back to Toronto. It's after midnight, and we're all tired, and I have signed and posed for pictures for an hour, but this is important. Jen is looking cute in her pink tracksuit, and Peter somewhat anxious, and John his usual calm self. Skip is present, and Gilli sits with her pencil poised. After all her hard work I am proposing to change it all again. We all agree that the opening is not working very well. The problem is that it is all new material, and the audience simply prefers familiar material. There is no getting away from this fact. As soon as we slip into Nudge Nudge they are happy. We have to try and get to this stuff sooner. John valiantly performed "I Bet You They Won't Play This Song on the Radio" with me, manfully providing hundreds of silly sound effects.

I bet you they won't play this song on the radio
I bet you they won't play this new XXXXing song
It's not that it's XXXX
Or so controversial
It's just that the words are so XXXXing strong

You can't say XXXX on the radio
Or XXXX
Or XXXXX
Or XXXXX
You can't even say I'd like to XXXX you someday
Unless you're a doctor with a very large XXXX

So I bet you they won't play this song on the radio
I bet you they won't even dare program it

ERIC IDLE

I bet you their XXXXing old program directors
Will think it's a load of horse XXXX

It works okay, but it is still a fairly unfamiliar song and it's not hitting the way you need at the start of the show. So it's cut. Cut, too, is Peter's entry from the audience into Strip Quiz. This quiz game is only mildly amusing, and so it goes. We start making swift changes to act one, shaking it up and reordering it. "Galaxy Song" comes in from act two to follow the Pepperpots on the Moon skit, and Peter and I decide to have a go at the classic Argument Clinic. I hadn't wanted to do too much Python on this tour to avoid making it too similar to my last tour, but there seems no doubt that Python stuff is what they want. My real anxiety is Toronto. Will they feel cheated or short-changed if there is too much of the same stuff as before? I figure that's a risk we simply have to take. After Toronto the rest of the gigs in Canada are at places we have never played before. We simply must get the show right here and now and risk it. We decide to get into the theater early and work on the enormous changes as fast as we can, and cross our fingers we can get it all done in time for the curtain at eight. It's a union hall, which means we don't have the stage after five, so it's going to be a race against time. No doubt it will be a very scary day, but that's showbiz, folks. Everyone feels these changes are great and will work, but just to add to my anxiety Skip hands me the schedule for tomorrow's interviews. Tiarra has scheduled two and a half hours from ten until twelve thirty, when I am scheduled to have lunch with the Greedy Bastard promoters, who *want to ask me to do more interviews!* Ironically I shall have to interrupt this lunch held to persuade me to do more interviews in order to do an interview for CBC News.

Sphincters crossed for tomorrow.

DAY 10

MASSEY HALL, TORONTO

WAS UP TILL TWO WORKING ON THE SCRIPT AND THEN ROSE AT SEVEN TO COMPLETE IT AND GET IT TO SKIP FOR PRINTING AND DISTRIBUTION. TWO HOURS OF INTERVIEWS, A WORKING LUNCH WITH THE GREEDY BASTARD promoters, a quick interview for CBC outside the bus, and then we race to Massey Hall to work onstage for a couple of hours. *Now that's a full working day, lad, and don't you forget it.*[4] It's a beautiful, warm, springlike day in Toronto, perfect weather for sitting in a hotel room giving interviews. [*Don't start with the fucking irony.*—Ed.] Last night there was a fire alarm at the hotel. Major alarms went off, people descended to the lobby, fire engines arrived clanging. I was so shagged out[5] I slept right through it.

I bitch and moan about the interviews, but sometimes they can be quite interesting, if only to find out what I think about things. Today, for instance, I absolutely deny that Canadians are boring. I say it's only because they live

---

[4] Working Class sketch.
[5] Sleepy.

next to the Americans and are a little backward in homicide that they seem comparatively dull. In response to a question from Steve Colwill about Arnold on the radio, I hear myself say that I think Americans have gone mad and shouldn't be allowed to be in charge of the world anymore. They should be diagnosed by the U.N. as legally bonkers. There is a shocked silence.

"Have I gone too far?" I ask.

"No. I absolutely agree with you," he says.

▽

Between interviews I jot down some notes for my diary. Here, by the way, is a list of things to avoid saying to the Pythons.

a) *How did you get together?*

b) *How did you come up with the name Monty Python?*

c) *What is your favorite sketch?*

d) *Are you the gay one?*

e) *Which one are you?*

f) *Will you ever get back together again?*

g) *Are you Mike?*

Massey Hall is a very pleasant old venue to play, a high, scalloped room with many tiers and pillars like an old music hall. Nowhere is very far from the stage. Peter and I sit in the empty theater rehearsing the Argument Clinic sketch. It is one of the finest of the Cleese-Chapman sketches and is the most fun to play, as it is so precisely written. It's like a Tom Stoppard play in its cryptic use of logic. It's probably the best sketch they ever wrote, but can we memorize it in time? It has some tricky bits. (I once played it with Michael Palin in French on French television.) Jen holds the book and we sit running the words until fatigue overcomes me and I have to go take a nap. I awake refreshed and lift weights and have some dinner. It's a make-or-break day for this show. If we can make Toronto laugh and keep them laughing, then the tour can take off and fly. But tonight is the real test.

Somebody up there likes us, because everything works. It's a triumph. We pull it off. All the changes, all the new stuff, all the reordering, everything hits. The show takes off like a rocket. We get them early, and we hold them, and we run with them to the intermission. They are noisy, happy, bright, and hugely responsive. I would say it was one of the best shows we have ever done. After all the hard work it is very satisfying. The reaction is better than we could have hoped, cheering and shouting and curtain calls, and we all feel very good about ourselves. What clever children we are. Only one thing goes wrong. The local promoter surprises us and hands out a free program that kills stone-dead the sales of our elaborate and expensively printed souvenir program. I have to sign hundreds of the damn freebies instead *and* grubby ticket stubs, too. The tight-fisted Torontonians! How is a Greedy Bastard supposed to live?

DAY 11

TORONTO TO OTTAWA

LAST NIGHT MY HOTEL ROOM OFFERED ME A MOVIE, *MOST GLAMOROUS BLOW JOBS OF THE WORLD*, BUT IT WAS A LITTLE THIN ON PLOT, SO I WENT FOR THE BASEBALL. AS I'M ON MY WAY OUT OF THE HOTEL, IZZIE THE DOORMAN *tips me* twenty dollars. I'll repeat that. Izzie the doorman tips me twenty dollars. He slips the money into my hands with a big thank-you card, and he won't hear of me taking it back. I explain to him it's supposed to be the other way round but he won't listen. You're my favorite man in the world, he says, "after Jackie Mason." Oh my God. Has he seen through my disguise of being a Greedy Bastard? Is my secret identity revealed? Has he seen that I am really Super Nice Guy? Izzie has always been very kind and helpful to me, but to have doormen around North America tipping me is a bit much. Well, this is Canada, and they are much nicer in Canada, you know.

▽

I need medication now because I am definitely Sir Limpalot. Don't mistake the limp in that word. I'm referring only to my silly walk. The Viagra

prescription is not yet necessary, as I could tell from my few moments with the movie. After this many days away from the wife even baseball looks erotic. It has been determined that I do not have gout, but there are certain species of *faux* gout that have not been ruled out. Ersatz or pseudonymous gout? I guess that's like *mock* turtle. My doctor says there is a particularly painful test to determine this. Fuck off. I'm not going to submit to a particularly painful bone marrow test just so we can give it a name! It's a real drag being gimpy, and I've had to send for my bloody irritating surgical boot, which is being shipped to Burlington. I think my ballet days are over. I promised my daughter that I would dance at her wedding. It was going to be an interpretive dance as well. . . .

▽

J ennifer Mather, a radio interviewer in Vancouver, asked me whether we were all whacked out of our skulls when we wrote Monty Python. This is a persistent myth about Python among Canadians, who seem to have been whacked out of their skulls when they watched it. As a matter of fact it is almost impossible to write good comedy when you are whacked out of your skull, as I discovered when I worked on *Saturday Night Live* in the seventies, a show that *was* written by people whacked out of their skulls and, at times, showed it. ("What's the difference between life and a *Saturday Night Live* skit?" "Life doesn't go on forever.") Talking of radio interviews, there's a legendary story of one of the Monty Python boys being interviewed on a tape recorder by a pretty Canadian journalist while actually in flagrante, but wild horses would not drag the name of the recipient of this *in-depth* interview from my lips. To talk seriously on the radio about comedy while porking the questioner is still something of a high spot in the history of irony. Speaking of irony, it is a cliché of British journalism that Americans have no sense of irony. I have never bought into

ERIC IDLE

this British myth, and wonder how it arose. Does it go back to Dickens, who was very bitter after his tour of America? Is it something Oscar Wilde said? He was, after all, superbly ironic. Indeed his whole life was irony. Whatever the truth about American irony in the nineteenth century, and surely you can't ignore Mark Twain, it seems to me that a country that has produced Lenny Bruce, Nichols and May, Gary Shandling, Larry David, Steve Martin, Chevy Chase, and Jack Benny, all masters of the form, can hardly be accused of lacking irony. Perhaps the Brits are just being ironic?

P eter Crabbe, in an e-mail rant he expects me to post on PythOnline, raises the bathroom issue. Let me broach this sensitive subject in Peter's own ranting words.

"Look, do you really want to know what's going on here? The bottom line: We have two 1.3-million-dollar tour buses with digital TVs, huge showers, kitchens, PlayStations, master bedroom suites, and two toilets—yes, we have TWO bathrooms on each bus—and yet we aren't allowed to take a shit in any of them! Four thrones—no sitting! Oh, we can pick up groupies of the foulest nature imaginable and have them perform the sickest, most twisted things that would make Cirque du Soleil performers wince,[6] but basic human functions on the bus? Not on this tour, mate! No, not on these million-dollar buses. What? Do we need to get the 1.8-million-dollar buses for the bowel movement package?"[7]

Well, he has a point. We were asked at the beginning of the tour to avoid number twos on the road. I was going to address this issue in a slightly more circumspect way than a Crabbe rant, but I think it best he gets his bile out in some form. Ordi-

---

[6] Dream on, baby.

[7] Actually, yes. They have a "grinder." I don't propose going into explanations. . . .

narily it's not a problem, as we have hotel rooms and theaters to take care of our needs, but now, as we are living on the bus, it is an issue. Skip, our tour manager, explains that while the waste disposal system on these buses would be adequate for one or two people living in the master bedroom, six adults producing poop makes the whole thing smell, well, like a toilet. It is basically an airplane system, but one that does not dispose of the waste outside in the form of blue ice. (Wait, I thought that was a myth?) We can indeed use the toilets for poopery (which my spell-check just autocorrected to *popery*) but we would have to stop immediately and evacuate the tank onto the roadside. I'm not sure the good citizens of the U.S. and Canada ought to be exposed to this. Bad enough they have to watch our shit onstage.

Last night's second show in Toronto was another smash. The audience was with us from the start, singing along and cheering happily. I felt really tired going in and was worried I had been interviewed-out, but the moment I felt the enthusiasm of the audience, I perked right up. It is a strange drug and no mistake, this support and comfort of strangers, and it really lifts you as powerfully as a jolt of caffeine. I wonder if there is some survival use in it, the approbation of the tribe in moments of stress? I can understand the necessity of encouraging great performances under arduous conditions, in hunting or in warfare, but in comedy? Nah. Perhaps people just like comedy. But people just like sex, and there is an obvious benefit for DNA to encourage them in all that messy business. Is comedy connected to sex? It always makes me laugh. . . .

Whatever the reason, the encouragement of the audience was highly effective. Toronto was our best

Why do gays want to get married, by the way? Are they tired of sex?

ERIC IDLE

reaction so far. Richard of York, my entertaining old codger of a publicist, said that while the previous night was a ten, this night was a nine and a half. The bastard. I thought he was going to say ten and a half. He has a dry wit and no mistake, and sends me e-mails with pithy quotes from obscure Lancashire comedians like this from Manchester poet Les Barker: "Always borrow from pessimists: they don't expect it back."

I feel relieved that we have finally nailed the show and can now play it anywhere with confidence.

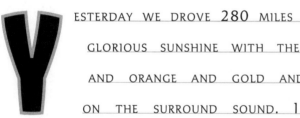

CASINO DU LAC-LEAMY, GATINEAU, QUEBEC

YESTERDAY WE DROVE 280 MILES TO OTTAWA THROUGH GLORIOUS SUNSHINE WITH THE LEAVES TURNING RED AND ORANGE AND GOLD AND BEETHOVEN PLAYING ON THE SURROUND SOUND. I FELT THE PASTORAL Symphony was an appropriate choice. Or as the sex therapist once described it: the Past Oral Symphony. At a gas station while reloading the Greedy Bastard buses we all piled out and took photos. It's Thanksgiving weekend in Canada, and the roads are packed. We are going up to Gatineau to play the Casino du Lac-Leamy. A French casino. A first for me.

Ottawa is a glorious city situated at the confluence of the Rideau and Ottawa rivers. The latter separates Quebec from Ontario and, more important, the French from the English; and, like so many other things, it sounds better in French: la Rivière des Outaouais. This magnificent old city of massive gray stone, castellated buildings with elaborately carved Norman windows, capped by steeply angled roofs of green copper, is filled with

**ERIC
IDLE**

fountains and squares, markets and malls, and a big, broad river spanned by many bridges. It feels more like Europe than North America. This morning the view from my gabled windows in the Château Laurier hotel is breathtaking. In the faint, pinkish blush of dawn, a perfect pale hunter's moon hangs over the stately river; three huge plumes of steam from a power station on the far shore fill the middle distance with haze; the bright oranges and reds of the turning leaves bisect the powdery greens of the trees, giving a tinted picture-postcard look to the entire scene. As if on cue, the rising sun lights up the waterfront, adding highlights and reflections while the moon fades gently into the morning.

Everywhere this city is draped in the improbable red-and-white maple leaf flag of Canada. Canada itself is improbable. The only other collaboration between the French and English (apart from the Hundred Years War) was Concorde. Mercifully, they have soccer here, which is what Americans call football. We like to call it football because, unlike American football, it is played with the *feet*. We go to an English pub to watch England play Turkey, an important European football qualifier that promises to produce high anxiety. Thank heaven they had toilets.

The basement of the Duke of Somerset pub was rapidly filling up as game time approached. The England supporters were out in force and in great voice.

"You're shit, and you know it," they sing loudly at the Turks on the screen thousands of miles away in Turkey. It is an extremely tense game, a needle match, and the winner qualifies automatically for the European finals next year. A draw (tie) will put England through in first place. A loss will result in a potentially nasty play-off. England have a very strong team and play magnificently. They are all over the Turks for the first twenty minutes, until they finally wake up and remember it's their pitch. Then they look menacing, but wait, the fabulous Steven Gerard dances into the box and is blatantly tripped. Penalty. Got to be one–nil to England as David Beckham steps up. But what's this? The goalkeeper dives the wrong way, Becks slips on the wet grass, and the ball is skied sixty feet over the bar. A most unusual sight.

"Blow it like Beckham," says Peter.

The Turkish players rush over and taunt Beckham as he lies on the ground, yelling in his face. This is not cricket. It is not even soccer and the nastiness continues into the tunnel at halftime, where a mini riot breaks out. Later on the Red Sox and the Yankees re-create this incident, but thoughtfully remain on camera so we can all enjoy it.

There is tension as the two teams return to the pitch and Pierluigi Collina, the huge, bald Italian referee, is everywhere, his determination to leave this thing at nil–nil to avoid a riot becoming increasingly evident. In the last quarter England are content to soak up the pressure, and you get the feeling that the Turks have lost heart. They have never scored against England and this magic spell seems to dominate their thinking. The final seconds tick away agonizingly, and suddenly it's over, and England are through. The pub erupts like a volcano. The crowd, many in England shirts, begin jumping up and down and singing *"Always look on the bright side of life— duh-duh, duh-duh, duh-duh, duh-duh, duh-duh."* Normally I hide at moments like this, but, dammit, England have just qualified in first place over the wily Turks and I rush forward to the singing crowd and give them high fives. Even a few Turkish supporters come over and shake my hand. Now the pub starts

ERIC IDLE

to sing "One Eric Idle, there's only one Eric Idle" and after a chorus of this ego-boosting massage the only thing I can do is announce there are TWO Eric Idles, though one is called Michael Palin. Then, blow me, if they don't start singing "Philosophers Song": *"Immanuel Kant was a real pissant . . ."*

Time to leave, or Peter and I should just stay and do the show right here.

The bus drivers say the difference between the French and the English sides of the city is that on the French side the lap dancers don't wear panties. Good to know these things. The Casino du Lac-Leamy is on the French side, though I still wear panties. It was a good show, though I was rotten, well at least until act two. I couldn't focus, perhaps due to the large amounts of steroids my doctor is cramming into me to try and reduce the foot pain. If this is what it does to *my* brain, God help California under Arnold. I was all over the place. I managed to skip an entire sketch in act two, but my cast are very bright and wonderfully alert people, and they segued right along as if nothing had happened. They did this so efficiently, even I didn't notice.

DAY 13

CENTENNIAL HALL, LONDON, ONTARIO

A SLIGHT SPRINKLING OF RAIN. IT'S THAT INTERMITTENT, TINKLY KIND OF ENGLISH RAIN LIKE FINGERS DRUMMING LIGHTLY ON THE ROOF OF THE BUS. IT'S SIX IN THE MORNING AND I'VE ALREADY BEEN UP AN HOUR: THE curse of the early riser. I slip between the heavily curtained sleepers in their bunks to make myself a cup of tea, disturbing English, our driver, who is crashed out on the sofa. We have rattled through the night and are parked in a very odd neighborhood. To our right are what seem to be crack houses, once very beautiful old homes, bright yellow brick Victorians that are now all boarded up. Black squirrels run about the lawn and gray doves sit on the scalloped roofs moaning softly. We are very close to the loading bay of Centennial Hall, our gig for tonight, and here we must sit for fourteen hours until it's time to do the show. Should be a good day for Dickens. I am rereading *Hard Times* and very much enjoying it. Dickens is so funny. I think I have spotted a direct antecedent of the Four Yorkshiremen sketch:

*"We used to dream of living in a corridor! Would have
been a palace to us! We had to go and live in a lake!"*

*"You were lucky to live in a lake! There were a hundred and fifty of us living in a shoebox in the middle of
the road!"*

"A cardboard *box?"*

"Aye!"

"You were lucky!"

I always understood that Marty Feldman got the idea for
this sketch from a Stephen Leacock piece, in which case Leacock must have got it from Dickens.

*"Cold? I was born with inflammation of the lungs, and
of everything else, I believe, that was capable of inflammation," returned Mr. Bounderby. "For years,
ma'am, I was one of the most miserable little wretches
ever seen. I was so sickly, that I was always moaning
and groaning. I was so ragged and dirty, that you
wouldn't have touched me with a pair of tongs. . . .*

*"My mother left me to my grandmother," said
Bounderby; "and, according to the best of my remembrance, my grandmother was the wickedest and the
worst old woman that ever lived. If I got a little pair of
shoes by any chance, she would take 'em off and sell
'em for drink. Why, I have known that grandmother
of mine lie in her bed and drink her four-teen glasses
of liquor before breakfast! . . .*

*"She kept a chandler's shop," pursued Bounderby,
"and kept me in an egg-box. That was the cot of* my
infancy; an old egg-box."

Luxury! We used to *dream* of living in an egg box.

DAY 14

MONTREAL

T'S TRUE, I DO LIKE THE FRENCH. I LIKE THEIR FRENCHNESS. I LIKE THEIR LANGUAGE; I LIKE THEIR STYLE; I LIKE THE WAY THEY HAVE OF LIVING THEIR lives through their senses, paying attention to the important things like food, clothing, sexuality, wine, and even movies. Everything is about enjoying life and that applies to all classes of French society, not just the wealthy bourgeoisie. By comparison the Anglo-Saxon obsession with duty and the endless American pursuit of money are simply second-rate ways of being. I live from time to time in Provence (someone has to do it), and there are times when I really miss it, and today is one of those. I am having huge *nostalgie*. I can smell the lavender, hear the buzzing of the bees and the chirping of the cicadas and the clicking of the *boules* in the square.

I like the French. Someone should be doing the job of the Democrats.

ERIC IDLE

Jen and I escape for lunch at the magnificent café L'Express on the Boulevard St-Denis. It is perfectly French, from the paper tablecloths on the small square tables to the handwritten menu in its glossy wrapper with its huge list of wines. The food is delicious, freshly cooked, and excellently served, and we succumb to the temptations of dessert: a fine almond chocolate thing for her and an unhealthy but delicious orange crème caramel for me. Tomorrow we are back in the land of the Big Mac. The people at the next table are drinking Sancerre, and that always reminds me of Michael Palin. We used to drink buckets of it and swap cases as presents back in the days when I was a trainee alcoholic. Sadly I never qualified. Who could rival Graham? Now my inebriated days are over and I sip unhealthy diet colas in hope of a minor caffeine buzz. I wonder where Mike is now? Probably halfway up a Nepalese mountain wishing he was on my tour.

Commander Palin's Diary

Mount Everest. Sunday. Sherpa Biggles says he can get me to 2nd Base. But sadly he doesn't seem to have tits. Wish I was on Eric's tour having to have lunch with cute blond actresses in French restaurants in Montreal.

Jen and I discover a treasure trove of tiny bijoux shops and manage to cram in some shopping before limping lamely back to the theater. Last time I appeared at the Théâtre St-Denis was in the Just for Laughs Festival in the summer of 2000, when I hosted one of their galas. The magnificent Terry Jones joined me onstage and we did Nudge Nudge together for the first time since 1847. The show was great fun and at the end I was whisked away by limo to a deserted private airfield, where a tiny light in the sky landed and picked me up. It was Robin Williams, celebrating his birthday, and together we flew to Paris for the final day of the Tour de France, to watch his pal Lance Armstrong ride in to the Champs-Elysées for his second consecutive victory. The sun was shining, and the tree-lined boulevard was filled eight-deep with fifty thousand Frenchmen on their bleachers, and Paris was at its most glorious. Blue skies, tiny streets, big wide Napoleon III boulevards. Ah, oui, ça c'est la vie. On the last day of the Tour the riders, who have just cycled three thousand kilometers around France in three weeks, ride proudly into the center of Paris, sipping Champagne and waving to the crowd. One of the U.S. Postal team even wore a woman's wig. They complete the race by circling the Champs-Elysées eight times on a two-mile course that takes them in front of the Louvre.

▽

Michael J. Fox, a very sweet and brave man, was there with his family. Robin of course was being irrepressibly hilarious, among a bunch of Lance fans from Texas, including the mayor of Austin and some representatives of the Lance Armstrong Foundation. We were having a blast enjoying the sunshine and the occasion, knowing that the race was over and Lance, ahead by six minutes, had effectively won.

▽

Robin and I were interviewed by OLN, the Outdoor Life Network (which should really be called the Outdoor Death Network, since most of their programs seem to be about killing as many living creatures as possible). We say we are not interested in who has won the yellow jersey, we are concerned about the *pink* jersey, awarded to the cyclist with the cutest butt . . . and, well, you know Robin, half an hour later we are still demonstrating effete pedal pushing . . . swish, swish.

ERIC IDLE

The tour is down to its last two laps when we are invited to ride in one of the lead cars. We climb over the barriers and jump into a small red Renault, which pulls out onto the Champs-Elysées. Now we are on the course! We drive slowly up the cobblestones toward the Arc de Triomphe, the vast crowd on either side of us chattering and listening to their portable radios, awaiting the arrival of the *peloton*—that's about a hundred and fifty cyclists pedaling in unison—and as I look behind me I see the bright headlights of the gendarmes, heralding the approach of the race.

"Erm," I say to the driver, "you'd better watch it. I think they are coming."

The driver gives a Gallic shrug of immense proportions. I am clearly an English idiot who knows nothing, so we sit by the side of the road as this huge flotilla rapidly advances on us. I am getting very anxious now. We are definitely in the way. Suddenly the blue cars of the gendarmes flash past and there, quite clearly, is the big wide line of cyclists approaching like a cavalry charge. At the very last moment our driver guns the car and we pull out *directly in front of them!* Oh my God. The riders are fifteen feet away. We can practically touch them. We are leading the riders around the final stage of the Tour de France! Normally, this privilege is reserved for French presidents. The television cameramen, standing up on their motorbikes, grin at us and laugh at our astonishment. This is unbelievable. We are all yelling out in excitement as we belt up the Champs-Elysées, around the Arc de Triomphe and back down the big wide boulevard, pursued by a bunch of brightly colored cyclists. A squealing tire noise as we slide round a big wide bend, past the enormous Ferris wheel, and then a stomach-lurching dive into a sudden underpass. Behind us we watch the breathtaking sight of a hundred and fifty peddlers streaming downhill after us.

"It's like a dream," says Michael, "a dream where you are being pursued by a hundred bikes."

Now, as we come sprinting past Hôtel de Crillon we clearly hear the bell for the last lap. No time to stop now, we are going to be on the final lap of the Tour de France. We are so close that on TV you can see us in the same shot as the leaders! They are on their final sprint, and our driver has to accelerate sharply to prevent them running into us. This is the most exhilarating thing in the world. We are kneeling backward on our seats, looking through the rear window of the Renault, cheering, yelling, and screaming at the top of our lungs. We are like three kids in our unabashed joy at this unbelievable ride. Now, two leaders have broken from the pack and are dueling it out behind us, their bikes shifting furiously from side to side as they stand up on their pedals. They angle dangerously around the corners, skim the curbs, and slide perilously over the cobblestones, racing for the finish. It's the final stretch and we lead the entire Tour under the finishing line and then pull in. There is a pause. We are all utterly shocked, our minds completely blown by what we have just experienced. Then Michael says, "Well, we'll always have Paris!"

DAY 15

MONTREAL TO BURLINGTON, VERMONT

AFTER THE MONTREAL SHOW WE DROVE OVERNIGHT BACK INTO THE STATES. THE MONTREALIANS (THE MONTRALEEZE? THE MONTRESQUES?) WERE A GREAT AUDIENCE. JEN SAYS IT'S THE BEST SHOW I'VE DONE. THE Greedy Bastard Tour organizers have moved us here to Burlington for a day off instead of leaving us to enjoy some respite in Montreal. There was no time to sleep on the bus till Vermont, so I broke out my little Taylor guitar and thumbed through some old favorites in a fake standards book. It was like camp with Jen and Gilli singing along lustily. Even Skip joined in, though bitching that it was not in his key and he doesn't know these songs. Well hello, if you tour with the Sex Pistols, what chance do you have to get to know real Broadway songs?

"Where are the homosexuals when you need them?" I asked, as we broke down for the third time on a chorus.

Two great shows in a row. Last night Montreal and the night before we kicked ass in London, Ontario. I was determined not to lose two in a row and I tried extra hard to be on my guard against the steroids coursing

through my manly body on their way to my Achilles' heel. I beefed up with some weight training, a shower, and a hot cup of tea, which is three out of four for maximum happiness. (Do I need to spell it out?) I was pumped and ready, and I'm glad to say that London took off like a rocket and we never let them go till we had them out of their seats screaming and stomping for more. God bless 'em. There was a nice cover story in London's entertainment paper *Scene* that says the Nudge Nudge sketch is "a classic, right up there with Abbott and Costello's Who's on First," which is praise indeed.

The Radisson Hotel Burlington is a bit of a comedown after the Château Laurier in Ottawa, even though I am in their best suite: the Ethan Allen suite. I thought that was a furniture shop, but no, he is apparently a local Vermont hero who saved the state from becoming part of New York. The walls are paper thin, and I can hear the couple next door bickering. The Ethan Allen suite has a great view of the car park, but as I am leaving for the elevators I see, through a picture window, an unbelievable view of a wide blue lake with flags snapping in the wind and sailboats tugging at their moorings. Across the choppy water lie long lines of pale orange hills. This glorious sight is Lake Champlain, a mini–Great Lake. So *this* is Vermont. What a glorious day. There is fresh air out there, and fabulous views and adventures to be had, and I am to be stuck inside all day talking about Monty Python. In the cafeteria I can feel Mister Grumpy settle in beside me. Muzak pollutes the air. Secondary music is really bad for you. It's worse than smoking. At least smoking doesn't stop your thinking, but Muzak makes me resentful and gloomy. I stare at the tiny tin jug of warm water and the tea bag that is offered as a tea experience and I feel Mister Grumpy getting nearer.

"We could have been in Montreal," he says, "smelling the fresh bakery smells and watching the endlessly fascinating French girls going about their bijoux shopping. But no, we are stuck in a cafeteria listening to someone whine on about how they've got a friend." Not in here they haven't.

▽

When I was writing *The Road to Mars,*[8] I became interested in wondering what exactly *is* comedy? Is it something unique to our species, or would we expect any other intelligent life-form to have a sense of humor? (*The Search for Intelligent Laugh in the Universe*?) Does comedy have evolutional value? Did it help us evolve? These are interesting questions because they are close to what being human is. Personally, I think comedy *is* a survival tool. Comedians tell the truth through a sense of moral outrage. They're the first to point out that the elephant is in the room, that the emperor has no clothes. They say the right things at the wrong times. Laughter is a recognition of the accuracy of their observations. This bottom-lining is invaluable for our survival, for unless we learn to interpret what is really going on in the world we cannot avoid danger; we will always be trapped by rhetoric.

▽

Comedians are not normal people. It is not a normal thing to do. You don't become a comedian without some early traumatizing experience, so comedy is also a coping mechanism. People make jokes when they are in peril, or at heartbreaking moments such as funerals. It happened to us at the memorial service for Graham Chapman. It was a very solemn and sad event, and then John Cleese started it.

"Graham Chapman is no more. He has ceased to be. He has rung down the curtain and joined the choir invisible. He is an ex-Python. And I say good riddance to him, the free-loading bastard."

---

[8] 1999 novel. Part sci-fi thriller, part mock-thesis on comedy.

John didn't stop there. He went on to be more and more outrageous.

"In conclusion, I would like to be the first to say 'fuck' at a memorial service."

The reaction was uproarious as he became funnier and funnier, and in the end the spirit of Graham was released, and we all felt liberated. Yes of course everyone was sad and in tears, but we were laughing. After that, the hardest thing I ever had to do was sing "Always Look on the Bright Side of Life." For a moment trying to sing it was just terrible for me, because music makes you weep, while comedy makes you weep *and* laugh, but because of all the earlier laughter I got through it.

> *Always look on the bright side of death*
> *Just before you draw your terminal breath.*
> *Life's a piece of shit*
> *When you look at it.*

DAY 16

DAY OFF, BURLINGTON

THE RADISSON HAS MOVED ME OUT OF ETHAN ALLEN'S BEDROOM INTO A BUSINESS-CLASS ROOM THAT OVERLOOKS LAKE CHAMPLAIN, SO I NOW HAVE A SPECTACULAR BUSINESS-CLASS VIEW. I CONTEMPLATE asking for a lower-middle-class room with a view but settle for this neat box with its huge picture window. I am gazing due south over Lake Champlain. It looks very cold. Seagulls flap about, fishing. Fingers of light shift spectacularly through the clouds, illuminating the bright white of the sailboats as they race about the bay. Across the water lie low, bumpy hills in orange and green plaid. Here and there tiny islands sprout masts of sailboats against the skimming clouds. A sleek, low ferry hoots mournfully and slides away from the dock, its fresh white-and-blue trim glistening in the low-angled sunlight. Long lines of stone breakwaters bisect the dark gray of the waves. The sun lights the islands, dusting the tips of the trees with gold and brightening the far shore. You can see the whitecaps as the wind whips everything to the right across my view. Beneath

me, the low line of the breakwater is buffeted by big waves, sending plumes of spray barreling over from the power of the driving wind. The yellow trees are thinning rapidly as the wind carries away the dying leaves. The low hills slip in and out of silhouette, sometimes appearing as dark blobs starkly outlined, sometimes gray mounds veiled with rain. The mountain disappears and is replaced by a great burst of light. The hills appear like humpback whales and then disappear again. Now the water is dark, now light. All the time I'm nattering away about Monty Python and why I'm a greedy bastard. One minute I'm in Edmonton, now I'm in Calgary, now downtown L.A.

The weather has changed since yesterday. It was very stormy and blowy last night, the wind hurrying directly off the water, sweeping down from the Adirondacks and shaking the hotel. Provincetown was hit by very bad weather, which serves them right, since their promoter pulled out of our gig. It's time to pull the woolies out. It looks and feels like Scotland with the low, flat islands in the lake and the lowering clouds pushing fast across the slate gray water. Small beads of rain pepper the window, collect, and then trickle swiftly down. I sit and gaze at the view for hours while being grilled by journalists on the phone. In case you think I am a totally spoiled bastard, let me show you what a day off looks like:

Wednesday, Day Off

Schedule	Activity	Notes
8:30 AM	P	Eric is to call Kevin and Pete. This is to support the Poughkeepsie show.
station: WPDH		
DJs: Kevin Karlson & Pete McKenzie		Wake up live on the radio.
9:40 AM EST	P	Eric is to call Tom. Interview is live. Last time through the market the interview helped ticket sales dramatically.

ERIC IDLE

Schedule	Activity	Notes
station: KQRS interviewer: Tom Barnard		Let's hope it works this time, Tom, the greedy bastards are tracking you . . .
1:00 PM	P	Eric is to call Bob and Brian. This is to support the Poughkeepsie show. Station leans 60/40 women, 25 and up.
station: WCZX Mix 97 DJs: Bob Miller & Brian Jones		This one was canceled. Which is sad because I too lean to women of 25 and up.
1:15 PM EST station: Clear Channel interviewer: Jay Wulff	R	Eric is to call Jay. Stations that will use the interview: WRKW-FM, WKIP-AM, WELV-AM, and WRNQ-FM.
1:30 PM publication: *Edmonton Journal* (major daily) interviewer: Todd Babiak	P	Eric is to call Todd. This is to support the Edmonton show.
1:45 PM publication: *Edmonton Sun* (major daily) interviewer: Mike Ross	P	Eric is to call Mike. This is to support the Edmonton show.
2:00 PM station: JACK FM station contact: Matt O'Neill	P	Eric is to call Matt. This is the presenting station, #1 in the market. This is to support the Calgary show.
2:15 PM station: 96X (FM radio) DJs: BJ & Shannon	P	Eric is to call BJ and Shannon. Ask for Mike McKenn's studio when placing the call. Live to tape for morning show.
2:30 PM publication: *Calgary Sun* (major daily) interviewer: Lisa Wilton	P	Eric is to call Lisa. This is to support the Calgary show.
2:45 PM publication: *Fast Forward Magazine* (weekly magazine) interviewer: Martin Morrow	P	Eric is to call Martin.
3:00 PM publication: *Gauntlet* (university paper) interviewer: Jeff Kubik	P	Eric is to call Jeff. This is to support the Calgary show.

Schedule	Activity	Notes
3:15 PM station: CBC Radio interviewer: Bill Roach	P	Eric is to call Bill Roach.
3:30 PM EST station: Mundo LA/La Guia Familiar interviewer: Gabriel	P	Eric is to call Gabriel. This is to support the L.A. show. Gabriel is an Argentinean Monty Python fan.
3:45 PM EST station: IGN FilmForce interviewer: Ken Plume	P	Eric is to call Ken. Feature piece—Web site receives approx. 400k unique visitors per day. Interview will be 30 minutes.

You can see why most people in showbiz are mad. They spend their lives doing interviews and promos every day. It's enough to drive anyone mad. Being interviewed is anti-therapy: all questions and no answers. It's just not healthy for a human being. Add a posse blowing smoke up their ass all day, managers and agents on the gravy train telling them how marvelous they are, doctors offering them surgery to become flawless, photographers flashing pictures, and the public fawning over everything they say, well, you're breeding monsters, aren't you? No wonder we like to see them in trouble in the tabloids. I have thought of trying to leak my own sex life to the tabloids to gain a little publicity, but I think MAN WATCHES TELEVISION is just not going to fly.

After the endless hours of interviews, I took an autumn in Vermont tour with John, my musical partner. We drove around for a couple of hours, looking at the spectacular foliage, the russets and oranges and spectacular bloody reds of the maples. We visited Ethan Allen's shack (he wasn't in), the university campus (apparently the biggest party school in the States), and saw the local sights, chauffeured by Tim, an ex-

ERIC IDLE

deejay from New York who grumbled mildly about the current state of radio. He dropped us at the waterfront at a delectable eatery, where John and I have the high-cholesterol diet of oysters and sweet Maine lobster. The food at Shanty on the Shore is excellent, and the young people who serve it are very friendly; the only criticism I have is that the bathrooms are labeled "Sailors" and "Mermaids," which is a bit twee for me. *Do mermaids go to the bathroom? Don't they just pee in the sea?* Most women I know pee in the sea anyway, and they aren't even half fish. I suppose if you are looking for a bit of tail you can't do better than a mermaid. What's that old gag? "My girlfriend is a mermaid: her figures are 36, 24, and five dollars a pound."

Always remember the words of W. C. Fields: "I never drink water because of the disgusting things fish do in it." I took a risk and visited the Sailors room, a little anxiously, as we all know what sailors get up to in the bathroom. I should know, since I once wrote a very rude novel called *Hello, Sailor*. But it's a great restaurant, and we're going again tonight.

DAY 17

THE FLYNN CENTER, BURLINGTON

A POSTCARD FROM PALIN! HE IS NOT IN THE HIMALAYAS SWATHED IN FURS STRUGGLING UP BEN MCFOREIGN (A SCOTTISH CLIMBER); BUT SWEATING IN AMRITSAR, INDIA, AT THE GOLDEN TEMPLE. HE SAYS IT AIN'T HALF hot in Punjab, but he is not sweating as much as Basil Pao, who has seventeen cameras to haul. ("Don't ask me why," adds Mike.) Basil is from Hong Kong and follows Mike all over the world taking his photo for the calendars and books that are the real money behind these tours. You think *I'm* the only greedy bastard? You haven't heard the half of it. Wait till I get on to the tall one,[9] whose love for the odd nickel leads him to be constantly yearning for a hammock, an island, and a book, but who we all know will never make it. He has been saying this since 1968, but he works so hard, he'll never stop. In fact he is in so many movies with "two" on them that we

---

[9] I believe the Greedy Bastard is referring to the elegant, hilarious, and unquestionably funny John Cleese. It's glib bits of ribbing like this that gets the GB in such trouble with the U.K. press, who, ironically, seem to miss the irony.

ERIC IDLE

have labeled him *The First Among Sequels*. John once told me he would do anything for money, so I offered him a pound to shut up, and he took it.

▽

Michael writes to tell me he was thinking of me when he learned of the death of Peter West, a quirky BBC commentator I used to impersonate. Can you be so far behind when your subjects start to kick? By an odd coincidence the postcard is dated September 29—the very day I set out on my voyage and wrote my first diary entry. So that's weird and synchronistic, isn't it? I guess Mike and I are interchangeable after all. I miss his comic writing. He wrote some of my favorite Python bits. "Not to leave the room until I tell you" in *The Holy Grail* is my particular favorite, that and the hilarious jailor scene in *Brian*.

> *"Crucifixion? Good. Out the door, line on the left, one cross each. Next—crucifixion?"*
>
> *"Ah no, freedom."*
>
> *"Hmm?"*
>
> *"Ah, freedom for me. They said I hadn't done anything, so I could go free and live on an island somewhere."*
>
> *"Oh, jolly good. Well, off you go then."*
>
> *"Nah, I'm only pulling your leg. It's crucifixion, really."*

The brilliance of Michael Palin. I do hope he's being mistaken for me in Amritsar. Thinking of *The Life of Brian* reminds me of Graham's brave full-frontal-nudity shot on that long-ago day in Tunisia. Graham had to open a window stark naked to find an enormous crowd outside shouting "Look! There he is!

The Chosen One has awoken!" We had just started to film the scene, and Graham flung open the window and the crowd went "Look!" when Terry Jones yelled, "Cut!"

"Er, Graham," he said, "I'm afraid that we can see that you're not Jewish."

"Props!" yelled Michael.

With no moyl in sight, a small rubber band was procured, et voilà, an impromptu circumcision; the scene could continue. Graham flung open the window again, but this time, big problem: the crowd had run away. This was Tunisia, an Arab country, fairly liberal by Arab standards, but most of the women have never seen bare-assed British men, nor are they allowed to, and Graham's appearance caused consternation and then pandemonium as the women were dragged away. To be fair, most were laughing hysterically, but the scene could not continue until religious rules were satisfied. The men could be part of the crowd, but the women could only be present for the reverse shots without the full frontal nudity.

Interestingly, since Graham's demise, I am now the second tallest Python, but Graham, at forty-eight, has become the youngest. The former youngest, Mike Palin, is now over sixty, and John, well, I realize with a shock that he'll be sixty-four in a few days' time. No wonder we're getting to be such cranky old bastards.

I got a parcel from home. Das Boot is here. I can now limp around more comfortably in my surgical boot, though I'm afraid interpretive dance is out. In-

I'm a limey bastard as you can tell. I'm married to an American. I like to think I've been invading America for almost thirty years. In fact, I've trained my wife to yell out "The British are coming, the British are coming."

ERIC IDLE

side the package are the sweetest notes, cards, and gifts from my daughter, Lily. She is missing me. I feel bad. I know a thing or two about abandonment issues. It's tough to have an absentee father. I wish I'd blown all the publicity they lined up and flown home to see her. I kick myself for not doing this; my ridiculous English-boarding-school sense of duty again. Lily and I chatter away on the phone, but it's not the same as having a dad around. Her basketball team is on a winning streak, and she wishes I could see her. Me, too. Guiltily I pillage the gift shop for souvenirs and send her a package.

We do another really good show at the Flynn Center, Burlington. They are a very noisy and appreciative crowd, and we get 'em up on their feet yelling for more. The encore bucket was in almost constant use, people coming up throughout the evening whenever a favorite piece played, walking shyly or brazenly up to the front and dropping in dollars, particularly during the songs. ("Public panhandling," Jen called it!) At the end I was shocked to find more than eighty dollars in there. Wow, what a difference from Canada. And real money, too, none of those Canadian tire dollars.

I have relaxed into act one and now feel comfortable doing stand-up. I am still learning, but it is fun talking directly to the audience. I am looser and trust my instincts and follow my own thoughts. I can stop my spiel and point out strange people from the audience. Last night I brought onstage a man wearing enormous antlers with a British flag wedged between the horns and "The Duke of Rutland" painted on the ivory. Quite a sight. Almost the entire audience stayed to have something signed. The line in the lobby was huge when I came hobbling in. You could tell it was a college town, as copies of *The Road to Mars* were flying off the piles. Tom, our powerfully built merch guy, was doing roaring business. One young man came up to me at the table and said, "Baweep, granaweep, ninabong!"

I stared at him blankly.

"Surely you remember *Transformers*," he prompted.

And then it came back to me in all its horror. It was a Japanese animated movie, and they offered me tons of money to fly from London to New York on Concorde to record my voice. But nothing is ever for nothing. They tortured me for days recording this one damn line. I was even called back for another session in London, because they weren't satisfied.

"No," they'd say through the control booth window, "Baweep, *granaweep*, ninabong!"

I'd try it again. And again. And again. I tried it in every single way I could think.

"Baweep, granaweep, ninabong!"

"You're still not getting the sense of it."

I tried it in every single accent I knew—Scots, Midlands, Norwegian, French, German, Spanish, Tongan—but they were never satisfied.

"Try it again," they would say. "This is a key plot line, so emphasize the *ninabong*."

I hadn't a clue what they were talking about.

"Do another eight," they'd say. "This time, make it *funny*."

What?? I tried, believe me, I tried everything I know, but I could never manage to make any sense out of that damn sentence. Still, I am in a movie with Orson Welles.

We say farewell to our stowaway. Jennifer Usher has come along for the ride since Rutland. A fine, young blond woman, she decided that she had had enough of her life and would hit the road with us for ten days. I guess living on a bus

ERIC IDLE

with a bunch of chaps will make your own life seem better in no time, but we have all been spoiled rotten by having her along, as our wardrobe is freshly cleaned and pressed nightly, and she is always waiting in the quick-change booth with socks prerolled and brown shorts waiting to fling on me for my swift change into the Bruces' costume. Oh, by the way, can you believe this: She did it all for nothing! So a huge thank-you, Jennifer. Greater love can no man inspire than that a young woman stands in the dark handing him his socks.

DAY 18

BARDAVON OPERA HOUSE, POUGHKEEPSIE, NEW YORK

 WAKE UP IN A CAR PARK IN POUGHKEEPSIE. THE DICE HAVE BEEN GIVEN ANOTHER ROLL, AND WE HAVE LANDED IN UPSTATE NEW YORK. TOMORROW NEW HAVEN, AND THEN ON TO BOSTON. I'M SITTING UP IN my bed in the car park with pale autumnal sunshine lighting a wan sky. The darkly veined acacia trees have almost lost their yellow leaves. One or two early risers are taking constitutionals. A lady in blue jeans with the face of Helen Mirren gets out of a gray Nissan. She smiles at her husband as she zips her coat against the chill. A dark-haired man in a leather jacket—who looks like he slept there all night—gets out of a small black car and brushes his hair with his hands. He lights a cigarette and heads off. A man with heavy eyelids, big cheeks, and soft protruding lips is taking a walk swathed in big old headphones. He has the face of James Baldwin. I once came face-to-face with that unforgettable face in the streets of St.-Paul-de-Vence, and his huge, intelligent eyes seemed to stare right through me—almost as re-markable a shock as seeing Salvador Dalí in the streets of New York. I re-member getting very excited when Graham Greene boarded my flight from

ERIC IDLE

London to Nice. I immediately wrote a postcard to Michael, saying "I am flying with Graham Greene." I have been happy to see quite a bit of Salman Rushdie. He is very funny in my Rutles sequel *Can't Buy Me Lunch* (still unavailable from Warner Television). When I was an undergraduate at Cambridge in the sixties, someone pointed out a very old man, bent over a walking cane, emerging from Kings College.

"That's E. M. Forster," they said.

Impossible: surely he has been dead for years? His last novel was published in 1926. But it *was* the great man himself. Even the famous are not averse to bathing in the company of the famous. Stephen Spender once told me frankly he preferred the famous: "They are more interesting," he explained. These were the days when I would have dinner with Gerry Durrell in his brother Lawrence's house near Nîmes, in Provence. (I might as well go all out if I am literary name-dropping.) But we are all fascinated by the famous, aren't we?

I get the runner to show me a bit of Poughkeepsie en route to lunch at the River Station, a nice bright pubby place with a spectacular view of the Hudson. The trees haven't yet turned here, save for a few outrageous maples burning bright orange-red against the placid Hudson below the picture window of the restaurant. Thirty years ago Poughkeepsie literally burned their bridges when the giant railway bridge caught fire.

How does a bridge burn? I ask.

"Wooden," they replied.

There are pictures of it belching smoke on the walls of the restaurant. It still survives, its massive black box girders spanning the wide river, mirrored half a mile away by an elegant suspension bridge called the FDR. There are plans to open up a walkway across the blackened remnants of the burned-out bridge.

"Suicide leap?" I ask.

"Something like that," says the lady in the restaurant.

The Bardavon Opera House is like me: old, elegant, and beautifully restored. The hall is packed with history, from Mark Twain to Harry Houdini, to George Burns and Gracie Allen, to Frank Sinatra. It dates from 1869 and has a wooden dome hidden upstairs and a ghost called Roger. Apparently he is an old stage manager who wandered onto the stage in the wild west days and was shot by one of the customers. He is a friendly ghost, and has on one occasion saved the theater from fire by pointing out its location to the stage crew. I wonder why ghosts aren't more friendly? For example, why are ghosts never nude? Either they have a silly sheet on, or they are fully clothed, or they are skeletons. Why not a healthy nude lady ghost?

"And over here we have naked Sal, the very friendly gal. . . ."

Heidi the headless lap dancer would make a very popular haunt. But no, it's all rattle your chains and flounce about in sixteenth-century costume . . .

We record our madrigal to donate to a charity CD to raise money for the restoration of the theater.

> *There was a ship that put to sea*
> *All in the month of May*
> *With a fa la la la*
> *With a fa la la la*
> *With a fa la la la la lay*
> *In the month of May*
> *The merry month of May*
> *And the ship that put to sea*
> *In the month of May*
> *In the month of May*
> *Fa la la Fa la lay*
> *The ship that put to sea in the month of*
>   *May. . . sank!*[10]

---

[10] "Madrigal." Written 1965 by Eric Idle and John Cameron.

DAY 19

SHUBERT THEATER, NEW HAVEN, CONNECTICUT

I was on a remote island with him when a man came up and said "George Harrison, oh my God, what are you doing here?" And he said, "Well, everyone's got to be somewhere."

That's a lovely line, isn't it? It's like a line from *A Hard Day's Night*. It totally captures his sense of fun and reality. I miss him every day. From the stage, I encourage people nightly to go and see *The Concert for George*, which is just out in limited release. It is a wonderful memorial concert performed by his friends Eric Clapton, Paul McCartney, Ringo, Jeff Lynne, Tom Petty, Joe Baker, and his son, Dahni. It is marred only by an appearance by the old Monty Python boys, who come onstage at the Royal Albert Hall and sing "Sit on My Face." Then they show their ancient asses. . . . So avert your eyes. It is a ten-Kleenex movie, so be prepared for tears. They play only George's music and you won't believe just how many great songs he wrote.

THE GREEDY BASTARD DIARY

We once planned to tease John Cleese by letting him discover accidentally that the rest of us Pythons were secretly getting together to rehearse his memorial. Cruel, yes, but funny, isn't it? We could be quite cruel with one another. John once hid in Michael's hotel room while he prepared for bed. He stayed silently watching him for twenty minutes, with his head poked over the back of a chair. Only after half an hour did Michael finally notice him, and then nearly leaped out of his skin. We used to play a game while filming that if we were on a life raft in an extreme survival situation in what order would we eat one another? Graham was often the first suggestion, because of being such a lazy old bastard, but he always got a bye, as he was a doctor and would be helpful in cutting up a body. Also, he was a bit of a chef so we felt he might usefully curry bits of us. Invariably the second choice was John, since he was so large he would feed us for days without having to kill anyone else for a while. No wonder John would get so grumpy with us. In Canada, on our stage tour, he would often dine alone at the same restaurant, sitting at a separate table for one. You've got to admire that sort of eccentricity, haven't you? The only other person I ever saw dining alone quite so comfortably was Harold Pinter. Once, when all we Pythons were having a big, loud lunch, he sat alone at the next table. No book, no pretense at reading a newspaper; Pinter just stared at us through his big glasses as though we were some kind of recorded entertainment.

I wake up parked outside the Samurai Japanese

George once said to me, "If we'd known we were going to be the Beatles we'd have tried harder."

ERIC IDLE

Restaurant, just a block from Yale. Breezy coeds go by in search of falafels. I decide to try this dining alone thing, and over lunch I begin a series of epigrammatic Zen *pensées* in the Japanese manner. I'm thinking a cross between La Rochefoucault, Lord Chesterfield, and Abba:

> *The further one travels, the less one gets any-where.*
>
> *If you don't get on the bus, then you'll miss it.*
>
> *Life is like a journey. We don't know where we're going to, we don't know where we're coming from and we won't know if we arrive.*[9]
>
> [*Not much like a fucking journey then, is it?*—Ed.]

I think publishers will lap this up. I must get on to my greedy bastard agent and see if he can't whistle up a couple of million advance. [*Dream on.*—Ed.] I continue to apothegmize over the cold raw fish:

> *Women have emotions; men have sport.*
> *Home was not built in a day.*
> *There is no time like the pleasant.*

Great stuff, eh? All it needs is some snappy title like: *The Four Disagreements* or *The Five Stages of Unbeing* or *Six of One and Half a Dozen of the Other* or maybe *The Seven Things You Learn When You're Dead*. Over lunch I notice I seem to have discovered the Cleese joy of dining happily alone and its benefit: Nobody disagrees with you. Afterward I bump into Jen and we walk

It doesn't matter how nice you are. Nobody says they love Shakespeare because he was a nice man, do they? They don't say, "We love Mozart, what a nice guy." Nobody said Beethoven was such a nice man. Beethoven was a total shit!

You don't hear them say that on classical radio, do you? You don't hear the announcers say, "And now here's the Fifth Symphony by that total shit Beethoven."

around Yale. Some of the buildings are very old. One ancient brownstone proudly boasts the date 2003.

The audience for our show was loud and smart, though frankly cheap. The previous night our merch flew off the table; these tight bastards, *though we gave them the very same good time,* kept their wallets in their pockets. The extremely amusing Rutland Isles calendars, which have been handwritten and magnificently printed and make the perfect gift for people you never quite liked, remain in unwanted piles. The programs, so witty and filled with gems and such good value at only ten bucks, lie idle.

After the show, barreling down the Massachusetts Turnpike at three in the morning I realize we have now officially become a rock-and-roll tour. We are on rock-and-roll hours. John and I stand with smoking breath in the cold air at a truck stop, gazing at the moon, talking about the show. Everyone is happy with the way it's going. We just need to tighten a few cues. We'll work on it today at sound check.

The bus swallows up the miles as we head into Boston. I ride shotgun, up front with 'Lish, our bus driver. At 3:00 A.M. the streets of Chinatown are jumping. The bars have turned out, and the clubs are doing heavy business; lines of young people buzz like wasps around a diner. The lobby of our hotel looks like the end of the world: young couples are crashed out everywhere on the floor, waiting for transport. The girls look spectacular in semiformal dresses; the guys, yobbish and a bit drunk. I have anxious thoughts about my daughter in a few years. Hopefully Showbiz Alzheimer's will have set in by then.

▽

I go to bed at four after watching Dave Chappelle be very rude and funny on HBO. I am woken suddenly by a horribly cheerful voice. It's an automatic alarm call. There is no real person on the line to abuse back. Carefully I dial the desk.

"Can you find out who set the alarm call?" I say in my most reasonable voice.

"Yes, sir."

"I want them eviscerated," I say.

"You want them killed?"

"No, I want them disemboweled, their entrails unwound, their livers extruded, their testicles removed, and their remaining bits burned and chopped into Boston Harbor."

"Right away, sir."

Politeness is best.

DAY 20

ORPHEUM THEATRE, BOSTON

BOSTON, HOME OF THE WORST TEA PARTY EVER. YANKS HAVE BEEN MAKING BAD TEA EVER SINCE. THEY SEEM TO THINK IT HAS SOMETHING TO DO WITH CHUCKING TEA BAGS INTO COLD WATER.

▽

I am cranky with everyone at rehearsal. Must be careful. Don't want to end up like Captain Bligh on this voyage. First I snap at Peter for asking me for the sixth time to put "Money Song" before "Penis Song." He is quite wrong, and I am quite tired of explaining why, but there's no reason to go outside the boundaries of civilized discourse. Then I go off at Gilli when she reasonably wants to tell me what lighting areas to get into. Snappy, snappy, snappy. I must be having feelings of abandonment. Quite easy to do when you've been abandoned. I apologize later to both of them, but that's not fucking good enough, is it? Back to being the twelfth nicest Python. However, we *do* get a lot done in the allotted ninety minutes of rehearsal and we

ERIC IDLE

Hmm, so this is comedy lap dancing.

sharpen the show and polish some things that were getting sloppy, and it's just as well, because it is a Sunday night in Boston, we are not full and though they are joyous and noisy we need to go after them and grab them. The encore bucket is busy from the start. I have to stop people coming up onstage before I can get on with the show. They are throwing money at me.

There are a dozen eBay winners in the audience who have been conned by the greedy bastard promoters into bidding outrageous sums for front-row seats, free merchandise, and "special opportunities." These usually involve some kind of backstage "meet and greet" that are currently all the rage in showbiz. I don't know why they don't just go all the way and let them buy tickets to fuck us. [*Because who would pay to fuck you, you geriatric old bastard?*—Ed.] I decide to bring them up at the end of the Bruces and have the audience abuse them. This is jolly good fun. The audience get right into it at once and yell abuse at these poor innocent folks who have paid so much to be here. To give them a break I get them to sing the Bruces' song, which they join in heartily. Jen takes a picture of them all onstage. Then I release the tiger. (Kidding.)

At the post-show signing, a man said to me, "Thank you, because I don't think you'll be coming back." And that sounded right to me. I don't want to be an old drama queen and start with the "Farewell Tour" and "That last chance to see" bullshit, but on the prednisone night, the night I felt off, I glanced in the mirror and had a sudden vision of myself as Archie Rice, a character in John Osborne's play *The Entertainer*. Archie Rice is a sad, old music hall entertainer, condemned to a declining life on the vaudeville circuit, endlessly repeating his old jokes. Magnificently and memorably played by Laurence Olivier in the movie, this vision was chilling enough to make me realize that I never want to get anywhere near there. I think this voyage is for me. It's about turning sixty, about nostalgia, about remembering old friends, and getting out and seeing the world before it's too late. Peter has already observed that we seem to be reviving vaudeville on this tour. At the moment the show is still new for me, elevating and uplifting, thanks to the audience. But there is that specter in the mirror, an old man wearing too much makeup. So yes, he's right. I probably won't be coming back.

A DAY OFF IN BOSTON

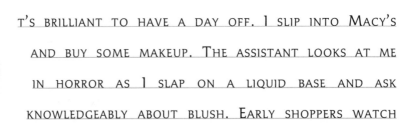

I'S BRILLIANT TO HAVE A DAY OFF. I SLIP INTO MACY'S AND BUY SOME MAKEUP. THE ASSISTANT LOOKS AT ME IN HORROR AS I SLAP ON A LIQUID BASE AND ASK KNOWLEDGEABLY ABOUT BLUSH. EARLY SHOPPERS WATCH askance as a very mature British man leans into a mirror dabbing on concealer. It's kind of fun. Appropriately, Eddie Izzard calls. He's in town. We neither of us are working tonight so we decide to meet for a movie. I love Eddie. I went to see him at the Aspen Comedy Festival in Aspen in 1998 when we were being honored, and I laughed so much I had to go back the next night and see him again. He walked away with the best-comedy award that year and waltzed onstage at the start of our reunion interview at the old Wheeler Opera House.

"Monty Python, how did it all start?" asked Robert Klein.

"Well," says Eddie, "I was in a railway carriage with John Cleese and Graham Chapman . . ."

"Fuck off, Izzard," we said, booting him off the stage.

I meet Eddie at the movies and we watch *Mystic River*. Afterward we cab for coffee and a Kaliber at the Parish Café, on Boylston Street. I remind him that the last time I saw him (about three weeks ago on the L.A. leg of his Sexie tour) he was sitting backstage with Sharon Stone talking about La Perla underwear. He laughs and raises an eloquent and ambivalent eyebrow.

"Well, you have to," he says.

Eddie seriously helps me. He is genuinely supportive of my shift into stand-up and filled with tips and ideas and helpful hints. He is very keen for me to improvise and gives me a couple of pointers. I explain my concerns, which are between balancing the needs of the genuine Python audience (who want and expect old favorites) and finding my own voice. I also outline my Archie Rice anxieties. He will hear of none of the latter. He sees a future for Idle striding onto the boards like Izzard and Connolly. (What it is to have friends!) We natter on till two in the morning and I am tremendously buoyed up. I am so rock-and-roll, living dangerously, out on the streets late at night, man, that I accidentally break a glass, and it *means nothing to me*. I am wandering into dangerous territory here. Will I become the Keith Richards of comedy? What's next, breaking a *saucer*?

Eddie riffs some very nice stuff about the warm-up man at Nuremberg who opens for Adolf, and the little S.S. stormtrooper who has to go off for a piss in the middle of Hitler's hysteria and can't find his way back to the troop: "Excuse me, Hamburg? Has anyone seen Hamburg?"

This has almost Chaplinesque qualities, and of course Eddie has already played Chaplin. He is obsessed with an idea to put the Pythons back together and have them do improv.

"No old stuff, you see, just fresh new improvised stuff. They'd come from miles."

"*Yards*, I think."

"You could start in little, obscure out-of-the-way places. You could work out in each other's homes."

ERIC
IDLE

"Yeah right, one day in Santa Barbara, California, the next in Brixton, London."

He seems so much in love with this idea that it is a shame to disabuse him, so I agree to it. Immediately he drops it. Only to return to the subject five minutes later.

"That's the beauty of the improv thing. It might be painful and unrewarding at the beginning."

I who am slightly more acquainted with the strange workings of the semilegendary snake have a different take on the chances of this coming to fruition. Just tonight my wife has had desperate calls from *Vanity Fair*: the Pythons won't return their calls for a photo session. Of course they won't. Mike's in the Himalayas, Terry Jones is filming in Lincolnshire, and Terry G. is under the Weinsteins in Austria. (Now there's a musical: *The Weinsteins in Austria: The Mound of Music!*) This photo session is never going to happen. Dream on, Graydon, baby.

▽

The very nice people at the Parish Café won't let us pay. The odds against *two* British comedians wandering in off the streets have clearly impressed them. Eddie's Sexie tour is doing very well. I tell him my next tour will be called *Fuck me, I'm British.* He said he liked the T-shirt.

CALVIN THEATRE, NORTHAMPTON

I N NORTHAMPTON WE DO THE BEST SHOW WE HAVE EVER DONE. IT MAY BE THE BEST SHOW I HAVE EVER DONE IN MY LIFE. THE COMBINATION OF A night off and a young crowd lifted us into somewhere really dynamic. We have up to now been playing to a theater crowd and this was our first real college experience and boy were we in the right playing field. The house was packed. They were on their feet doing "YMCA" before the "Spam Song." I felt loose and free at the same time, kept the pace going, and yet was able to wander off text at will. Thank you, Eddie.

I'm dreadfully horny. Perhaps it's the rocking of the bus. Perhaps it's the prednisone kicking in. When my lovely lady wife heard I was taking prednisone she warned me severely to behave myself. When she took it, things became incredibly steamy. (Thanks, Doc, by

All religions seem to dislike breasts, but it's just the opposite with me.

the way.) I miss her terribly. I wonder if Palin has these pangs, jigging about on the back of a camel.

▽

When my first marriage broke up I went off to Australia. It's where English people go to have emotions. It's summer in the winter and there are beautiful half-naked sheilas on the beaches. George said to me, "You're going to Australia?" Yes. "So you'll be flying over India?" Yes. "That's pretty heavy," he said. "I'm going to give you something."

Twenty-seven years now and I'm still nuts about Tania. Can that be healthy? I met her in New York on January 28, 1977, and it was lust at first sight. I had been in Barbados for Christmas with Lorne Michaels and Paul Simon, and stayed on for several weeks, after I met Ricky Fataar on a beach. He invited me to move into Heron Bay, a magnificent Palladian villa built by Ronald Tree in the forties, in which a year later we would write the final draft of *The Life of Brian*. It was currently being rented by a Baron Bingham, who did mysterious things for a living—for which he would eventually spend some time as a guest of the U.S. government. Mustachioed ex-Vietnam helicopter pilots would arrive in the middle of the night for mysterious meetings. Ricky and I carefully ignored everything that was going on and concentrated instead on drinking endless rum punches brought by a very old Bajan butler called Mister Brown, a small dark man as wrinkly as an old nut, who had served Churchill in this very same house. Ricky and I played guitar all day in the beautiful formal gardens and swam in the Caribbean and watched sunsets, while I totally transformed my life. Baron, a very generous chap, served no meat at his table, so during the four weeks I was his houseguest I became a fishetarian. I haven't eaten meat since. After my first marriage broke up, I am saddened to relate, I had not been an utterly chaste human being; indeed I had become in George Harrison's immortal phrase "a bit of a shagnasty."

I was happily unmarried for a while, helped in my irresponsible behavior by Carinthia, my beautiful, leggy landlady. She, very kindly, told all her friends that I was gay, and, one after another, they slipped downstairs to see if they could rescue me. No one seemed to notice just how easy it was. These naughty habits continued in Barbados, until one morning, I woke up on a beach with sandy knees beside a young Canadian of whose name I had not the slightest recollection and realized that this had to stop. It was obsessive behavior and not that much fun. I don't discount the advice and support of my spiritual chum George, from whose influence I wore an Ohm sign around my neck.

For all these very good reasons I suddenly abandoned all sexual activity and began to live chastely for the first time since maturity. So come the freezing January day I stepped onto the tarmac in New York I was long-haired, chaste, healthy, and bronzed. It was ninety-four degrees when I left Barbados and sixteen in New York, and Lorne Michaels kindly sent a car and an overcoat to meet me. I went straight to NBC for *Saturday Night Live,* hosted that week by Fran Tarkington. Afterward there were a couple of parties, one a chic uptown party filled with fashion models, where I sat, smugly thankful I had given up all that, and a second, downtown at Dan Aykroyd's loft. We arrived at Bond Street in the Bowery in Paul Simon's big white limo and took the rattly old freight elevator up to the superheated loft that Dan shared with some others. (They kept the sauna on all night and day since they had hooked their electricity supply into the car rental company downstairs.) Eventually Lorne and Paul said

So I'm on my way to the airport and a beautiful package arrives with a peacock feather—and it says "Not to be opened until over India." Wow!

So ten hours into the flight I look down and there's this huge brown land mass and I think, right, it's time. So I take down the package and I'm thinking this is great: the meaning of life from the spiritual Beatle—and I open it up and pull out a little card and there in George's handwriting it says, "Shag a sheila for me!"

93

ERIC IDLE

George was always on at me to be more spiritual. He'd say things like "Leave your dick alone."

I didn't like to leave my dick alone. It got lonely.

they were moving on and they would send the limo back for me. I wasn't tired, and I decided to hang for a while. I was standing by the sink when a tall, beautiful, dark-haired woman came up and introduced herself as one of the hosts. She asked me if I would like to dance. I had been on the dance floor all of twelve seconds when I became utterly overwhelmed. I am not exaggerating. I realized in a sudden, powerful, and utterly convincing moment *that I wanted to spend the rest of my life with her*. I can't explain it. It just came to me in a pheromonic flash that this was the woman for me, that I should on no account let her go until I had explained what had just happened and at least try and persuade her that I was serious. Love at first sight. Does it exist? All I can say is that I have never been as certain of anything in my life. Every gene in my body wanted this woman. I quickly hustled her out of her back door and well . . . we kissed. And kissed. And kissed. We were out there for about two hours. In fact we were out there so long some of her guests thought she'd left. I'm not sure that she really believed me, that this was completely crucial, but I did tell her that I was deadly serious and that there was no way I was ever going to leave her side. I must have convinced her, or perhaps she just fancied me, because I have never left her side since that night. Twenty-seven years ago. It still seems amazing to me. How could I know so overwhelmingly? She brought sense and balance into my life, and after a time she persuaded me that I could be a parent again and brought me a beautiful daughter and in a million ways changed my life, so that I am now the sixth nicest Python and not the nineteenth as I was then. And now where is she when I need her??? Grrr. I talk to my lovely daughter, Lily, on the phone, and she is happy she has won another basketball game. I have to hear her voice morning and night. I am a fortunate dad. My son, Carey, is a lovely chap, too, and he e-mails me sweetly from time to time. He is proud of me for being on the road, and though he lives in Australia he comes through at least twice a year.

Good evening, ladies and Bruces, my name is Bruce. This here is Bruce. And this here is Bruce. And we are all from the Philosophical Department of the University of Woolamoolloo, Australia, where we teach thinking and drinking. I teach Classical Philosophy, Bruce here teaches Hegelian Philosophy, and Bruce is in charge of the sheep dip.

DAY 23

THE EGG, ALBANY, NEW YORK

HOW BAD IS THIS? YOU'RE FEELING VERY TIRED THE MORNING AFTER A SHOW AND INSTEAD OF HAVING TO GET UP, *SOMEONE TAKES YOUR BED FOR A DRIVE THROUGH THE NEW ENGLAND LEAVES.* YOU HAVE YOUR FAVORITE CD on the stereo: *The Academy of Ancient Music by Request*; and Neville Marriner is revving up the best of Bach and Glück and Handel and blue suede Schubert as you float down the mighty roadsides of North America. You're being driven through the heart of New England in a queen-sized bed in a big, wide bus. I tell you, sometimes this trip seems like a magic carpet ride. We're traveling through deeply wooded country along the Mass Turnpike. Black slate cliffs plunge at crazy angles under the road. We're barreling through acres of woodlands of cranberry colors and yellow trees and the bright bark of the birches. Sudden still ponds reflect the sodden gray sky, and everywhere the knitting colors of the woods are interspersed with the dark peaks of the evergreens. Sometimes we churn through deep channels of forest to emerge briefly into wide pastures, where patient brown cattle stand in the damp meadows. In the distance misty mounds of hills are laced with light rain. We squeeze through endless tollbooths, James Taylor songs in mind: "And so was the Turnpike from Stockridge to Boston."[11]

▽

An English sky is low and lowering as we pull into the third truck stop this morning. Someone needs the bathroom. There's a huge, rusty semitrailer parked: MOBILE CHAPEL, it says on the side, TRANSPORT FOR CHRIST. He must be inside having breakfast, as it's deserted. It's starting to rain, slanting gray streaks across the windows, trying to snow already. Yoiks—it *is* snowing.

The Egg at Albany is ovoid. That's a clever way to say "egg-shaped." It was apparently built by Nelson Rockefeller to impress foreigners. It succeeds. This foreigner looks around for a huge cement Chicken theater nearby, but no luck. So clearly the Egg came first.

A gigantic egg is an unlikely shape to find sprouting among tall buildings on a hill above the Hudson. There were three Eggs in the world once and this is the last left standing. (You can't make a *Hamlet* without breaking Eggs?) It is referred to in all our tour notes as a U.S. government facility. Makes it sound like a prison. The theater is ultramodern; high-tech heaven, with an elliptical freight elevator that leads directly to the back wall of the stage and a couple of perfectly round elevators. Inside, the loveliest plush red auditorium folds around the inside walls and reminds us that the womb is a soft egg as well as very comforting. This is the Kitty Carlisle Hart Theatre. I once met her in Barbados, a lovely lady, very jolly and very funny. How nice to have a theater named after you. The Eric Idle Theater. The Eric Idle Egg. The Old Yolks Home. . . .

---

[11]   These words are from "Sweet Baby James."

ERIC IDLE

$\bigtriangledown$

Our buses are parked deep in the bowels of the loading bay; with a constant scream of cars zooming through an underpass all day—no place to stay. John and I reconnoiter Albany, which has historic buildings from the seventeenth century. This is the state capital and there is a nice graystone, turreted, castellated building, a classic Greek columned gallery, and of course the mighty Hudson River. We go to Jack's for oysters and clam chowder and then back into our routine:

4:30	Onstage for sound check and rehearsal. (Today we restage "The Getty Song.")
5:30	Dinner for cast and crew. Salmon and scallops in the Ladies Chorus Room. (Sadly, no ladies, just the scent of former intrigue.) Ribaldry and ribbing, banter and teasing with Scott, Skip, Peter, Jen, John, etc.
6:10	Nap for ten minutes.
6:30	Weightlifting and exercises to pump up and wake up.
7:00	Shower (bliss).
7:10	Makeup.
7:20	Larry Mah comes in at T minus ten to tape the radio mike to my back.
7:25	Final wardrobe check. Silk Prada dressing gown on. Yeah, baby.
	Beginners, please!

DAY 24

COUNT BASIE THEATRE, RED BANK, NEW JERSEY

 WAKE UP OUTSIDE A TYPEWRITER SHOP IN RED BANK, NEW JERSEY. I FEEL LIKE A CHARACTER ON A TV SHOW, A CROSS BETWEEN *THE FUGITIVE* AND "RIP VAN WINKLE." "THIS WEEK ERIC WAKES UP IN . . . ." I HAVEN'T EVEN HEARD of a typewriter shop in twenty years, but this one sells old typewriters and adding machines. We are parked yards from the Count Basie Theatre, which, in addition to me, is also selling the New Jersey Symphony Orchestra and Tom Jones. The sun is shining, though it looks chilly. A stiff wind tugs at the flags, making them snap. People go by, shoulders hunched, hands in pockets. Why am I here?

Well, love, why are any of us here?

No, I mean in a car park in New Jersey?

Well we couldn't get around the back of the theater until later.

No, I mean what am I doing here, on the bus, on a tour, doing this show?

ERIC IDLE

Oh. Right. Oh, dear. He's in one of his self-questioning moods, love. It's because you can, Eric, love. It's because you grew up as a boarding-school boy behaving well publicly, doing as you're told, and you learned all sorts of survival skills, how to surf life without being drowned, how to survive on a smile and a song and a bitter sense of humor. How to get through. How to maintain. How not to crack. It's because you went to Cambridge and fell in love with laughs. You liked being a bit of a toff. Dressing up in fancy clothes, copping the adulation of strangers. You became a bit of a laugh junkie, luvvie. You need that big noise of approval the intelligent apes make when you say something funny.

So this, then, is a quest?

If you like, love, it's a sort of search for your own internal Holy Grail. A spiritual quest of a man who has reached a certain point of life and seeks to explore his own response to that knowledge. Or.

Or what?

Or you just like showing off.

So why *did* I become a comedian? Try this for pathos. It's England. It's Christmas 1945. The country has just spent six years at war, an exhausting, crippling war, a war that has cost it every last ounce of will to survive. After several attempts my father, Ernest, joined the RAF in 1941, in the bleakest, darkest time, when his country stood alone in the world against the entire continent of Europe united under a Nazi Germany. Take a look at the map sometime. It's awesome. The Battle of Britain. Mastery of the skies, the few, the many dead. The sickening civilian bombing. London burning. The hammering sound of the planes at night. Cheer up, love, we can take it. Death from the skies. The boy Eric was born in 1943. He nearly didn't make it; a previous son died. His father came home on sick leave to give him blood. The absent father, always away in India, Nassau, New York, Canada, RAF stations around the globe, sitting in the most dangerous seat of a Wellington, the rear gunner, wireless operator. Just a Plexiglas bubble between you and the enemy planes. But he came through.

It was the end of the war. The country shivered under another winter of shortages, but at least the killing was done. No more the dread sound of planes in the sky at night, the awful banshee wailing of the air-raid sirens, the dreadful smell of rubber on his little Mickey Mouse gas mask. Eric was two years old. His mother was working as a nurse in the north of England. His father, Ernest, still in uniform, had nothing much to do but wait for his discharge. They had survived, that was their triumph. Now they flew odd sorties off Scotland to secret destinations with strange code words. He had found the words "Spam Exit" in his father's tiny handwriting, in his tiny RAF diary for 1945. He had also found a few references to himself, the choking words for July 7: "Eric's first paddle & trip to the Beach"; and a few days later, "Took Norah & Eric over U Boat."

Christmas was coming. The boy was not well, but maybe he was not that sick either. His mother yearned for her husband, locked up in those barracks. She sent a telegram: "Come home urgently. Boy very sick." What harm could it do? It wasn't as though they were still at war, and four years without your husband, who could blame her? Fate, that's who. The Fat Lady hadn't yet sung.

ERIC IDLE

Ernest was granted leave. Four days. It was just before Christmas, December 21, cold, foggy, freezing postwar Britain. The winter solstice, the shortest day, hardly light for more than a couple of hours and it's getting dark again. Wet roads, lights on, glistening, slippery tarmac. "Don't take the trains"—that's the advice to the servicemen; "hitchhike." Everyone stops for the men in uniform, our boys who have delivered us from evil.

Somewhere outside Darlington the blue-uniformed man gets a ride from a lorry with a load of sheet metal. Hop in the back, mate. No problem. Hitching home for Christmas. Nice one. Cold in the back of the truck, huddling down to escape the chill wind, blowing on his hands. Huddled into his woolly greatcoat, dreaming of Christmas by the fire, wife, child, and the war over.

Outside Darlington on a two-lane main road, a car, hooting in a hurry, tries to pass. There isn't room. Something is coming. A honking of horns. The car swerves in front of the lorry. The truck skids, a squeal of tires as it runs off the road. Dad in the back is trapped, crushed by the shifting load. Badly injured he is taken to hospital, and now it is her turn to get the telegram. "Come urgently husband very ill." Pausing only to find someone to care for the two-year-old, she takes the trains all night to end up by his, yes, deathbed. He lingers.

"I made a right wakes of this Norah, darling," he says to her.

He dies the night before Christmas Eve, the nurses in their red capes singing "Silent Night." Happy Christmas, everyone. Father's grave: in neat lined slabs they are drawn up in ranks,

forever at attention, name, rank, serial number, and date of death, 23 December 1945. And the sad Latin words of the RAF over each of them: "Per ardua ad astra."

▽

The mother works, the boy grows, she gets £756 compensation and a plaque from the King that says he officially "gave his life to save mankind from tyranny." The boy grows, but she cannot look at him without thinking she is to blame. Her guilt. Her grief. The shining future that they had dreamed, wiped out by telegram. Christmas by the fireside, the mother weeping, always weeping. Why always weeping, for look it is Christmas and how brightly the fire shines off the little tinsel tree, how prettily it reflects the shiny aluminum reds and golds. Surely that will cheer you up if I cannot? Why weeping, Mother, when we have a big bright food parcel from America with a little teddy bear for the boy? *Why are you always weeping?*

▽

The boy becomes seven and is sent away to boarding school. Here's the irony; he is sent to a school to grow up with boys *all of whom have lost their fathers in the war.* A single-parent half-orphanage that had been, until just before he got there, a full-blown Victorian orphanage with boys in blue coats buttoning from the neck to the ankles. A Victorian school with a dormitory 110 yards long, the longest in Europe they are told. A dormitory which is so cold frost can be found inside in the bleak gray winter mornings. Twelve years he spends there. He becomes a comedian. Why a comedian? To avoid the bullying? To escape the irony? They called it the Ophny, short for orphanage. Sad, isn't it?

"Are you happy at school?"

"Oh yes, please, sir, thank you."

Twelve years of happiness. Pure bliss in the longest dormi-

ERIC IDLE

tory in Europe. One hundred and ten yards—a powerful black athlete could easily run down it in ten seconds. They identified with the black slaves. They sang Negro songs on old banjos, plucking at cheap guitars and blowing into small harmonicas. Why should they identify with the black slaves of the American South? The music? No, the lyrics. The bitterness, the hopelessness, the despair, those endless years, those endless fourteen-week terms. Sonny Terry and Brownie McGhee, Big Bill Broonzy, the songs of Jim Crow . . .

> *If you're white, you're all right*
> *If you're brown, stick around*
> *But if you're black, oh brother*
> *Get back, get back, get back.*

The bitterness, the hopelessness, the despair.

▽

They were fed on a diet of British war films, of amiable RAF men locked up in cold Colditz Castle. No wonder they identified, walled up in their Wolverhampton monastery. Sad? A million sad tales I can tell you, repressed emotion recollected in tranquillity. A thing of duty is a boy forever. Per ardua ad astra. Through hard work to the stars. Could be the motto of mankind entering the Space Age. Or a young man entering show business.

DAY 25

WILLIAMSPORT COMMUNITY ARTS CENTER, PENNSYLVANIA

STEAMING DOWN THE HIGHWAY, BOB DYLAN'S *LOVE AND THEFT* CRANKED UP HIGH ON THE STEREO. LAST NIGHT WE PLAYED THE COUNT BASIE THEATRE AND WON. NOW WE ARE LEAVING NEW JERSEY, LAND OF SPRINGSTEEN. BYE-BYE, Bruce. Good disguise tonight, by the way. The fans never noticed. You *were* the woman in the twinset in the fourth row, weren't you?

I am gobsmacked[12] by the news that John Cleese is coming to Chicago to be photographed with me for *Vanity Fair*. This is totally unexpected and utterly surprising. If I were a betting man I would have given you 100:8 against. In fact, I can hardly believe it, but that is what they tell me. John is coming from Miami to Chicago simply for this photo, to celebrate twenty-five years since *The Life of Brian*, and then he has to go on to California. I think Graydon Carter must have something on him.

▽

---

[12] Verb, transitive. To gobsmack: to be startled or amazed.

ERIC IDLE

I met John forty years ago (dear God) at a Pembroke Smoking Concert. It was my first ever public appearance, and I was performing a sketch he'd written; this very lanky man came up after the show and was most encouraging. He's always been encouraging. I remember once, on his expedition up the Nile, we roasted him one night, and when it was my turn to speak he muttered softly under his breath, *"Be funny."* He himself was stand-out funny at Cambridge. You couldn't look at anyone else onstage. His control, his timing, his deadpan made him easily the funniest man of his generation. He went off to the West End in a Cambridge revue called *Cambridge Circus*; it eventually wound up on Broadway, because of which I got to take over some of his bits at the Edinburgh Festival, where I wound up meeting Terry Jones and Michael Palin. When John returned to England, after an improbable appearance in *Half a Sixpence* on Broadway (honest) I wound up writing bits for his radio show *I'm Sorry, I'll Read That Again* and then graduated to TV, where I contributed material to *The Frost Report.* He became a star overnight in this live TV show, appearing weekly in hilarious sketches he wrote with Graham Chapman. Terry Jones and Michael Palin also wrote for this show, as did the wonderfully eccentric and as yet undiscovered Marty Feldman. I then graduated to tiny roles in John's next show, which debuted Marty and Graham Chapman (with Tim Brooke-Taylor): the very silly and eccentric *At Last the 1948 Show*, which was the real father of *Monty Python*. The mother was *Do Not Adjust Your Set*, a highly successful award-winning kids' show featuring me, Terry Jones, Michael Palin, Neil Innes, the Bonzo Dog Band, and Terry Gilliam. When Marty Feldman went off to star in *Marty* for the BBC, John was offered his own TV series by the BBC, which for some reason he was reluctant to accept. Instead he approached Michael to hook up with him. Michael said he was with Terry Jones and me, oh, and Terry Gilliam, too. We had all been offered our own grown-up show: an ambitious forty-five-minute slot on ITV, the commercial network, the only drawback being we had to wait almost a year for a studio to be free. This was the deciding factor. We decided to slip in *Monty Python* first! So, almost accidentally the two halves of Python slid together—on the one hand John Cleese and Graham Chapman, and on the other the *Do Not Adjust Your Set* crowd. We would work together on and off from 1969 until 1983, slipping into movies and records and books and stage tours as well as the original TV series. John would also come along and guest-star in my movie *Splitting Heirs* and reunite with us all at the Aspen Comedy Festival in 1998. And now it's forty years later and we are to have our photos taken for *Vanity Fair*. Forty years ago. And me still in my thirties. It's a funny old life if you don't weaken.

The Williamsport Community Arts Center is a magnificent Moorish movie palace, beautifully restored and painted buttery leather, with red-and-blue glass Moroccan brass light fixtures and twisted columns guarding two great murals: one a lurid sunset over the hills of Spain seen between the colonnades of the Alhambra, and the other a full and misty moonrise. On the ceiling and over the exotic alcoves heraldic shields are emblazoned with colorful coats of arms. Moorish designs on the tiles and moldings complete this exquisite 1928 example of the power of the talkies. Now it is a tribute to the restorers' art, America proudly conserving her past.

Tonight a few heads dropped when we heard our crowd was down. It happens. Each promoter does what he can, in his own way, to sell the show. He has very limited dollars. This one only had three weeks' notice and consequently we are far from full. I gather the gang together in my dressing room before the show and warn them not to let it affect them.

"These people have paid," I say. "We are going to give them an even better show than they could possibly expect. We haven't lost a show yet, and I don't intend to start here."

The cast responds with enthusiasm. Yes. Right. Let's go. Let's get 'em.

▽

We needn't have worried. Most of the crowd fill the wide stalls, it's the upper tiers that are thinly peopled, and we can't see up there anyway. The audience is as noisy as ever, responding enthusiastically, laughing loudly, and singing along lustily. We don't lose a show at all. They stand and cheer and demand encores. I'm proud of the chaps. An extra rum ration all around.

DAY 26

STATE THEATRE, NEW BRUNSWICK, NEW JERSEY

THE SUN RISES GOLDEN OVER THE APPALACHIANS. AS WE PASS THROUGH LOYALSOCK (YES, HONEST) THE GRASS IN INDIAN PARK IS FROSTED WHITE. WE ARE SLIDING ALONG THE BANKS OF THE SUSQUEHANNA, THE RIVER THAT IN 1935 FLOODED the foyer of the theater we have just left. Five feet of water in the auditorium. Now *that's* a tough audience.

▽

We are heading east toward the rising sun, sliding between the long ridges of the Appalachians. Pale barley spears of dry corn catch the golden light. Round balls of pumpkins dot the fields like some recently abandoned game. Deer stand alert among the white rime of the fields. Scattered whitewood homesteads appear occasionally through the trees. Patches of wrecked cars. The roadside plants stiffened by frost. Farms and outbuildings and tall silvery spacecraft water towers slide by. There are farm machinery sales with shiny green tractors. This is Amish country, and

ERIC IDLE

there's a local fight about whether their buggies should have taillights: they're not in the Bible.

The landscape here is deeply scarred and wrinkled along a northeast angle. We head north for a while. We're in western Pennsylvania heading back to Jersey for the last of five shows in a row. We are a fighting unit. We can roll out the show, set up, play, and move on. Our two ships trained and ready. Our crew, under Skip, our ever buoyant Number One, always one jump ahead of the problems. Our tech staff, led by Gilli, who strides about where Teamsters fear to tread. Scott, on guitars, ever loyal, ever encouraging—"Have a great show, Boss." Tom, our merch guy, tattooed and dome-headed with his trailer packed with brown parcels, always counting. Larry Mah, quietly smiling and ever efficient as he wires us for sound and adjusts the balance in an empty theater. Larry sits out front. He is our eyes and ears. We rely on him not only for sound but to tell us what the audience is thinking and feeling. Then there is my magnificent cast: John, the stalwart, seated onstage all night with his handcrafted organ; Peter, the sneering, loud and always dependable; and Jennifer, the unflappable flapper.

▽

"Some people feel that 'The Penis Song' is a little sexist...."

"Well, that's right, Eric, but people do forget that there are more than four billion inches of penis on this planet at any one moment."

As we drive through the fall colors this morning I'm thinking of my mother's death. Perhaps it's the time of year, almost Halloween, when she came for her final visit to our old (1929) Spanish-style home in Hollywood. Like all northern mums she was very proud of what I had achieved and damned if she'd say anything about it to me. She lived in Shakespeare's Stratford, a pleasant town. This time she would come out for a few weeks and see Lily in the Halloween parade and then fly home. She was eighty-three, though sprightly, and it was good to see the way the fine October sunshine and the warm Jacuzzi brought a glow of health to her. We were getting on extremely well, and she was having a very good time, not always the case with our Norah, who could lapse into a gloom thicker than a northern fog.

I remember the day only too well. There had been some rain, and I took her arm as we took a little walk in the garden. Suddenly she slipped, and I turned and caught her, but not before she dashed her leg against the wooden railroad ties that formed the garden steps. It seemed to be so little, but when I looked down I was horrified. She was pouring blood, and I could see bone. Jesus. I lifted her bodily and carried her up to the lawn and sat her on a chair, grabbing towels to stanch the flow of blood, which was everywhere. She was losing consciousness, and I held her until she came back, and then I said, "Hang on," and went to dial 911. The emergency services responded instantly, and I heard the wail of the siren approaching from just down the road. They ran to her, and the paramedics stopped the bleeding. They lifted her up in a stretcher and carried her out of the garden to an ambulance. I followed in my car to St. Joseph's in the Valley, where she was patched up and bandaged and was soon comfortable in a pleasant room with a window and a little view of Disney. Next day I was booked on *The Tonight Show with Jay Leno* next door at NBC, and Jay was very kind about my mum and wished her well and sent her an enormous basket of goodies. (A very kindly man, Jay.) It seemed to be just a scare, but for one worrying thing: her skin was so old and thin the surgeon was worried about how to stitch her up. They were talking of a skin graft. Perhaps it was the anxiety; perhaps it was the stress; but a day later I got to the hospital, and things had got a lot worse. She was back in emergency.

"She's had a minor heart attack," I was told. "She is in discomfort, but we can't operate. She is just too old. We've given her something to help her heart."

The something was a painful bladder thing that she hated. Couldn't they operate? In the end it was Norah who decided. She was tired of the incessant medical procedures, the discomfort, the pain. She would call me in the middle of the night and beg me to ask them to give her something to finish her off.

"Please, luvvie, ask them to put me out of my misery."

"I'm not going to do that, Mum."

"Please, Eric, I can't take any more like this."

"Mum, it's a *Catholic* hospital. They're not going to switch you off."

And I'd drive over and hold her hand and ask for more painkillers.

I still remember the white-faced doctor, weary with exhaustion, telling me there was nothing they could do.

"What do you mean?"

"Well, we can make her comfortable, but she is going to die."

"What?? When?"

"A week or two."

They must see so much grief, these poor guys. Working night and day with death as a companion. We are a remarkable species, you know. I was, of course, overcome, but my family rallied, Tania, Lily, and our lovely nanny, Wee; little Lily bravely entertained her beloved Gran with pictures and drawings. We decided that since there was nothing to be done we would get her out of the hospital and at least let her die at home. St. Joe's have a very good hospice service and soon we had a hospital bed downstairs and an IV and a trained nurse to come in once a day, and Norah had morphine and we put on all her favorite music, *The Mikado,* songs of the thirties, "Pennies from Heaven." We would watch by her deathbed. She would go out surrounded by her loved ones. My son, Carey, flew in from Australia and by extreme good fortune, not only is he a Buddhist, but he had been working with the terminally ill. So he held her hand and sat with her, and she said all the things to me you could ever wish for. How she loved us all, how she was proud of us and thankful for everything—all the things she had trouble expressing in her life she now said. It was moving, and heartrending and wonderful because we all knew she was dying, and we even had *Holy Grail* badges saying I'M NOT DEAD YET. She died suddenly one morning. It was Tania's birthday. We had gone out for a quick walk, and when we came back Carey said simply, "She's gone."

We had a little ceremony in the garden to give thanks and say good-bye. No funerals. I hate funerals. Who would come? All her friends were in Stratford, and her family scattered in the U.K. and Canada. So we chose instead to gather in the garden and hold hands and say a few words from our hearts. It was touching and simple. Norah, born in South Shields, died in Hollywood. She would have liked that. And for me, well, it was blessed. She might have keeled over on her own in her flat in Stratford and not been found for days. I might never have seen her or ever experienced the joy of the things she said to me at the end. She made her dying one of the best things she ever did in her life. I was proud of her. She departed with dignity, at home, surrounded by her loved ones. She wanted me to sing "Always Look on the Bright Side." But I couldn't do that. I'd never get through it.

DAY OFF IN WASHINGTON, D.C.

AST NIGHT AT THE SIGNING A LADY SAID TO ME: "YOU LOOK MORE LIKE YOU DO NOW THAN YOU DID THEN." GOOD, ISN'T IT? I EVEN *FEEL* MORE LIKE I DO TODAY THAN I DID THEN. BEING AN EX-PYTHON IS WEIRD. I SUPPOSE we are all are mistaken for the people we once were, that's what the fossilization of fame is all about, but we're not really them, are we? Those young men are long since gone. We have to talk about them as though we still are them, but we're not, you know. They were smart, young, and terribly clever. We older, wider, and grayer men are their descendants. I used to be Eric Idle in Monty Python. But now I'm not. I'm not even like him. He drank and smoked and ate meat. He was married to a blond Australian. I'm none of the above. But looking at his pictures now I see he was quite cute, and mercifully, he didn't know it. He had a lot of insecurities which have since been ironed out by a jolly good shrink. I know the English disapprove of shrinkage, but then they still think smoking is a good idea . . . and look at their tabloids: *they're* completely bonkers. I think that's why certain interviews are so taxing for me: they only want to talk to him. And I'm not him, any more than Ringo is still Ringo. Sometimes I have to pretend to be him, and I can still do his material and sing his songs, but I'm clearly a totally different person.

After five nights on the road, a hot bath! Luxury. And now a day off. Last night in New Brunswick there was a great crowd and a wild reception. We had young people from Rutgers and neighboring high schools as well as the loyal ones who have been watching Python for thirty years. We had over a hundred walk-ins, which was excellent. I teased the audience with doing Eric the Half a Bee, and think I might well do that tomorrow for a change. No one gets Do What John. It is a very English thing.

Do what John?
Do what John?
Come again?
Do what?
Do what John?
Do what John?
Do what Do what Do what?
Do where John?
Do where John?
With what with whom and when?
Triffic really triffic
Pardon? Come again.

I have got into a rhythm now and am starting to drop weight. It's all the singing and performing. I shall be a younger, slimmer old bastard by the time my good lady wife comes into New York. I vaguely remember her. . . .

THE GREEDY BASTARD DIARY

People are always asking if there is going to be anything new from Monty Python—and the answer is no. We have discovered that the less we do, the more you pay.

NIGHTCLUB 9:30, WASHINGTON, D.C.

'M SLIGHTLY NERVOUS ABOUT TOMORROW AND SEEING MY BELOVED AGAIN FOR THE FIRST TIME IN FOUR WEEKS. IN MY EXPERIENCE IT CAN BE SLIGHTLY BUMPY PICKING UP RELATIONSHIPS AFTER A PERIOD OF SEPARATION. BOTH partners have got used to being 100 percent of their world and along comes this other person with demands and needs and expectations. So reentry can be a little rough. I'm not talking about the first ten minutes! Of course it's really good for you to be apart for a while, to experience who you are. If you can't live alone you can't live with someone else.

People ask me how do you make a marriage last twenty-seven years? Well, I'll tell you my tip: separate bedrooms. And that doesn't mean no nookie. Far from it. (It means you now have *two* venues, plus the kitchen floor.) It just means that a woman of a certain age no longer has to put up with a farting, burping, snoring, demanding old bear in her bed; and, by the same token, a gentleman doesn't have to watch *ER* and bad television till all hours of the night. I fall asleep easily and early. I like a little Chopin and a good book. The missus likes late-night TV, pottering around the bathroom, and sleeping late. I love to get up really early and write. This way I don't disturb her. We found that the only time we ever bickered was over what time the light went out. So we solved it. She has a boudoir, all silks and perfume, and I have an English room, all wood and fabric.

Everyone needs their own space. See Virginia Woolf's essay *A Room of One's Own* (apart from *Orlando,* the only tolerable bit of writing she did).[13] In a totally perfect setup I would share a bathroom, because I am terribly fond of casual female nudity. It's an odd thing, but I have never grown tired of looking at the naked female form. I have always thought it terribly unfair that artists can have nude models and not writers. In fact, I once asked Tania to pose for me as a writer's model to see if it would help me writing comedy. She took off all her clothes and posed naked on a sofa while I sat down at the typewriter: but, alas, I didn't get a lot written. Artists must have much more self-control. And *how did* Picasso paint with his penis? Or is that just a metaphor?

She is hilarious, my wife. After we had been to see a season of Japanese movies, whenever I entered the room she would throw herself on the ground and kowtow! I'd find her facedown, prostrate, behind me, and nearly leap out of my skin. She'd get me every time. I think she became pregnant shortly after that. . . . She has a way of saying very little and then coming up with the best line at dinner. It's very annoying. Once, when I said I was reading *The Shorter Pepys,* she asked me if there was a taller one. I remember filling in an immigra-

---

13   In the Greedy Bastard's opinion. But then he did write *Hello, Sailor,* and she only wrote *Mrs. Dalloway.*

ERIC IDLE

tion form for her and under "profession" I entered "gagster's moll." On the return trip she wrote "Occupation: Pillow."

▽

As you can tell I'm nuts about her. And she has learned not to listen at just the right times. If I'm grumpy and foul she simply feeds me. I think the art of marriage is trying to improve the lot of the other person. It isn't just having someone to blame. If it isn't better than living alone then you shouldn't do it. [*All right, enough marriage guidance. Get on with the fucking diary.*—Ed.]

▽

I'm in Washington, D.C. I think Washington, B.C., might be more appropriate with the dreadful Bushites in power. This is the town where the attorney general covered up the tits on a statue of Justice. Highly appropriate when you think that this lot only came to power by mugging the Supreme Court.

It's a rainy Monday so I hope we get a crowd as we are playing our one and only club gig; an experiment by the Greedy Bastard agent. After tonight's show we pile into the buses and head for New York City for three whole nights and a day off. Yea. Yesterday here was sunny and lovely, the Capitol shining, the big wide streets jammed with monumental buildings. Tania and I came with Lily a few years ago at cherry blossom time and did all the tourist sights, which is just as well, as they are all closed off today for a marathon. I always hated cross-country and spent the afternoon at Union Station, a rather elegant Roman building housing trains and shops and cinemas. I saw *Intolerable Cruelty*,

All men love breasts and all women love breasts—because they are our first meal. Breasts are God's Big Macs.

118

which made me laugh a lot. About ten years ago I made a movie (*Splitting Heirs*) with a relatively unknown Catherine Zeta-Jones, and she was lovely and clever and adorable then, and I'm thrilled she has made it big-time, because you can't take your eyes off her. We were all very taken with her on the set, and one day for a gag had our director's chairs remade with the names *Eric Zeta-Idle* and *Rick Zeta-Moranis*. In fact I even got to do a nude love scene with her. But sadly and disappointingly it was I who was nude.

DAY 29

DAY OFF IN NEW YORK CITY

T'S TWO IN THE MORNING AND WE'RE CROSSING A MIGHTY LONG BRIDGE. I THINK WE'RE JUST OUTSIDE BALTIMORE HEADING NORTH FOR NEW YORK CITY. WE JUST FINISHED A GIG IN WASHINGTON AT THE 9:30 CLUB, OUR FIRST-EVER nightclub. They put down seats and erected a large stage but it was essentially a rock club, and it was packed. They were hanging from the rafters, and we did great. Skip was here a couple of months ago with the Sex Pistols. I see myself now as a sort of elder statesman Johnny Rotten. Our Greedy Bastard agent is keen to expand the platform for this show and I must say he was right on with this club, as we did very well. We started later than usual and the bars kept them tanked up and in a great mood.

"The atmosphere's electric," said Larry as he wired me for sound. Sure was. They added about ten minutes to the show in laughter and ad-libs. I got the eBay winners to sing "Happy Birthday" for John Cleese. He turned sixty-four. Oy vey. Happy birthday, John.

Ron Devillier was in, but sadly I never got to see him. I intended to thank him publicly for all he did for us, but he had to run off early for babysitters.

Ron was the man who first put Python on TV in the States, when he ran PBS in Dallas in the early seventies. Now he sells the reruns of the Python TV shows for us. People are always surprised to learn that Python broke first in Texas, but there it is. A hit in Dallas. Just like JFK. [*A joke in very questionable taste.*—Ed.]

Rather worryingly I have started to lose my voice. I blame the Washington Terrace Hotel, which was like a sauna. It might have been Saudi Arabia. I had to put the AC on and open the window. Let's hope the voice thing is just a temporary glitch. Or I'll have to bone up on my mime.

We slide through the tunnel from New Jersey into NYC at four in the morning, where I sack out, exhausted, and when I wake up there is my lovely Tania for breakfast. We seem to get on okay. A spot of shopping and then lunch at Brasserie. A quick raid on Rizzoli's bookshop for the new J. M. Coetzee and a new Martin Amis, then we spot my pal Jim Piddock outside the hotel. Tonight a movie and *no show!* Tomorrow a return to the cheap hucksterism and low-life grubbiness of showbiz. Hey-ho.

THE
GREEDY
BASTARD
DIARY

I am a bit puzzled by your government, which does seem to be environmentally retarded.

I'm just a foreigner. My vote doesn't count. And with the new electronic voting machines soon neither will yours.

TOWN HALL, NEW YORK CITY

ISASTER. I'VE LOST MY VOICE. I'VE GOT LARYNGITIS. I CAN'T SPEAK AT ALL: I CAN ONLY CROAK. I WOKE UP WITH A VOICE SOMEWHERE BETWEEN DEMI MOORE AND HENRY KISSINGER, WHICH AT FIRST AROUSED, THEN TERRIFIED, MY WIFE. NOW I have twelve hours to recover. I'm on antibiotics and homeopathics and echinacea and ginger and vitamins and I have so much zinc in me I'm suffering from metal fatigue. I'm even swallowing phosphorus now, so I'll probably glow in the dark. Everyone, it seems, has their own recipe for this common showbiz ailment. Jim Piddock advised gingerroot with apple cider and honey. My friend Joe asked me if it was hysterical laryngitis, and I said it wasn't that funny. I'm aware of the psychosomatic effects of stress on the body, of course, but what do you do? Tell yourself "Don't be stressed, just get well"? "Fuck off," says your body, "I'll do what I damn well please." It's sod's law of course. First night in New York, all the *Spamalot* company are coming with the producer, Bill Haber, and the director, Mike Nichols, and several friends attending, and now this. Oh shit, shit, shit. It's just not fair, dammit. My wife comes all the way from L.A. to be stuck with a sick husband. I'm going to lie around all day not talking and hope to hell my voice comes back.

▽

I had the same problem one time when I was hosting *Saturday Night Live*. All week I had wanted to work on my monologue but Lorne kept saying "No, no, we'll write it later," and I knew we never would, and of course we never did. Just before dress rehearsal, with very little voice and feeling like shit, I grabbed Al Franken and Tom Davis, and they carried me in on a stretcher, and we improvised stretcher impersonations: me upside down, me at an angle, and so on. It worked out quite well, but I can't fake two hours without a voice.

It's a rainy day in New York. Patient pigeons are parked along the branches of the trees. Tourists scurry by with umbrellas. I keep falling asleep. Every time I do someone calls or comes to the door. It's like a French farce. Head down, eyes closed, ding dong. Finally I manage a sweaty nap and wake up feeling a bit better. Now I sound like Lee Marvin. Eight hours to go. It's going to be touch and go.

Recently I met the lady who discovered the G-spot. She said she'd show me how to find it. She curled my fingers into an O, inserted two fingers into the fist, and from inside pushed real hard on the fleshy part of my palm.

"That," she said, "is the G-spot."

And I was surprised, because I'd always thought it was in the vagina.

So be very careful, ladies, next time you shake hands with me.

DAY 31

NEW YORK CITY

W E ARE IN THE SUPERB RITZ-CARLTON HOTEL WITH A MAGNIFICENT VIEW OF CENTRAL PARK. THEY HAVE THOUGHTFULLY PROVIDED A MOUNTED BRASS TELESCOPE IN THE WINDOW, SO WE CAN CHECK OUT THE NEIGHBORHOOD high-rise bedrooms. Voyeurism is a sport in New York. Mike Nichols told me he once watched a particularly steamy bedroom scene across the park and when it was over and they snapped on the light he realized he had been watching an old man clipping his toenails.

I train the telescope on one of the lakes and watch a magnificent heron fishing, stepping gingerly on its elegant legs. The rain has passed and it's one of those brilliant blue New York days. The leaves seem late to turn and have not yet reached Vermont standards, but there are one or two magnificent magentas. I'm on a vow of silence. My laryngitis is still with me, but not bad. I got through last night, at Town Hall, though squeaky on the high notes and a little hoarse. The audience response was great and friends flattering, though that is the very least you expect of friends. If they can't lie convincingly to you after a show, why have friends? You don't really expect them to come back and say "Darling, you were shite." Mike (Nichols) tells me his favorite thing to do is go backstage, spread his hands wide, and say "What can I say?" Mercifully, he doesn't use this line on me, but only because I suspect he was catching up on his jet lag. . . . He was full of health concerns and strongly advised no whispering and no talking for the first two hours in the morning. So I'm talking to my diary instead of my beloved. We ran out of sign language.

Tania is off to lunch with Lauren Hutton, and I can't go because of my semi-Trappist vow of silence. I love Hutton. She is my adopted sister, and she's coming to the show tonight. I'll always remember her in Hollywood, mooning me on Sunset, sticking her ass out the window of a passing car. She asked me once what quote to use when she retired from being the face of Revlon. I suggested she say, "It's time for America to sit on a new face." She is my daughter's fairy godmother, having adopted her once when babysitting beside a pool in Hollywood. In our absence the baby Lily began to wail, and she has very powerful lungs.

"Give her dry suck," said Lauren.

"What's that?" the sitter asked.

"You don't know what dry suck is?" she said, and with a big grin, clamped the young Lily onto her exquisite nipple. Oddly, shortly thereafter, Lily developed a gap in her teeth!

THE
GREEDY
BASTARD
DIARY

Is your wife a goer? Eh? Know what I mean? Know what I mean? Nudge, nudge! Know what I mean? Say no more!

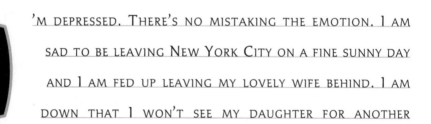

KESWICK THEATRE, GLENSIDE, PENNSYLVANIA

'M DEPRESSED. THERE'S NO MISTAKING THE EMOTION. I AM SAD TO BE LEAVING NEW YORK CITY ON A FINE SUNNY DAY AND I AM FED UP LEAVING MY LOVELY WIFE BEHIND. I AM DOWN THAT I WON'T SEE MY DAUGHTER FOR ANOTHER month, and I am pissed that I was sick for the first show in NYC and had no voice on the one day that all the people I really wanted to impress came to the show. Oh, bollocks. Sod's law in action. I am saddened that the New York show seems to have remained a well-kept secret, so that we are inundated with reports of people saying if only they'd known they'd have come. That's always been the trouble with this show: its hit and run. You have no time to build word of mouth, which is the only way to attract an audience without a large advertising budget. We don't stay around long enough to take advantage of all the people who came and loved us. If the promoters haven't reached our audience, we're screwed. They, in their turn, will only risk a limited advertising budget. Nevertheless, this is the third show in a row where my name hasn't even been up in front of the theater! No posters, no marquee, no billboards, no nothing. What kind of advertising is this? I am deeply frustrated by it all as I climb on the bus, and we inch out of town through the usual gridlock. We pass Carnegie Hall, where we played two nights on my last tour (Eric Idle Exploits Monty Python). You haven't really lived until you have stood onstage at Carnegie Hall in full drag singing "Sit on My Face."

We pass the Osborne, a magnificent old apartment building on West 57th Street where I first spent the night with my beautiful wife. Across the street is the diner where I last ate meat: a bacon sandwich in 1977. How long ago all that seems, the seventies: Studio 54 and Andy Warhol, and Mick and Bianca Jagger; trips to watch Muhammad Ali fight Ken Norton at Yankee Stadium, where there was chaos in the streets because the police were on strike. "Just like Arsenal versus Chelsea," I said cheerfully as I tried to hover protectively over Paul Simon. On a visit to Madison Square Garden to see Ali fight Jerry Quarry, I rode downstairs in an elevator with Henry Kissinger, while Ronnie Wood stood directly behind him, making silly faces behind his back. Kissinger was staring at me puzzled as I was trying desperately not to crack up. All the time a gigantic black bodyguard stood staring impassively at Ronnie, utterly perplexed as to how to deal with this situation. Ought he to attack, to defend? I think he was enjoying it. But I was almost shaking with laughter at the sheer childish naughtiness of the whole thing until mercifully we hit the ground, Kissinger left, and we collapsed howling in a heap on the floor.

Henry Kissinger
How I'm missing yer
You're the doctor of my dreams
With your crinkly hair and your glassy stare
And your Machiavellian schemes
I know they say that you are very vain
And short and fat and pushy

ERIC IDLE

But at least you're not insane
Henry Kissinger
How I'm missing yer
And wishing you were here

Henry Kissinger
How I'm missing yer
You're so chubby and so neat
With your funny clothes and your squishy nose
You're like a German parakeet
All right so people say that you don't care
But you've got nicer legs than Hitler and bigger tits
  than Cher
Henry Kissinger
How I'm missing yer
And wishing you were here!

I met Paul Simon in the line waiting to get into Bette Midler's dressing room to congratulate her on her brilliance in *Clams on the Half Shell.* We had to wait quite some time, as Elton John was inside giving her diamonds. Well, you have to. Paul and I struck up quite a pleasant friendship. We both had sons of the same age and were both currently separated. Later he would kindly throw a party for my wedding to Tania.

In 1980 I was on holiday with Paul in the West Indies when, late at night, we heard that John Lennon had been shot. Paul later wrote a song ("The Late Great Johnny Ace") saying he was standing on the streets of New York when he heard John Lennon had died, and I teased him about this. I said I could understand that it didn't make such a good lyric to say "I was in Barbados on holiday with Eric Idle when I heard John Lennon had died."

Tonight it's the Keswick Theatre just outside Philadelphia, and we're pulling into a car park behind a redbrick building.

Hey-ho. Another day, another dollar. Only two months, and we'll be home. . . . But I should be there now, watching the kids trick-or-treating, enjoying their joy in dressing up, their squeals of delight as the Hollywood ghouls spring out of their coffins. Oh, bollocks.[14]

It's certainly a roller coaster this tour. After the disappointment of the size of the crowd in New York, the theater at Keswick was packed. A delightful, noisy, and appreciative crowd turned out, dressed to the nines in all kinds of fancy costumes. It's Halloween of course, and I'd been half expecting the theater to be empty, but no, they came along in droves in fancy dress. Quite a few trollops were out in tarty red-and-black skimpy things plus several healthy-looking serving wenches, with the slutty, bosomy look that encourages you to admire the merchandise. God bless dear Nellie Gywn. Many very beautiful women then, complemented by an assortment of pirates, monks, and Mounties. Some people were even in *Holy Grail* costume, which can now, apparently, be bought on the Web. There was a Sir Robin, a King Arthur, a Sir Bedevere and a Black Knight. I think this dressing-up festival is America's favorite holiday, and it seems to do everyone a great deal of good climbing into costume and pretending to be someone else. There is a sense of carnival in the air, and a high level of sex. I suspect many of the couples are not going home to watch television. Rather worrying for Attorney General Ashcroft and his Puritans. Americans will insist on pursuing happiness.

I get frequent compliments during my signing, and several ladies want to shake hands with me after my G-spot bit. A large part of men performing comedy is clearly sexual signaling—and the message certainly seems to get through. The female rewards laughter with sexual favors. Men seem more threat-

---

[14]   English slang: meaning *Oops*, or *Oh, dear.*

ERIC IDLE

I like older women: they're more grateful.[15]

ened by funny women than attracted. You never hear men say I have this girl with a great sense of humor. No, it's always her breasts, isn't it, not her brain. Are we really that shallow? [*Yes.*—Ed.]

There have been several instances recently of kind ladies leaving little love notes and billets-doux in the encore bucket. I'm assuming they were trying to contact a younger and more available Eric Idle, but of course it is still tremendously flattering to be flirted with by younger women at my age; in fact by any women of any age.

---

[15] Frankie Howerd, c. 1966.

NEW YORK TO NORFOLK, VIRGINIA

T'S THREE IN THE MORNING AND WE ARE ROLLING THROUGH THE FORESTS OF VIRGINIA ON OUR WAY TO NORFOLK. I HAVE TURNED OUT THE LIGHTS IN MY LITTLE BEDROOM IN THE REAR OF THE BUS AND LIE BACK WATCHING THE BRIGHT stars as we zoom along the highway.

Last night a professional astronomer told me he calculated that I must have been in the latitude of Bombay or Calcutta when I wrote "The Galaxy Song," as that is the point on the planet where the rotational speed of the earth is nine hundred miles an hour. He points out that the speed of your rotation alters with how far north and south you are. At the equator your rotational speed is fastest, at the North Pole it is zero. I thought I had given the optimum rotational speed at the equator, but not apparently so. I have had to revise my "Galaxy Song" lyrics several times since I wrote it more than twenty years ago, because, even in that brief time, our estimation of the size of our galaxy has changed considerably. It is amazing how quickly our speed of knowledge is increasing, and very important, too, since our speed of efficiency at self-destruction has also increased.

ERIC IDLE

*Just remember that you're standing on a planet that's
     evolving
And revolving at 900 miles an hour.
That's orbiting at 19 miles a second, so it's reckoned,
The sun that is the source of all our power,
The sun, and you and me, and all the stars that we
     can see,
Are moving at a million miles a day,
In an outer spiral arm, at 40,000 miles an hour,
Of the galaxy we call the Milky Way.*

*Our galaxy itself contains five hundred billion stars;
It's a hundred thousand light-years side to side;
It bulges in the middle six thousand light-years
     thick,
But out by us it's just a thousand light-years wide.
We're thirty thousand light-years from Galactic
     Central Point,
We go 'round every two hundred million years;
And our galaxy is only one of millions of billions
In this amazing and expanding universe.*

*Our universe itself keeps on expanding and
     expanding,
In all of the directions it can whiz;
As fast as it can go, at the speed of light, you know,
Twelve million miles a minute and that's the fastest
     speed there is.
So remember, when you're feeling very small and
     insecure,
How amazingly unlikely is your birth;
And pray that there's intelligent life somewhere out in
     space,
'Cause there's bugger all down here on Earth!*

Backstage I was visited briefly by Ann, a British folk singer from Renaissance who reminded me of the first time we met at Warner Brothers Records in Soho in the late seventies. I had popped in with Carrie Fisher for a social visit to see my pal Jonathan Clyde when in came Chrissie Hynde and the Pretenders, totally elated that their song "Brass in Pocket" had just gone to number one. They insisted we join them in an instant celebration. Champagne corks began to pop, and there was some very odd behavior as the party grew riotous. I remember Chrissie fiddling provocatively with the front of guitarist James Honeyman-Scott's pants, which seemed to inspire Carrie into a kind of testosterone challenge, and soon both American girls were in each other's faces seeing how wildly they could dance *at* each other. It was odd and strange and kind of wonderful: two of the ballsiest American women engaged in a wild contest from which neither would back down. The party drifted on to my house in St. John's Wood as parties in those days tended to, and we drank on and danced to my jukebox. At some point the news came through that Paul McCartney had been arrested and thrown in jail in Japan on charges of possessing marijuana, and Ann reminded me that I instantly got on the phone to the Japanese embassy to protest this. I demanded that unless he was released at once we would all boycott Japanese restaurants. That should have scared them.

It's 5:00 A.M. and I'm riding shotgun with 'Lish as we head east toward the dawn. It comes up green with red streaks and dark black clouds. The navy blue of the waters of Chesapeake Bay glow weirdly as we roll along a wide causeway. The deck lights of fishing boats flash past on either side. Venus is high in the sky and Mercury prominent as we cross, appropriately,

ERIC IDLE

Mercury Boulevard. There are many British place names all improbably jumbled: Portsmouth, Norfolk, Suffolk, Newmarket, Aberdeen. I see that Powhatan, Pocahontas's dad, has now become a major highway. This is where the real first colonists came four hundred years ago. Can we imagine what it will be like after four hundred years? Now tangles of cranes are silhouetted against the sky, and we pass the shattered remains of an amphitheater, its roof shredded like tattered sails, torn apart by the last storm. Gray navy ships are everywhere as we slip by the Elizabeth River, its flat, calm water reflecting the lights from a large hotel. A scurry of ducks are taking to the water as the light becomes first muddy yellow and then brilliant gold bars in a Krishna blue background. At six thirty in the morning I climb off the bus and check into the hotel with the ever vigilant Skip. No one else is up. I'm expecting a junior suite, small and compact. The joke is on me. I'm in the presidential suite. It's massive. The bedroom has a four-poster bed and an escritoire and a sofa. The vast stateroom contains a dining table for twelve and a real fireplace, complete with a three-piece suite and an enormous panoramic bay window where, as I enter, with perfect timing, our nuclear neighbor the sun rises straight ahead, bright fiery red. It's a breathtaking view of the bay as beneath me an early catamaran slips out toward the sea. Sun up and the birds are heading south for the shoreline; it's definitely time to go to bed.

DAY 34

THE NORVA, VIRGINIA

TODAY IS ANOTHER BEAUTIFUL, SUNNY DAY IN VIRGINIA. I'M MAGNIFICENTLY INSTALLED IN A PENTHOUSE OVERLOOKING PORTSMOUTH AND NORFOLK AND THE NAVAL DOCKYARDS. I WENT FOR A WALK AND TOOK A SHORT FERRY RIDE ACROSS the Elizabeth River. A fine sailing ship called the *Rover* was at berth, packed with naval brass in full dress uniform. Some family members emerged looking solemn, and I realized that a memorial service was in progress, a reminder that these ships and the lives of the sailors and servicemen are in daily danger. Speaking as a war baby, I wish they weren't. I don't want any more kids to lose their fathers.

The Norva is a blast. It's a nightclub, only the second we have played, and is even more rowdy than the first. The audience are jumping. They are already having a good time before I even get onstage. They are a much younger crowd; the bar is open and they are all buzzed. The owner has never tried comedy before in this rock-and-roll venue, and Bill Reid is very excited by the success of the show. They have never put in seating either, but when the seats are installed, with the packed gallery above, it is very

ERIC IDLE

much like an Elizabethan theater. Since the audience is so close our type of intimate revue plays really well. It goes so well that we add twelve minutes on act one over New York just from laughter alone. Amazingly the promoter had only two and a half weeks to sell this show and he did a great job. My name is out front on the marquee—wow, what a concept!—and as the Norva is opposite a huge shopping mall, we picked up a ton of passing trade. Backstage we find the most luxurious quarters we have ever encountered. There is a huge Jacuzzi and a very warm sauna as well as nicely appointed dressing rooms with huge leather sofas to stretch out on and big TVs and carpets and nice-smelling candles. These rock-and-roll people really know how to look after themselves.

I spent the morning walking the streets of the Old Town of Portsmouth. Every house bore a plaque of antiquity like a badge of honor. There were big gardens and flowers and old trees with blackbirds squawking noisily. The crickets chirped and the scent of magnolia hung in the air, which was balmy and warm. I wanted to buy a home and live here in these quiet old streets. I could see myself installed on a comfortable swing on the verandah of one of these beautiful 1870 white wood houses. Nobody was about the streets at all at eleven on this Sunday morning. Perhaps everyone was in church.

I found a lovely courtyard with a café and took a leisurely brunch at Sassafras.

"Are you someone famous?" they asked.

This is a terribly loaded question. If you say yes and they've never heard of you, you feel about six inches high. I said I was John Cleese and left it at that.

A DAY OFF IN BALTIMORE

A HALF GLOBE OF AN UPSIDE-DOWN MOON IS SINKING AS WE HEAD NORTH AT MIDNIGHT, THIS TIME FOR BALTIMORE AND A DAY OFF. I'VE GOT THIS ROCK-AND-ROLL ROUTINE DOWN NOW: INTO THE BUS AFTER THE SHOW AND ON THE ROAD BY midnight. A couple of mouthfuls of pizza, a down or two of football on the telly, and I retire to my chamber where I bash out a few e-mails on the old laptop before crashing. I wake up around four as we slip into the new city. Today, if it's Monday, it must be Baltimore. I stumble past the bleary-eyed bellman as he looks with alarm at the size of our two huge buses. Today a junior suite in a corner tower, on the twenty-second floor, a bit of mindless television and I fall asleep around five, waking again about ten.

It's another glorious Indian summer day, with temperatures in the high seventies, and as soon as I dispatch my journalistic duties I head for the streets. My entire knowledge of Baltimore is garnered from two sources: the movies of Barry Levinson and *The Wire*. I first met Barry back in the seventies in London when he was a writer for *The Marty Feldman Comedy Machine*. I

ERIC IDLE

I think it's interesting that women never went to the Moon. I think it's because the Moon controls their periods, and if they were on the Moon they'd have a period all the time.

love his movies. He is a very funny man and has what I now think of as a Baltimorean cheerfulness. (Everyone seems very cheery here. Maybe it's because the sun is shining.) *The Wire* was my favorite TV series of the last two years. Impeccably acted, written, and directed, it has for two years been absolutely gripping television at its finest (HBO, of course). How can I reconcile these two Baltimores? The middle-class neighborhoods of the fifties and the crack 'hoods of today?

▽

A cheerful Haitian taxi driver gives me a preliminary tour, up Charles Street to the George Washington monument, then down again to Camden Yards, the home of the Baltimore Orioles. We cruise past Little Italy, and he drops me in Fell's Point, whose tiny cobbled streets, old buildings, and place names (Thames Street, Shakespeare Street, Lancaster Street) remind me of Olde England. I pick up a water taxi and cruise the bay. It's like Venice. Except for the view. Sunlight dances on the water in points of brilliant light, and the fresh air blows in my face, ruining my hairdo as we bounce from Captain James Landing to Tide Point. I'm reminded of other cities I have toured by water: Sydney, Dubrovnik, London; this is just as pleasant. Except for the view. So what about the view? Well, frankly, it's butt ugly. Brutal rotting wharves, ancient peeling warehouses, and broken-backed iron structures tumbling toward the waterline. Venice it ain't, but it is, well, *almost* beautiful in its seedy magnificence, in the same way that the ruined dockyards of the Thames can appear almost beautiful. It has a Dickensian beauty. The rot, the decay, the smell—especially the smell, which turns to sweet sickly molasses as we ap-

proach the Domino sugar plant. I decide that's enough of the water-taxi experience. Maybe next time I should take a water limo.

▽

I join the tourist throngs hanging around the sailing ship the U.S.S. *Constellation* in Harborplace and grab a bite at City Lights Seafood. Two Peruvians are playing amplified Gypsy Kings music to a small crowd. This is the brave new world of the tourist, listening to ethnic music from another continent while a newly constructed shopping mall sells plastic souvenirs imported from China. But I like tourism. Better tourism than armies. We are all essentially tourists on this planet, aren't we? [*Oh God, here he goes. The Planetary Tourist again. Where's the delete button?*—Ed.] (1,541 words later) So that is why I think we must all look after the planet.

I dine at the Don Shula Restaurant. The menu is on a football. I don't point out to the wide-shouldered manager that the football is the wrong shape for a limey. It should be round. Football, what I call football, is my addiction. I love it and have done all my life. Now, sadly, I have to call it "soccer" here.

I head out to the Charles Street Theatre to see a movie. The streets are deserted. A large brother spots me, crosses the street, and heads straight toward me. I brace myself. Do not give in to white panic. He probably just wants some cash. Wrong. He is a huge Python fan. Himself a comedian, Tom tells me he is going to make it big doing stand-up in L.A. and can he be my bodyguard tomorrow night? He needs it for his résumé. I tell him to put down he guarded my body tonight instead, and he goes off happily.

I live in California. I have a stretch Prius. I send all my garbage to Ed Begley. And now we have the Governator: the man who popularized the sport of waitress lifting.

ERIC IDLE

I watch some people catching up on their smoking in the Voodoo Bar. Smoking seems to be popular here still, the man in the hotel room next to mine has been kindly sharing clouds of it with me for twelve hours now. Ironically a sign tells me that this is a no-smoking room. Virginia was the place for smokers. That figures, I guess. It did introduce the foul practice to Europe. In Portsmouth at the restaurant where I brunched, people would hardly pause long enough in their coughing to suck in more tobacco. My cabdriver lit up the moment I got in. *Thanks for sharing.* It's a puzzling habit. An addiction without reward. It kills you off without getting you off. I hope it dies out before we do. At George's funeral I had the bad taste to thank Marlboro, "without whom we wouldn't be here today."

I got e-mail from Liv the other day saying she thought George performing "The Pirate Song" on *Rutland Weekend Television* was the bravest thing he ever did and that she wanted to be a pirate, too. Well, his dark sweet lady was the love of his life, and I know how much he loved her; a braver, finer, lovelier companion no man could ever find, and it breaks my heart to think of these last two years.

The Pirate Song

I want to be a pirate
A pirate's life for me
All my friends are pirates
And they sail the BBC
I've got a jolly roger
It's big and black and vast
So get out of your skull and crossbones
And I'll run it up your mast

With a yo ho ho
And a yee hee hee
And a yo ho ho ho hum
With a yo ho ho
And a yee hee hee
And a yum yum yum yum yum

I've got a jolly roger
It's big and black and vast
So get out of your skull and crossbones
And I'll run it up your mast!

SHRIVER HALL, BALTIMORE

THE YELLOWING ACACIA TREES DROP LEAVES INTO MY SOUP. I AM SITTING UNDERNEATH THEIR SCRAWNY BOUGHS OUTSIDE THE LEGAL SEAFOOD RESTAURANT (I KEEP THINKING IT SHOULD BE CALLED THE BARELY LEGAL Seafood Restaurant). Unfortunately, I am about to pass out. I forgot to eat. Damn. I walked all the way down to the harbor and was so pleased with the progress of my foot that I ignored the early warning signs, the sweating, the light-headedness, the shaking hands. Now the light keeps changing as though there are clouds scudding by in the sky on a windy day. Trouble is there are no clouds and there is no wind. These are my eyes. I'm blacking out. I'm going to lose consciousness right here in the busy Inner Harbor. This happens occasionally when I forget to eat. I remember my wife's advice: "Put your head between your knees." I remember my reply: "I'd rather put my head between your knees." How can I make gags at a time like this? I am sweating, and my mind is clouding over. I was overcome in Banana Republic, and not just by shopping anxiety. I barely made it across the street, my mind on stage one of survival strategy; ordering massive amounts of food. Now I'm watching the light disappear from the corners of my eyes. The world is strangely out of focus. They're going to find me passed out on the pavement: EX-PYTHON IN BIZARRE SIDEWALK INCIDENT. In the nick of time my waitress arrives with hot food and caffeine. I fight off the temptation to pitch headfirst into the cioppino and attack the food, chugalugging the Pepsi, and swallowing the hot black tea. Wow. Just made it. I'm a little uncertain at the end, but the sweating has stopped, and I finally crawl back to crash at the hotel.

I wake up feeling fine to discover on the bus to Shriver Hall that John has been having a bad day with vertigo. Fortunately we are playing Johns Hopkins University, so soon our kindly promoter is calling in doctors and John goes off for a wrestling match with a medic. He is literally thrown around and held down for eight minutes, while his ears realign. Apparently the crystals in his inner ear are out of balance. I hear to my alarm that he may be being bounced around too much in the back of the bus. I must talk to Mike, his driver. John is the rock around which we plant our invasion force. He anchors the whole show around his ever reliable keyboards. We discuss what we must do if any one of us is sick from here in. Gilli will attempt to cover for John, Jen and Peter will cover each other. I of course am irreplaceable. (I kept trying to tell my wife that.) I must time my voiceless days to nights off.

I was crucified once and frankly I don't recommend it. There's something a bit chilling about turning up first thing in the morning and finding a cross with your name on it. Thirty-foot crosses they were, too, with a neat little sign on the back: Mr. Idle.

DAY 37

CARPENTER CENTER, RICHMOND, VIRGINIA

"WHO WRITES YOUR DIARY?"

A DEEJAY ASKS ME THAT ON THE RADIO ON THE DRIVE INTO RICHMOND.

"EXCUSE ME?"

"Do you have someone who writes your diary for you?"

Expletive deleted.

I explain patiently that I write my own diary. He seems surprised. I tell him I also wipe my own bottom and tie up my laces unassisted. Are people so conditioned by the thought of stardom that they expect everyone in show business to be spoiled, brainless wonders? Frankly I am amazed when . . . (paragraph deleted).

We are back in Virginia. Named after Virginia Woolf. [*Actually, after the Virgin Queen Elizabeth I, you spoiled, brainless wonder.*—Ed.] We love Virginia. They have been wonderful to us. A snobby person from somewhere up north said to me after a show, "Good luck in the South." Well, snobby person, you were talking out of your butt, the South loves us. I think it's the same Yankee prejudice that is always shocked to learn that Python broke first in Dallas. That's right, *Texas*. Not New York at all. The Richmond crowd were roaring noisily before the curtain. They were engaging, smart, and hugely receptive. I felt loose enough to add some lines from somewhere inside my filing cabinet of a brain and they were kind enough to scream and yell for more.

We are a jolly gang for dinner downstairs underneath the stage: Peter, John, Jen, Skip, Gilli, and Scott are joined by our promoter and the catering staff, an attractive blond lady with an adorable accent. Here are the serious subjects we discuss:

> *a) What is the Mason-Dixon Line, and who are Mason and Dixon? Someone suggests two members of Pink Floyd but Darren, our new replacement sound guy, has the answer: they were surveyors. (He knows this because he is a Civil War re-creator.)*

> *b) Lyle Lovett's menu for his show here next week. Some kind of tart is suggested.*

> *c) The Confederacy.*

> *d) Richmond's history as the capital of the South.*

> *e) Banana pudding. With examples.*

The Carpenter Center for the Performing Arts is a highly painted Moorish movie palace with an improbable rococo exterior, like a baroque Bavarian church (except my name is in lights). I suppose we have Rudolph Valentino in *The Sheik* to thank for all these twenties Moroccan harem–style movie houses. This one comes complete with nude statues of classical antiquity, you know the sort of thing: discus throwers

ERIC IDLE

draped in a hankie and nude ladies throwing children into the air to see if they can fly. There is a perfect naked Greek boy just to the right of the stage. We throw a spotlight on him during "The Getty Song" as I sing these words:

> *There's a Greek boy there whose ass*
> *Is made of solid brass*
> *In the Getty*
> *And the air-conditioning*
> *Has shrunk his little thing*
> *In the Getty.*

It gets a huge roar and a round of applause. Wish we could take him with us.

DAY 38

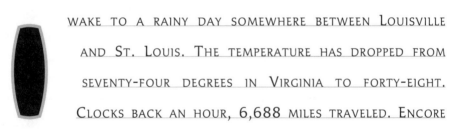

RICHMOND TO ST. LOUIS, MISSOURI

WAKE TO A RAINY DAY SOMEWHERE BETWEEN LOUISVILLE AND ST. LOUIS. THE TEMPERATURE HAS DROPPED FROM SEVENTY-FOUR DEGREES IN VIRGINIA TO FORTY-EIGHT. CLOCKS BACK AN HOUR, 6,688 MILES TRAVELED. ENCORE bucket last night a record $128. That's more than a thousand bucks for charity in the encore bucket so far!

▽

The Westin Hotel has heavenly beds. They are truly heavenly, too. Unfortunately it also has a poltergeist that raps smartly above my heavenly head at two thirty in the morning. When I complained about this unfortunate noise to the "executive bellman," the engineer tracked it to an upstairs fan, which he turned off. Now it's on again and banging away happily. Perhaps it is an executive poltergeist. This is a very smart, new executive hotel, downtown in the ancient executive parking district of St. Louis. There seems to be nothing here but a baseball ground. The hotel has been rebuilt from old brick warehouses and is all blond wood and Swedish furniture.

ERIC IDLE

Very nice, too. Its only problem is that to get to the executive suites you have to cross a bridge and they are chary about posting directions to this glass-and-steel appendage, so that I wander minotaurlike through a maze of executive corridors before giving up and starting over. The nice lady at the desk deserts her post and leads me to my destination, giving me a local paper for the movie times. I am startled to find myself on the cover as Nigel Spasm. I note from the interview inside that I have now progressed from comedy legend to comedy god. I think the cycle goes: wannabe; cult; legend; god; has-been. Anyway at the moment I'm an executive comedy god. Perilously close to executive has-been.

Deification doesn't seem to have improved my looks. Or my mood. I think I must have that sunlight deficiency syndrome, since my spirits sink in the cold gray of the day. That's really why I left the U.K. I need the sun or I'm back in the Ophny at Wolverhampton. This afternoon I fail to appear on a heavily promoted live radio interview in Edmonton thanks to an executive PR error: someone failed to notice we have changed time zones. They seem very pissed off at me in Edmonton. But what can I do? Tiarra has dumped me in it again. To cheer myself up I go out to the movies with Peter. John is there, too, but absolutely refuses to join us in seeing *Kill Bill*. Seeing the lovely Uma Thurman reminds me inevitably of the six months we spent together on *Baron Munchausen* in Rome and Spain in 1987–88. This Terry Gilliam movie dragged on for six months and provided many extraordinary memories, all of which are better in hindsight. I love Terry, but the filming was a multilingual mishmash, dogged by confusion and miscommunication at every stage, culminating in a shoot in Spain where Spanish assistant directors and extras tried to work with English actors and an Italian crew. It was worse than the Crusades! How he finished it at all is a mystery.

Terry cast Uma to play Venus, rising naked from a clamshell. She was a very young, extremely beautiful seventeen-year-old, and everyone adored her. She was also smart as a whip and very intelligent. She had legally divorced her parents at the age of fifteen and gone off to live in New York, where she began modeling. Her father was a famous Buddhist lecturer and my pal Timothy Leary was her godfather. I took to her at once. Little Sarah Polley was about eleven then and has since turned into Uma. The cast were an odd bunch: Jack Purvis, the little guy from *Time Bandits;* big Winston Dennis, the overweight bouncer from South London; the engaging and brilliant actor John Neville, constantly wondering what he had done to deserve this; Charles McKeown, who wrote it; and me, freshly bald. When he persuaded me to shave my head Gilliam swore he would shave his, too, but reneged on the deal the minute I submitted, the bastard. It was an odd experience to be suddenly bald and I enjoyed the menacing new power it gave me. In those days only lunatics and skinheads shaved their heads. When they saw me coming in Italy, people stepped off the pavement to avoid me. It was quite fun. Until my wife arrived. At the airport she took one look at me and burst into tears. Later when I came into the bathroom she screamed and almost jumped out of her skin. Not good.

We were very quickly in executive hell, as the picture had only a third of the budget it needed, and soon the producer, Thomas Schühly, wasn't even talking to Gilliam; he retired to his suite, where he entertained interviewers by showing them his gun and his fully equipped boxing gym. He would pose for photographers with his boxing gloves on, while the film snowballed into the red. Filming itself, with its daily grind of three hours' makeup and at least nine hours' waiting around, was a form of daily torture, mitigated only by our presence in Rome, which is a truly wonderful city to live in. Every morning on the way to Cinecittà I would watch the sun rising over the Coliseum. Now *that's* a commute.

Tania and I found quarters in the Palazzo Ruspoli, a sixteenth-century palace at the junction of the Corso and the Condotti. At the weekends we spent wads of per diem on Quinzi e Gabrielli's fresh seafood and visited new friends Franco Amurri, the director, and his then partner, Susan Sarandon, at the seaside. Old friends came by, too, and we were able to get away for a couple of weekends in my fabulous turbo Citroën, with Marsha and Robin Williams on what we called the "Big Jobbie Tour" (named after a memorable monologue of Billy Connolly's about a "floater," the turd that never sinks). We drove hilariously down the Appian Way to Naples and Sorrento, visiting Pompeii en route. You can only imagine what it's like to visit Pompeii with Robin pretending to be an Italian tour guide! "Theesa poor people a not able to leeva the toilet, frozen heer, taking a poop for eternity. . . ."

▽

We took a boat across to the island of Capri, where I relived the chairlift experience that had moved me at fourteen to write a purple passage of prose about what I did during my school holidays. It was as glorious as ever to float silently, feet dangling over the grapes and backyards of the houses, gazing across the magnificent Bay of Naples to the smoking mountain of Vesuvius. We saw the phosphorescent waters of the celebrated Blue Grotto, where Tiberius held his orgies. We went

The Greedy Bastard Tour bus with the author. *(Skip Rickert)*

Onstage, live at the Keswick Theatre. *(© 2003 by John Angelini)*

On tour. *(Courtesy of the author)*

Cast and crew at a rest stop. Back row: Peter Crabbe, Mike (driver), Scott Keeton, English, Tom (merch), and John du Prez; front row: Skip Rickert, Jennifer Julian, Jennifer Usher (costumes), Eric, Larry Mah (sound), Gilli Moon. *(Larry Mah)*

Performing "The End of the World" with Peter and Jen at the Keswick Theatre. *(© 2003 by John Angelini)*

Act Two: the story continues . . . *(Larry Mah)*

The Bruces with eBay winners, Boston. *(Skip Rickert)*

I was lucky enough to perform in my hat at beautiful spaces like the Williamsport Theatre. *(Larry Mah)*

With the Finnish Terry Gilliam. *(Courtesy of the author)*

Jennifer and Peter perform "The Getty Song." *(© 2003 by John Angelini)*

Sound check: John at the piano, Peter, Jennifer, and I. *(Larry Mah)*

The expensive set. *(Larry Mah)*

Performing "I Like Chinese" with Skip. *(Larry Mah)*

Singing "Killing for God." *(Larry Mah)*

In Toronto. *(Larry Mah)*

The expensive merchandise. *(Courtesy of the author)*

for a carriage ride pulled by a scrawny mule and we laughed and laughed and laughed. Later, after Robin was suckered into joining the movie to replace the suddenly unavailable and very canny Sean Connery, we drove up to Florence, where Robin and I shopped like gay men, swishing through the stores, screeching about how fabulous we looked in our new shoes.

"They're keepers, duckie!"

"Oo, get you in the pumps. Who are you trying to appeal to: Michelangelo's *David*?"

We visited Gore Vidal and Howard Austen in their Roman apartment, where we sloshed martinis and went off for a very drunken dinner. Olivia and George Harrison came out to visit, and to celebrate his forty-fifth birthday we made a big cake saying *Revived Forty-five*, a reference to his *Thirty-three and a Third* album. Long gone is the world of albums, LPs, EPs, singles, 78s, 45s, and 33⅓s.

There was intense speculation about who would succeed in dating Uma, and she sailed serenely through it all, effortlessly resisting the drunken lurches of the rather wonderful Oliver Reed. There was a famous old Italian actress called Valentina Cortese, who constantly made Uma's life hell. Valentina's idea of acting, no matter what the scene or how it had been rehearsed, was on the word "action" to bump Uma out of the way and then head straight for center screen. It was like a football play. No matter who was between her and her goal she would always end up in the middle waving her arms around dramatically. For the rest of us it was amusing. For Uma it was a nightmare. Robin got revenge for all of us. Fully aware of her tricks, he stepped firmly on the hem of her robe to prevent her moving, then squashed fruit into her mouth to prevent her protesting. He earned all our applause.

THE GREEDY BASTARD DIARY

151

ERIC IDLE

So here we are, then, in St.Louis with its big McDonald's arch. Tonight is our twentieth show! After that we pile into the buses and head north for Buffalo. Foul weather is on the way. Oh, to be young and in Roma again!

DAY 39

TOUHILL PERFORMING ARTS CENTER, ST. LOUIS

AFTER BREAKFAST I GO FOR A RIDE ROUND ST. LOUIS, UNDERNEATH THE IMPROBABLE GLEAMING ARCH, WHICH LOOKS A LITTLE LIKE SOMETHING SADDAM MIGHT HAVE BUILT IN BAGHDAD. THE TAXI DRIVER TELLS ME JOKES IN AN impenetrable accent. I can't even tell when they are over such is his accent. He is half Hungarian, half Italian, about sixty, and boasts he has a twenty-three-year-old girlfriend. He doesn't pause for breath. He keeps twisting around to see me and hammer home his humor. Not reassuring when he's driving.

"I hate Hungarians," he says, "we are so bloody depressing. And I work too hard. One week I work eight days!"

▽

He finally dropped me at Union Station. It's an odd mall, new and quite pleasant, but the shops are weird. There are endless funny shirt shops and fast-food places. A new Hyatt hotel uses the old station hall as a lobby. This comes as a total surprise. It's like walking into Bavaria. From a typical

American mall I'm suddenly in a vast, barrel-shaped room with an arched ceiling in art nouveau green and gold, stained glass, and statuesque goddesses holding torches aloft. It's magnificent and glorious and reminds me of the stately dining halls of European stations. I expect large ladies in Bavarian hats with arms like hams holding huge steins of beer to step in at any moment. And where's the little German band? It reminds me of the time I was in Munich with Terry Jones scouting for the second Monty Python German show sometime in the early seventies. It was Mardi Gras, and we were taken to the Knockebacker Bier Festival. It was freezing weather in February, and we were invited to visit a vast vaulted Bier Keller so large there was a German band at either end of the hall. To celebrate Carnival they brew a special, thick black beer that is so potent even the Bavarians stop serving it at ten thirty: otherwise they begin killing one another. People are very rowdy, drinking away at long refectory tables, and in one corner there are real Nazis. I kid you not. They are saluting and singing marching songs. As two English boys it feels like we just escaped from a prisoner-of-war camp and are trying to work our way home. Low-profile is clearly the order of the day. The main band has a feature where if you pay enough marks they will let you conduct. It's late in the evening, the beer has done its work, and I look around for Terry. I am startled and not a little disturbed to see him walk out onto the stage. He has paid his ten marks and is intent on conducting the German band, whose conductor, I notice, has no hand, but a kind of metal claw in which he clasps the baton. Terry has a quiet little dangerous smile on his face and conducts nicely for a while, bowing politely to the crowd and nodding. Then he begins to strip. Oh no! He starts doing a striptease, wiggling his bottom and slipping off his jacket provocatively. The audience begins to notice what is going on and turns its attention to this strange man performing a striptease onstage. The band, unsure what to do, plays on. Terry bumps and grinds like a pro, popping the buttons of his shirt like a stripper, then removes his shirt and twirls it around his head, flinging it into the wings. Next he turns to his trousers. He starts lowering his zipper to shouts of encouragement. He pops open his belt, flirting with the crowd. He is just about to drop his pants when the clawed conductor decides enough is enough, races onto the stage, rugby tackles him, and drags him off into the wings to cheers and vast applause. It was the funniest and the bravest and the maddest thing I have ever seen anyone do. I felt quite relieved to get out of there alive.

It rivals Graham's mad moment, when he was sent to pick up a Sun TV award for Monty Python. It was presented to him by the Home Secretary Reginald Maudling, a high official in the government of Britain. Graham took the award, popped it into his mouth, went down on all fours, and exited the stage through the audience barking like a dog. You don't see that at the Oscars.

Further down the mall in St. Louis there is a Beatle souvenir shop, though sadly they have no Rutles stuff. I made some Rutle merchandise for *Can't Buy Me Lunch,* but I gave it all to George, who adored all Rutle memorabilia. I think the most successful present I ever gave him was a Rutle guitar, which Danny Ferrington made for me. It was shaped like a limo and featured the Rutles looking out of the windows. George was thrilled with it. As well as customizing several ukuleles for George (one in fake leopard skin), Danny also made George's final guitar to his precise instructions. He wanted an Australian guitar. It was a beauty, a work of art, custom built with the sound hole a perfect map of Australia, the bridge was the

ERIC IDLE

Sydney Harbor Bridge, and the headstock the Sydney Opera House. On the back and front and sides there were aboriginal designs in mother-of-pearl, with further illustrations of rare birds and animals on the neck. I had it (for safekeeping) for about a year after George died and am still kicking myself for giving it back.

George once gave me *the* most spectacular present. It was Christmas 1975 and my marriage was breaking up, and I was very sad, and it was snowing, and my little two-year-old son and I were alone on Christmas Eve. There was a ring at the door, and we stood on the stoop, bewildered, as two men unloaded a heavy, bulky object from the back of a large truck and carried it inside. Carey and I looked at each other, puzzled. What on earth was it? It was wrapped in corrugated brown paper and tied up with string, so we set about ripping the covering off. To our amazement and utter delight it was a jukebox filled with rock-and-roll classics! There was a note on it that said "Every home should have one, Happy Christmas, love George and Liv." Well, we plugged that thing in, and it glowed and throbbed and pulsated with sound, and we danced madly to it all that Christmas. What a great gift.

DAY 40

ST. LOUIS TO BUFFALO, NEW YORK

WELL, I FINALLY DID IT. LAST NIGHT I BROKE THE TOM JONES BARRIER. A VERY ATTRACTIVE GIRL CAME UP AND PUT HER PANTIES IN THE ENCORE BUCKET! SO THAT'S IT, THEN. THE PINNACLE OF A GREAT CAREER. FORGET CARNEGIE HALL, THE Hollywood Bowl, Broadway, the English National Opera, and the Houston Grand Opera. I have finally achieved panty status! Now I can rest in peace. My life's work is done. Fuck knighthoods. Fuck Oscars. *Girls put their panties in my encore bucket!* Well, panty. But can you doubt that this is just the beginning? I foresee a whole selection of Victoria's Secret lingerie in there by the end of the tour.

I was in the mood for something like this. I had been watching an interesting film kindly provided by the hotel about two girls rubbing each other's breasts. They didn't say a lot and they weren't wearing a lot either, but they did seem to enjoy it. I enjoyed watching it, too, but then switched over to the Lakers game. It was fun to watch a film about breasts in Attorney General Ashcroft's home state, since he himself has such a problem with them. Probably an early breast-feeding issue, don't you think? Perhaps if they put

ERIC IDLE

By the way, I know Victoria's Secret: She's a slut.

baby bottles on the naked statue of Justice outside his window instead of breasts, he'd feel more comfortable. We're in Missouri, where he lost an election to a dead man, a singular mark of achievement for which Bush instantly rewarded him by making him Attorney General. Odd he should become a general as he set some kind of record with seven deferments from Vietnam, while Cheney had only five.

It was quite a flirty day. A woman called Heidi Decker interviewed me on the radio. She told me she loved *A Fish Called Wanda,* that it was her favorite film and she had seen it about a hundred times.

"That's very interesting," I say, "but I'm not in it."

Later I blurt out that I am looking forward to appearing in Boise.

"That's very interesting," she says, "but this is Spokane!"

We have a delightful chat filled with misunderstandings and single entendres. I say that to get to Spokane we are going to have to come over the Rockies in our tour bus, and if we get stuck, we may have to eat one of our party. I tell her we shall eat one of the girls, as it's more fun to eat a woman. She says she doesn't know, she hasn't eaten one since college! Sadly this jolly lady will be out of town when we come through.

DAY 41

UNIVERSITY OF BUFFALO CENTER FOR THE ARTS, BUFFALO

HERE IS NOTHING EXTRAORDINARY ABOUT NIAGARA FALLS," SAID OSCAR WILDE. "IT WOULD BE REMARKABLE IF IT WENT THE OTHER WAY."

YOU MIGHT SAY THE SAME THING ABOUT OSCAR WILDE.

I wake up to a sunny day by the shores of Lake Erie, which looks like a big blue ocean. Tonight we play the University of Buffalo Center for the Arts and then on to Ann Arbor, whoever she is. It's a freezing morning here in Buffalo. There's ice on the water of the fountain in front of our strangely named hotel, which is called Adam's Mark. It doesn't say who Adam's Mark is. I never knew Adam was gay, but with all the rumors swirling around about poor Prince Charles, you never know who they're going to out next. Last night Geraldo Rivera was positively out of the closet with joy, as he stirred up the rumor mill with the usual Brit rent-a-comment experts. Gerry, who looks more and more like a refugee from the Village People, was squirming with barely suppressed joy. Listen, take it from me, a man who believes that the royals should be let go for their own safety, Prince Charles is about as gay as a minesweeper. He's about as bisexual as a buffalo. He's a son of a queen, not a queen of a son. I've met Prince Charles on a few occasions socially—"Hello, Charlie boy," Eddie Izzard said last time—and he strikes me as a very nice, interesting, decent man trapped in hell. That's why I think all the royals should be let go, *for their own mental health*. Stalking royals has replaced deer stalking in the U.K. It's a tabloid sport. Fox News has replaced fox hunting. Incidentally I think the correct way of punctuating that should be Fox *News*? (Italics and question mark compulsory.)

▽

Peter, John, Skip, and I take a trip to Niagara Falls. It's about a thirty-minute drive from the shores of Lake Erie where our hotel sits, athwart a constantly Dopplering freeway that sounds like a twenty-four-hour Grand Prix. You can see the smoke of the falls several miles away, a white cloud rising higher than the skyscrapers of downtown Niagara. We crossed a low bridge spanning the river, which churned beneath us in strong skeins of white water, and drove onto the island that separates the two branches of the falls. The water was moving very fast, occasionally interrupted by big black rocks, until it suddenly became ominously smooth, rushed forward, and then plunged into nothing. The river simply disappears. As we leave the car and walk toward the thunderous noise, the ice-cold water droplets in the air dampen and then chill us. It's freezing, about twenty-two degrees here. We reach the viewpoint where we get a first glimpse of the dizzying white feathery falls. It's a breathtaking sight, powerful and impressive and unforgettable. The constant sound of the rushing water, the strong updraft of the water clouds, the ever present rainbow, and the faint echoing shadow of a double rainbow just beyond it leave us speechless. The freezing-cold water from Lake Erie

is tumbling down the Niagara River toward Lake Ontario on its way to the sea. Excited Japanese tourists race past us, snapping away. Although you don't get the full, wide-angled panoply of the Canadian view here on the American side, nevertheless you are much closer to the water's edge, and when we walk over to the larger Horseshoe Falls, the prospect is extraordinary. The sun is shining through the rising mist, making the river gleam as it races to its doom. On the tiny islands that divide the stream, the ferns are etched with white frost. At this point we are within five yards of the water as it ceases to become a river, and suddenly becomes a shower. You can barely see the Canadian side for the swirling clouds of mist, but way below, on a rocky promontory, tiny tourists in yellow raingear are strutting about like Lilliputians. At the base of the falls, the river turns sharp right into a steeply etched channel, where it is joined by the bubbling froth from the secondary falls and sets off bravely for Canada. Can you believe someone went over this last week? It's madness to even step into the river it's so cold. But to voluntarily go over the edge? Yet they survived! We step into the gift shop to get warm. The cold has gone into my bones, and my ears are frozen. It's like being twelve again. They are selling daredevil videos of the people who make a living going over Niagara. It makes comedy look a very soft option.

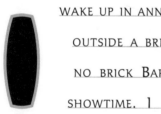

DAY 42

MICHIGAN THEATRE, ANN ARBOR

WAKE UP IN ANN ARBOR. SHE'S VERY COLD. WE ARE PARKED OUTSIDE A BRICK BAPTIST CHURCH ALTHOUGH THERE ARE NO BRICK BAPTISTS AROUND. HERE WE MUST SIT UNTIL SHOWTIME. I ANSWER E-MAILS. HANS TEN CATE, THE PythOnline Webmeister, tells me that in response to my picture of the Finnish Terry Gilliam, a fan from Finland left this on the message boards yesterday:

In Eric's Greedy Bastard tour journal on PythOnline he posted a funny picture of Finnish Terry Gilliam look-alike. Being a Finn myself I immediately recognized the man. He is Vesa-Matti Loiri posing in an ad for Finnish gossip-weekly. Loiri was very popular TV and film comedian in Finland in the 70s and 80s and still works as an actor and musician. He has made many recordings (serious and comedy) and represented Finland in the Eurovision Song Contest in 1980 with a song called "Huilumies." Sadly he got 6 points and ended up as number 19 of 19 entries.

THE
GREEDY
BASTARD
DIARY

Not a bad choice for a Gilliam look-alike! Though in real life he doesn't look as much as Gilliam as in that ad.

But the picture raised another question: When did Eric Idle visit Finland and why didn't I know about it?

Fabulous. So Terry Gilliam snuck off and represented Finland in the Eurovision Song Contest, finishing last in 1980. So *that's* what he was doing then. I am jealous, I have always wanted to represent Finland and score "null points"! Maybe next year. Michael Palin has even written songs about Finland:

Finland Finland Finland
The country where I quite want to be
Pony trekking or camping
Or just watching TV. . . .

You're so sadly neglected
And often ignored
A poor second to Belgium
When going abroad.[16]

Incidentally, you Yanks are missing out on this very silly contest, which is a high point in hilarity as each European nation competes annually to see who can write and produce the worst pop song. There is nationalistic voting so people get cross with one another politically. I'm surprised you haven't tried to copy it yet, but you should certainly try and see it. Monty Python's parody "Bing Tiddle Tiddle Bong" was exactly the sort of song that wins.

Bing tiddle tiddle bong
Bung tiddle tiddle bang

---

[16] "Finland." Words and music by Michael Palin, from *Monty Python Sings*.

ERIC IDLE

Bung tiddle tiddle tiddle tiddle tiddle
Bung tiddle tiddle bong. . . .

How they fared:

1st Monaco with "Bing Tiddle Tiddle Bong"
2nd Italy with "Si si Boing Bang"
3rd Germany with "Nein Bong Uber Tiddle"
4th U.K. with "Bang Bang Bang Bang"

As to my visit to Helsinki, I was there with Martha Stewart two years ago. Well not just Martha, alas, although I think she has a smoldering sexuality, and I'm sure she would have one or two very useful tips in the bedroom, which would not be confined to the décor. I was also with Deepak Chopra, although he mistook me for Jim Watson (honestly, Deepak, do I *look* eighty?). Dr. Watson *was* there, but sadly Sherlock Holmes was missing. It was an honor to meet the great discoverer of the structure of DNA, and a very fine and funny companion he is, too. Also, let's see: Dave Stewart, Dan Aykroyd, Robin Williams, George Lucas, Laurence Fishburne, Gina Gershon, Harry Shearer, Robbie Robertson, Tracey Ullman, and Meg Ryan, to name-drop but a few. It was a fabulous weekend party given by Paul Allen, who unbelievably and unforgettably took us all to St. Petersburg, where we were entertained royally in that extraordinarily beautiful city. We flew first to Helsinki, where we walked around and shopped and then got on a boat that took us overnight across the Baltic to St. Petersburg.

Now that is the way to travel. On a luxury liner. Gorgeous women in their finest clothes, the funniest companions, the most agreeable and educated people on a fabulous freebie. *That's* showbiz, son, and don't you forget it.

St. Petersburg is a city of pink and pastel palaces linked by bridges and more waterways than Venice. It has been lovingly and brilliantly restored after two years of siege by the Nazis during World War Two. The state has spent billions replacing in exact detail even the original fabrics from the Louis XIV manufacturers in France. Ceilings, floors, roofs, woodwork, tapestries, gold leaf—all repainted, replastered, and reupholstered in minute and exact detail in a dozen palaces. The irony is, only communism could have done this. No capitalist society would ever have undertaken such a massive work of public restoration. To think that state socialism spent billions of dollars restoring a tribute to Russian royalty! St. Petersburg is itself an improbable act of will, a city created by decree. Peter the Great decided he must have a Baltic port, departed Moscow, and insisted his court join him in building expensive palaces and a vast capital city out of a mass of swamps. How they must have loved him. . . . We modern courtiers, however, are thrilled to be transported everywhere by boat and barge and hydrofoil, hymned and fed and entertained by hordes of Russian caterers and choirs and costumed ladies, pampered, photographed, and heavily protected from the envy of the locals by ex–KGB officers with Kalashnikovs.

DAY 43

BYHAM THEATER, PITTSBURGH, PENNSYLVANIA

So it's a rainy day in Pittsburgh, and I sit in bed in the bus gazing out of the window at a couple of mustard suspension bridges that float over a mud brown river. I can see the modern ballpark of the Pittsburgh Pirates and a little farther downstream the stadium where the Steelers play. We are parked outside the Byham Theater and I have nothing much to do all day except read and sneeze and give exciting interviews. Our team has been magnificent. Every one of them. We have been working very hard on the road shifting this show from city to city, and I have to say I don't know how they do it. We drive into town overnight and set up a complete show in about six hours: that's set, sound, lighting, props, instruments, merchandise, and wardrobe. We stage a full two-hour musical review, sign merch for at least half the audience, and then pack the whole thing up and hit the road within an hour and a half of the curtain falling. It's incredible, really. People are looking a little tired, but their spirits are magnificent. Gilli is irrepressible. Skip can work twenty-nine hours a day and then say, "You know, I had a really great day." They have used the Internet to organize "street teams" of fans to spread posters and leaflets around their local towns. I am breathless with admiration. And gratitude. If I had an extra ration of rum I'd break it out.

I used to say when I lived in France that the meaning of life was to find a decent plumber, which I eventually did, though he turned out to be Dutch. Now I think it is to surround yourself with people who are better than you are at what they do. And I am a very fortunate man. I am a fortunate man with a cold, alas. I woke up streaming. I suppose that's the drawback of too much audience contact. But I do like meeting the audience after the show. They are touching and tender and affectionate.

I am enjoying my friend Bruce Wagner's new Hollywood novel *Still Holding*. It's very funny and beautifully written, though it makes me slightly anxious, reminding me of the nutty place in which I live, but then I always think of myself as living in *California* and not *Hollywood*, which is a bit saner. The book is about celebrity. He writes about both look-alikes and real stars. Cameron Diaz and Drew Barrymore both feature, and the central character is clearly based on Richard Gere: a Buddhist movie star with a charming smile, although hopefully with a different story line, since Kit Lightwood is casually bashed on the head by a vindictive fan and undergoes severe trauma. The book is also a discussion, and a very erudite one, about

I am an Alzheimer's agnostic. I can't remember whether I don't believe in anything or not.

167

ERIC IDLE

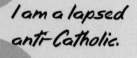

I am a lapsed anti-Catholic.

the arcane world of Buddhism, and it reminds me that though I claim onstage to be a bullshit Buddhist I am really nothing of the sort.

It's the hierarchies of heaven that bother me. All those lost souls waiting to swim into the vagina to be reborn. Who *runs* all that? And it's the same with the western religions; it's the sheer size of the bureaucracy required to monitor everyone's behavior every second that bothers me. Why would anyone go to all that trouble? Why not just let them die and have DNA modify behavior over time? Both Eastern and Western philosophies seem to believe in the perfectibility of the individual soul, the one through reincarnation and the other through rebirth in Heaven. The Hindu goal is to escape the misery of rebirth, but I never really understood what was quite so bad about living in human form on this planet. The Christians, similarly, want us miserable sinners to escape from this vale of tears and sit in Heaven enjoying milk and honey. Well I quite like it here. I think it's quite good, don't you? Yes, we fuck up, but wouldn't you rather be *here* than sitting around for eternity on a diet of milk and honey (yuck) surrounded by the self-righteous? I like a nice miserable sinner now and again.

I have to confess that I am a *praying* atheist. Each morning before I do my yoga I invoke the five major religions of the planet: Christianity (Lord's Prayer), Buddhism (*Om mane padme*), Hinduism (*Hare Krishna*), Judaism (*Shalom*), and Islam (*Allahu Akhbar*). But who do I think I'm talking to? Is this just superstition? They can't *all* be right, can they? Religions are ancient attempts by mankind to come to grips with some of the great moral questions of life, as we evolved from our animal state and before we had any clear idea of what was going on in the universe. I don't wish to be circumscribed by two-thousand-year-old philosophical ideas any more than I would want to be cured by two-thousand-year-old medical practices or be forced to agree with the scientific ideas of Nought B.C. So, why am I here?

Why are we here?
What's life all about?
Is God really real?
Or is there some doubt?
Tonight we're going to sort it all out
For tonight it's the Meaning of Life.

DAY 44

SOUTHERN THEATER, COLUMBUS, OHIO

 OPEN THE CURTAINS TO AN OVERCAST, IRISH SORT OF DAY. THE SKY IS LEAKING. NOT RAINING EXACTLY, BUT IT'S DAMP. MY DRIVER LAST YEAR IN IRELAND SAID THEY'D HAD A VERY GOOD SUMMER.

"It only rained twice. Once for six weeks and once for twelve."
He had another follow-up line ready.
"What has the Irish weather and Cher got in common?"
"I don't know."
"Neither of them has been fucking sunny in a long time. . . ."

▽

Hills and white wooden farmhouses. In the dark woods advertising hoardings stick out. A large sign says ADULT SUPERSTORE 17 MILES. How come when they use the word "adult" it always means "childish"? An "adult bookstore" means books with only pictures. We pass the Zanesville Pottery and cross a muddy river. There are signs for Ohio State University. Small clapboard housing. A railhead. Fields of shorn stubble next to the pale gold

of the uncut corn. Patches of flooding. The eyesore of a gravel works, and everywhere forests, brown sticks of bare trees with no leaves. The wispy woods flash by and give way to gently rolling hills. We are heading east on I-70 toward Columbus. We pass dark red Dutch barns. One more show in this run of four and then a break. I'm beat. We left Pittsburgh at six in the rainy predawn, with a hiss of brakes under the sodium lights. I opened an eye and a curtain and then went back to sleep. We had spent the night in the theater parking bay. Most of the company ventured out after the show, but I was too knackered. What *am* I doing here? No, I don't mean on the planet. I mean on the tour. I raised this question yesterday and I think it's time to try and answer the question.

▽

First of all there is a *testing* aspect to this tour. Can I still do this? Can I really get through the whole journey? About eight years ago I could hardly move for Epstein-Barr. I was losing two or three days a week to debilitating depression and flulike lethargy, but thanks to the miracle of modern doctors my chum Kipper got me to try out a new treatment, and it worked! Now, although I have to take a shot every day (one small prick for man, one giant leap for mankind), I have all this newfound energy. I feel younger than I did at fifty. (Thanks, Kip.) So I do it *because I can.* Life is the art of the possible.

Secondly, it's my métier. It's what I do. I know how to make people laugh. It may even be the *only* thing I know how to do. It is rewarding, and I don't mean financially. (Just as well—see later.) Making people laugh pleases me and meeting them afterward is inspiring. I used to dread meeting Python fans. I felt unworthy and embarrassed, but now I like it. We have made them laugh, often touching them in significant ways at important times in their lives. I know how important *Beyond the Fringe* was in my life, so I can understand that. I can't take

ERIC IDLE

credit for it, it's not what we were trying to do, but it is certainly an effect. We did a good job. We cheered people up.

Thirdly, *it's something to do in the evenings*. It is more exciting than just staying home. There is the sheer adventure of touring America on a bus. Hey-ho, the open road, the traveling circus, the medicine show. It ain't a bad way to see North America, and it's not forever.

Fourthly, it is really good for writing. I always had this fantasy of sitting in a Winnebago, banging away on a laptop while Tania drove me around America in a G-string. A fantasy not at all shared by my beloved. And while it is true that 'Lish, the large English gentleman who drives me, is not the same thing, even without the G-string, still I would never be sitting at home writing my memoirs like this. There's just something about the constant sound of the motor, the long, unwinding road, the many different places we visit, and the sheer time available that invites introspection. Each night I stare at my face in the mirror as I do my makeup. What an odd thing to be doing, I think, but *what would I rather be doing?* Do I miss being on film location stuck in some trailer, trying to memorize someone else's lines? Do I, hell. I'd far rather be preparing to sing "The Galaxy Song," or performing Nudge Nudge with Peter. The show goes by in a rush: one minute I'm walking out for my stand-up and the next it's the intermission. Act two shoots past as I talk directly to the audience about my life. I move them, and they move me, and suddenly we're all singing "Always Look on the Bright Side of Life."

So there you are, I'm halfway home: twenty-eight shows done, twenty-seven to go. It'll soon be Thanksgiving in Chicago, then the wintry leg up in Edmonton and Calgary and then over the Rockies and down the West Coast and then home for the holidays! It's a doddle.[17]

---

[17] English slang. A doddle = a piece of piss; easy.

DAY 45

DAY OFF IN BATTLE CREEK, MICHIGAN

LOOKING INTO THE WINDOW OF VICTORIA'S SECRET IS NOW THE CLOSEST I GET TO SEX. JUST GAZING AT THOSE SLINKY UNDERGARMENTS HAS me remembering there is something missing in my life, and it all fits into those clever little bits of fabric. Well, you know how guys are, and it doesn't seem to go away with age. It just gets slightly less frequent. Yeah. Like once every twenty minutes. I finally had to do an intervention and walk myself away from the store window. Surely Victoria's Secret is sexual harassment? I'm walking through the mall happily whistling Mozart and contemplating the meaning of life (which is shopping, natch), then boing! I'm staring helplessly at the exquisite buttocks of a half naked beauty bent over in a wispy thong, having unwanted lustful thoughts about shagging her senseless. Am I not being

> You know you've been on the road too long when you find yourself gazing into the window of Victoria's Secret for over an hour.

exploited? Am I not quite powerless to prevent my DNA urgently wanting to plant my seed all over her? Aren't they using my male programming to entice me into their store to flash my credit card and pull out my pocketbook and plonk down my fifteen dollars, while wondering wistfully what the lovely assistant is wearing underneath? Is exploitation okay if it's disguised as commerce? [*Yes. That is the point of America.*—Ed.]

▽

I announced on Bill Maher's show I was thinking of suing Victoria's Secret for exploiting me by bombarding me daily with shameless catalogues. Sometimes I can hardly make it back from the mailbox. I have to bend over double to prevent embarrassment. As if the sight of young women in satin skimpies was something I *wanted* to see.

▽

So I am having a day off in Battle Creek, Michigan, wrestling with lustful thoughts in a shopping mall and shortly after my return to the McCamly Plaza there comes a knock at my hotel room. Thinking it's my dinner I open the door to find a cute young blonde in a very revealing, eye-catching black lace shirt, showing a lacy push-up bra and a very healthy display of chest.

"Oh my gad!" she says. "It's *you!*"

"No it isn't," I say.

"Yes it is," she insists.

Philosophically this argument is becoming hard to maintain, so I try another tack.

"Who are you looking for?" I ask in my pleasant British way. Note, I don't say "whom."

"Steven Tyler," she says.

"I'm not him!" I say triumphantly.

"I know that." She is unflappable. "You're that English guy. My sister loves you. Can I have your autograph?"

I hesitate.

"Please," she says.

Dear God, lead us not into temptation. Surely just a quick . . . couldn't hurt . . . no, no, no. . . . I try to avoid staring at her breasts as I sign. But I fail miserably.

"This is so sweet of you," she says, not going away.

I decide silence is the safest course. I nod resolutely and close the door firmly. I'm practically sweating. Perhaps it was a succubus. (No, no, no, that doesn't mean a blow job on a bus. Succubi were medieval devils. Sexy little spirits that tempted you at night and were, probably, a medieval way of accounting for wet dreams.) Succubus or not, I close the door determinedly and return to my diary. Just then my wife calls. How do they do that? Women *know*, you know. They have these antennae. It's extraordinary. She says she likes my diary entry about the God thing and I say, "Oh good. I thought I might have gone too far."

"You always go too far," she says.

She cracks me up. I tell her about the blonde and, God or no God bless her, she believes me.

DAY 46

KALAMAZOO STATE THEATRE, KALAMAZOO, MICHIGAN

E ARE IN THE HEART OF KELLOGG'S COUNTRY: BATTLE CREEK, MICHIGAN. HOME OF CEREAL KILLERS. WE CAME BATTLING IN EARLY THIS MORNING AGAINST STRONG HEADWINDS AND A FLURRY OF SNOW. THE WEATHER DROPPED THIRTY DEGREES between the start and the end of our show in Columbus, Ohio. We were performing at the exquisite Southern Theatre, a gem of an old opera house that has been perfectly restored and reopened only five years ago. Backstage it is clean and efficient and very cozy, and front stage it is all royal blue velvet seats and hardwood flooring and gold Napoleonic wreath carpeting. It is a joy to play, and the crowd are noisy and very responsive.

e are finally heading west. We have been doodling around in circles and swoops all over the East Coast, what 'Lish calls "a dartboard tour," with a sudden dash across country to St. Louis and then back up to Buffalo. Our course makes sense only to a greedy bastard William Morris agent. But I have to say that at least hairdresser Marc has steered us clear of all bad weather, so perhaps he knows what he is doing. He is a little upset that I talk too freely about the promoters. *It's a fucking diary.* You're supposed to tell the truth. That's the whole bloody point. Peter says he has to watch what he says in case it ends up in here. . . . What is it about Yanks and freedom of speech?

Hans the Webmaster is away for the weekend, so of course, I'm late with my diary. It's like being back at school. You don't have to hand in your prep, as the master's gone off for the weekend, so you don't do it. You had to be quite tough as a teacher to survive the kids at my school. Many masters suddenly departed with nervous breakdowns in the middle of term.

I was dumped in my boarding school in Wolverhampton at the age of seven. I knew that a suitcase had been packed, with carefully marked items, but I still felt I had some choice in the matter. I was playing happily in the playground when a loud bell rang. Uh-oh, better go now. Don't want to stay here overnight. But no, too late! My mum had already gone, slipped away "to avoid creating a scene." No farewell. No fond "see you." Just "You boy get along inside and change your shoes." It was twelve years before I managed to escape.

That's really what we did all day: change shoes. To go inside, you put on your indoor shoes. To go and play outside, you take off your indoor shoes, put your indoor shoes inside a cage, and then put on your outdoor shoes. When you come in, you take off your outdoor shoes, put your outdoor shoes in the cage, and then put on your indoor shoes. To go upstairs, you take off your indoor shoes and put them in the cage

> At seven I was sent to a bleak English boarding school in Wolverhampton. That's not quite the end of the world, but you can see it from there.
>
> I was there for twelve years. You get less for murder.

ERIC IDLE

> *Boarding school didn't do me any harm. It made a man of me. And it made a man of my wife.*

with your outdoor shoes, and then you put your slippers on. When you have finished in the dormitory, you come downstairs, take off your slippers, and put on your indoor shoes, unless you are going outside, in which case. . . . Four years of that and you are ready for the senior school. Here you can become a fag. Stop there! A fag is not the same thing as in America. Not at all. So stop all that snickering.

While there was a lot of sexual tampering with the young, and I certainly didn't escape it, a fag in a British boarding school is an honorable tradition. As a fag you were a slave, a skivvy, to a prefect. You fetched him toast, you pressed his army uniform, polished his boots, shone his brasses, blancoed his webbing, cleaned his shoes, washed his sports kit, brought him books from the library—basically waited on him hand and foot. Bullying was endemic, beating common. You could be beaten for anything—being late, being early, being tired, being funny, for silent insolence (my favorite), or for simply being a boy. Beating by prefects was by slipper on the ass. Masters could beat you with canes, usually six of the best across the backside from the headmaster. In the junior school one of the worst beatings was on the hand with a wooden ruler—that hurt like hell—or, even worse, across the back of the calves with a ruler. A sadist called Mrs. McCartney beat me so badly in junior school because I got a math problem wrong that forever after I was hopeless at math.

The first night at school I remember the sound of abandoned kids in their beds sobbing. "Blubbing," it was called, and we soon learned to avoid it, the punishment being intolerable mockery from your peers. In this way we learned to hide our emotions. All good training for adult British life. I remember the freezing cold walk to "the petts" at night, the urinals that constantly overflowed on the cold stone floor, so to "take a slash," you had to leap about barefoot, dodging the pools of piss. Naturally we turned to gangs to defend ourselves from this harsh environment. Our form (class) became a highly evolved gang in the senior school, efficient and cynically corrupt. For instance, we never took a straight exam. They locked the exam papers in a heavily padlocked cupboard, but overnight we simply unscrewed the back of the cupboard and removed the question paper. We never touched the lock! We stole the special answer paper, too, so some kids stayed up all night writing out their answers in a neat hand. Then they smuggled the completed papers in under their sweaters and swapped them over when the master wasn't looking.

Once, the science master, a man we called Heap (because his real name was Everest, and Everest is a big heap), suspected that there had been cheating in an exam. So he made us sit it again and he brought the paper in at the last minute so we didn't have time to steal it like we usually did. We thought resitting this exam was jolly unfair (i.e., the big bullies were fucked), so we made a plan to simply screw it. The entire class sat and stared at the Heap for an hour and a half without lifting a pen, until he finally cracked and said, "All right, you made your point, just answer the final question." So the cheats were never discovered until GCE finals, which were outside exams and couldn't be stolen, since they arrived by special mail on the day of the exam. Of my class of thirty-two, only six made it through to the next term! I, who had had my answers constantly cribbed for four years, turned out to be top, passing all eight "O" levels with flying colors. The rest of the boys simply disappeared.

The strangest thing is that my school was founded as an orphanage in 1850 by a man called John Leese (!). Our school hymn went

> *Honour to John Leese our founder*
> *Builder he in bygone day.*

How weird is that?

QUAD CITY, IDAHO

OKAY, I FINALLY ACHIEVED TOUR BLINDNESS: I WAKE UP IN THE MORNING, AND I DON'T KNOW WHERE I AM. I DON'T KNOW WHAT CITY I AM IN, WHAT HOTEL I AM IN, WHAT FLOOR I AM ON, OR WHAT THE ROOM NUMBER IS. THIS IS IT. PURE Zen. Or Alzheimer's. They woke me up and dragged me out of the bus at about four in the morning and tumbled me into this mystery hotel in this nameless city. I'm not sure why. Usually they let us sleep if we want to, and last night I really wanted to. I think the bus has to go in for a fix, something about the pee tank being full.

So I wake up in a strange hotel room in a strange city. I do notice that the hour has changed and we are now on Central Time. I know we played Kalamazoo last night and it was a very good show, so we are somewhere within five or six hours of Michigan. And I know we are west of Chicago. I know this is Saturday and a day off, because I was hoping to watch soccer; but there aren't any Premier League games on, dammit. So today I am in, well, *where* exactly? I can see a big river. There's a watercolor gray wash sky and triangulated box girder bridges spanning a very wide, fast-flowing river, but I haven't a clue as to what it is, and I'm starving. I look at the room service menu. A clue. They are serving the Idaho breakfast, so I'm guessing we're in . . . Idaho? Also from the menu I deduce it's a Radisson Hotel (very good, Sherlock!), and when my poached eggs arrive, the newspaper they send up is the *Quad City Times,* but I've never heard of Quad City. Aha, the telephone gives an address in Davenport. I search the Web; there is nothing listed for Davenport but endless cut-price hotels and escort services.

Always take a cab if you want to find out what's going on. As I climb in the cabdriver says to me, "You look just like you!" He fills me in on the gaps in my knowledge. Turns out Davenport is the largest of the four cities that make up the Quad Cities. We're on the border with Illinois. That's it just across the river, which turns out to be none other than the Mississippi! He shows me downtown, the police station, the courthouse, the crack house, and the whorehouse. Actually there are two whorehouses. I'm guessing that's why they call it *I'd a Ho*.[18]

This is where the streetwalkers line up," says the cabbie, but jeez they'd freeze the tools of their trade on a day like this. It's a cold gray day with very little light.

"The local crack house," he says, "conveniently located directly across from the courthouse." No one seems to be about. He completes his tour by telling me there are three local sights

---

[18] This has been nominated for worst old joke in a book.

he always suggests first-timers to Davenport visit: the pizza parlor, the ice-cream parlor, and the John Deere factory.

"So much to do," I say. He doesn't notice my irony. He is keen for me to visit the tractor factory. Dear God, I feel I am in an episode of *A Prairie Home Companion*. He proudly points out the armaments factory "where they made the bunker blaster that killed Saddam's kids." I promise to visit.

There is an extraordinary statement from von Rumsfeld in the papers today.

"We are going to outlast them!" he claims proudly. It probably sounds better in the original German.[19] Of course you're not going to outlast them, *they live there.*

> *Killing for God*
> *Is thrilling for you*
> *Each drop of blood you spill*
> *Is by the good Lord's will*
> *If they don't believe*
> *Then why should you grieve?*
> *Just take their breath away*
> *And give them death today*
> *God wants those bastards dead*
> *So shoot them through the head*
> *It's atheist blood you shed*
> *When you're killing for God.*

After the show last week a young couple told me that their favorite thing to do is watch my episode of *Laverne and Shirley*. They watch it at least once a week. Now that is weird. In case you didn't know, I *married* Laverne. I was a guest star on the series back when because Penny Marshall was a friend and in-

---

[19] Nominated for best recycled old joke in a book.

vited me. In the story line I was part of a British rock group called London with Peter Noone (Herman's Hermits) and Stephen Bishop. Laverne and Shirley, big fans of this group, meet us at a party. We all get inadvertently stoned on hash brownies, so stoned in fact that we go off to Las Vegas to get married. I married Laverne. NBC were so unhappy with the suggestion that hash might be enjoyable that they banned this episode on reruns for many years!

▽

I'm not a big fan of sitcom, and I'm not very good at it. I played a ghost in the eighties in a very short-lived series, *Nearly Departed,* for NBC. They wouldn't go with my suggestion to have me haunt an African-American family. I loved the idea of a black family having to live with a poncy white English professor.

"No way, too dangerous," they said.

The executives wished to avoid conflict. But comedy *is* conflict.

▽

A very wealthy executive at a movie studio once told me to make all my characters nicer.

"But that's not funny," I protested. "Comedy is about dysfunction. If you have a perfectly nice family behaving perfectly well toward their perfectly pleasant relatives, *where's* the comedy?"

▽

For a year I was on Brooke Shields's NBC show *Suddenly Susan.* They enticed me with the notion that as her boss, my character would do nothing but abuse her. He would tell her she was a hopeless writer and quite useless. I thought it was hilarious. Brooke and I read together for the executives and it seemed flat-out funny. Two episodes in, as a result of a random "focus group" (five housewives and a questionnaire) I was informed that the "audience" didn't like Susan's being insulted (even though she gave back as good as she got) and so, sadly, my character spent the rest of the year being nice to her and telling her what a great writer she was. I gnashed my teeth and took the quite enormous amounts of money they paid me not to be funny. It was out of this experience that I decided to return to my roots and perform live again, in 2000, singing healthily refreshing filthy songs onstage to big laughs. I think it was a form of penance. Now I'm in Quad City. Just how much penance can you do?

THE
GREEDY
BASTARD
DIARY

ADLER THEATRE, DAVENPORT, IOWA

DAVENPORT IS A BIT OF A SURPRISE. THEY EXCEED ALL RECORDS WITH THE ENCORE BUCKET, AND THERE'S $142 IN THERE BY THE END! THAT'S OUR RECORD AND PER CAPITA IT IS MILES AHEAD OF ANYONE, SO I THINK WE PLEASED 'EM. THIS is before I tell the audience that the money is for charity, so it's impressive and there is clearly a future for me in comedy lap dancing. They really enjoyed the show, a good crowd and wildly enthusiastic. We are very high energy and there are loads of laughs.

▽

My wife's a bit worried about my returning home. She's been reading my diary and is concerned about how I am going to adapt to normal life after all these standing ovations. I tell her I can't wait to get home and, if she likes, she can give me standing ovations. It isn't easy to slip from one life into another, there is bound to be a small period of readjustment. We've all had to adapt to living on a bus and constantly being on the move, but she has a point, it might seem a bit dull. But that is the very point of home. I'm really looking forward to it. I can't wait to be dull. She has helped me through these times before. After I had been on *Munchausen* for six months I had per diem withdrawal. Per diems are weekly cash payments on movies to cover your expenses. In Italy they came in fat brown envelopes stuffed with thousands of lire. A cup of coffee was about ten thousand lire, so a couple of hundred bucks meant a huge wad of Italian cash. It was about as rich as I have ever felt, and I became so addicted to these envelopes that for several weeks after filming ended Tania would fill a fat brown envelope with English cash for me. Now that's a wife. . . .

I'm missing Kevin Nealon's birthday party. He is turning forty (at least that's what he's told his adorable young girlfriend) and is having a big celebration. I call him, and he teases me that all my friends are going to be there, Billy Connolly and John McEuen (the Nitty Gritty Dirt Band) are coming to play banjo. Later I see Billy on CNN flogging *Timeline.* I'm a bit bummed that he mentions Kevin Nealon and Steve Martin and John McEuen all sitting around playing banjos, but he *doesn't mention me.* That's the trouble with fucking banjo players. As a guitarist you're just invisible. You sit around for hours playing three chords so that their strangulated instruments can sound vaguely tuneful, but you might as well not be there. I once spent an evening with five of them—it's a nightmare for a guitarist. They always have one more fucking plaintive lament to play involving E minor, dead miners, and a cat. Banjo players hate all other musicians. They can only tolerate other banjo players. What's the line you never hear at a recording studio? *Will the banjo player please move his Ferrari.* I once saw a decal in the back of a truck with a picture of a banjo with a red line through it. It read "It's the law. Play a banjo, go to jail." John McEuen told me that someone said to him, "If banjo playing

ERIC IDLE

was a good idea the Beatles would have done it." Clint Black tells a gag about an unhappy banjo player: someone broke into his car, where he kept his instrument, and left nine other banjos. In the Rutles sequel *Can't Buy Me Lunch* my narrator says, "The banjo: the last resort of the antisocial." It does seem weird to me that three of my friends who are all comedians, all play the banjo. I wonder if John Cleese is a secret banjo player?

DAY OFF IN MADISON, WISCONSIN

E N ROUTE TO MADISON WE PASS THE LEGENDARY HORMEL FACTORY, THE HOME OF SPAM. JEN, SKIP, AND I GIVE EXCITED SHRIEKS AND BEGIN TO SING "THE SPAM SONG," BUT GILLI IS TOO INVOLVED WITH HER iPOD. WE CHECK INTO the very smart Madison Concourse Hotel, and there is a can of Spam in my bathroom. I can't decide whether it is just for me or whether this is clever product placement by a wily local company.

Cleaning your teeth? Why not a quick mouthwash of Spam first?

After shaving your legs, why not use Spam as a soothing aftershave balm?

Before you go out, don't forget, a quick dab of Spam under the armpits can really attract the opposite sex.

I have more electronic spam than ever on my computer this morning. How much Viagra can I take? Half of America seems to be engaged in selling the other half Viagra. It does seem excessive and intrusive. I don't go barging into corporate offices showing them my dick. Why should I have to put up with this endless huckstering? Erectile dysfunction seems to be the key-

ERIC IDLE

Internet spam is weird, isn't it? First they bombard you with offers to enlarge your penis, then they offer you Viagra, presumably so you can fill up the monstrous engine, and then they offer you another mortgage.

Well, if there is one thing guaranteed to shrink your dick, it's the thought of another mortgage.

stone of modern America. How long before Congress acts?[20]

We get in very late (3:00 A.M.) and I am awakened at eight by a symphony of door slamming, noisy vacuuming, and loud foreign lingo. It's the artillery of the artful maid. Wake 'em up early, and you can go home sooner. I had checked for that old trick, the cunningly set radio alarm, but I hadn't prepared for this early-morning barrage, and I wasn't wearing earplugs. In my best John Hurt voice I protested volubly to the charming staff.

"After all," I argue, "I don't have a DO NOT DISTURB APART FROM DOOR SLAMMING, SHRIEKING, AND VACUUMING sign on my door."

The hotel is offering something called a Wisconsin Brat Breakfast—rather appropriate with my own bratty behavior. It describes this as a State Fair Blue Ribbon brat patty. I am none the wiser. I plump for the lox and bagel. I think I may be turning Jewish. Idell is clearly a Jewish name. I am certainly becoming more and more Jewish on this trip. My daughter has a play-off basketball game today and last night I wished her "Mazel tov."

"*Mazel tov??*" she said.

"I know," I said. "I meant *break a leg.*"

During my time in *The Mikado,* an orchestra member came up to me. "Tell me," she said. "Are you Jewish, or just very talented?"

Madison seems to have grown some new features since we were last here. To begin with there is a

---

[20] Two hundred years. Congress is another word for Intercourse.

magnificent domed state capitol building which would not be adrift in Rome or Venice. Now that wasn't here last time, I swear. And this morning I opened my curtains to find a huge lake. That *certainly* wasn't here before. Jen and I both agree these features are new. And what is the name of this new lake? Can this be the legendary Lake Huron, the Great Lake that no one mentions?[21] John has been wondering why there are no references to Lake Huron. It is like the elder Osbourne child, something never mentioned in public. John is concerned by this. He wants me to write a lyric about it. Obviously we all hear a lot about Lake Erie and Lake Ontario, and Lake Superior is almost overbearing in its name and attitude, but of Lake Huron, nothing. No PR. No T-shirts. No posters. No songs. Of course only a pianist could want his lyricist to find rhymes for Huron. (*You're on?* Forget it.) We have been working on a new song that we intend to try out soon. It's called "Fuck Christmas." It has a lovely melody. We're thinking of using the Canadians as guinea pigs after Thanksgiving. When Peter hears us rehearsing it he says, "Is nothing sacred?" Then he goes off singing "Sit on My Face."

---

[21]   As anyone with half an inch of sense knows, Madison is nowhere near Lake Huron. It is situated on an isthmus between Lake Mendota and Lake Monona in southern Wisconsin.

DAY 50

THE BARRYMORE THEATRE, MADISON

A RAINY DAY. THE LAKE HIDDEN IN A WASH OF GRAY LIKE A JAPANESE PRINT. NO SKY, NO SHORE, JUST THE FAINT BRUSHSTROKE OF AN ISLAND. PAVEMENTS WET, THE STUDENTS, COCOONED IN THEIR WINTER GEAR, SCUTTLE INTO their buildings, ballooned like Michelin tire men. Yesterday on these same streets the crack dealers in their hooded sweats pushed their girls around and threw mock punches at one another. Today it's too cold. They're huddled somewhere in their cars waiting for trade. I curse their activity, looking cool and hip while selling misery to somebody's kids.

▽

My spirits are gray today, too. My mother, with impeccably bad timing, died on Tania's birthday, and that's tomorrow. I don't think she meant to. I believe her intention was to be gone long before, but when we went in to tell her it was Tania's birthday she gave a great sigh and said, "Oh no." We left my son holding her hand and went for a quick walk in the nearby canyon on a bright sunny day, and when we came back Carey said, "She's

gone." And she had slipped away. I remember two men carrying a tiny load in a white sheet up the stairs and out of the front door. That's what we become. Garbage disposal. Now she sits in a box on the shelf in my library. People say, "Why haven't you buried or scattered her remains?" but this is much closer. Why is one place better than another?

▽

Tania and I collected her ashes from Forest Lawn, and as I went to put the box in the trunk of the car Tania said, "You can't put your mother in the trunk." So we put her on the front seat. Driving home we became hysterical. What if I had to brake suddenly and the ashes flew all over the car windshield? What would we say to the police patrol man?

"What's all that in there, *drugs*?"

"No. That is my mother."

▽

I think laughter in the face of death is a perfectly appropriate response to grief. At Harry Nillsson's funeral, just as they were lowering the coffin, Alan Katz said, "Oh, I spoke to Harry last week, and he said he wanted me to have his royalties."

▽

The bad news from Camp Cleese is that the tall one is horizontal with flu. So poor John is sick, and our shoot in Chicago is canceled. I e-mail him good wishes and confess to disappointment. I was looking forward to seeing him, though not to the photo shoot itself. *Vanity Fair* e-mailed last week and asked for my sizes, and terrible visions of costumes ran through my mind—are they expecting us to dress up? Mind you, now that I think of it, it might be hilarious if we were all photographed in *drag* at our ages. A group of pissy old women, made up to the nines. Wouldn't that be funny?

ERIC IDLE

▽

Tania is sick, too. She has laryngitis and has completely lost her voice. She has a deep, husky, sexy voice on the phone, but sadly I can't keep her on for long—it's too painful for her. Tomorrow is her birthday and then on Saturday she flies to see me in Chicago. I have now been with her more than half her life. Poor thing. She must be a saint. But a Scorpio. So watch it. According to that pseudoscience called astrology, Aries and Scorpios never get along. Well, twenty-seven years says "crap."

▽

Even my greedy bastard agent is sick. He has the flu. I wish him well, but he seems more concerned about the show's numbers. Now *that's* a real agent. Normally flu season starts around Thanksgiving. Indeed this festival is responsible for spreading germs throughout America. Everyone flies around kissing and catching something and then returning sick. Planes are the ideal vehicles for spreading disease. People are crammed together for hours sniffling and coughing, breathing in the air of their sick neighbors (recycled but not resanitized), and then they get off the planes already ill. The airlines give a free ride to every hitchhiking virus in North America. After Thanksgiving everyone is out of action. I have labeled this the "Idle Thanksgiving Effect" for the convenience of future medical science. It is particularly noticeable in L.A., where people are a little healthier for longer, since the depredations of winter are later and less harsh, but after Thanksgiving they all go down like ninepins. So get your flu shots today and fly masked! Better to look stupid than get sick. I am thinking of adapting some kind of burka. This female Muslim headgear seems ideal and would also protect against bad airline movies, but how to read underneath it? There's the rub.

DAY 51

THE PANTAGES THEATER, MINNEAPOLIS, MINNESOTA

I HAVE SLEPT UNDER THE STARS. I WAKE UP ALONGSIDE A BLACK WALL PAINTED WITH THE NAMES OF ROCK STARS. WE'RE IN MINNEAPOLIS, THAT'S GREEK FOR "SMALL APPLES." [*PLEASE DON'T LISTEN TO HIM.*—ED.] WE'RE ON A MAIN STREET opposite the Target Center, and I am looking at the names of those who have played here: Cyndi Lauper, Billy Idol, Eurythmics (my pal Dave Stewart), and the Reverend Horton Heat (recently deceased). It reminds me I once had a fictional group called the Self-Righteous Brothers. I also liked a Rutles gag about Crosby, Stills, Nash, Young, Gifted, and Black. For a Python record I created a silly fictional group called Toad the Wet Sprocket, and one day I was driving along the freeway in California and heard the deejay say, "That was Toad the Wet Sprocket," and I was so shocked I nearly drove off the road. They eventually sent me a platinum album by way of a thank-you.

I have been reading Otto Friedrich's excellent book *Before the Deluge,* a history of Berlin before the Nazis. The book reminds me of my own visit to Berlin at the height of the cold war in 1963. It was summer and I was hitch-hiking through Germany with a friend. We were sleeping out in fields and at

ERIC IDLE

Rex Stardust, lead electric triangle with Toad the Wet Sprocket, has had to have an elbow removed following their recent successful worldwide tour of Finland. Flamboyant ambidextrous Rex apparently fell off the back of a motorcycle.

"Fell off the back of a motorcyclist, most likely," quipped ace drummer Jumbo McClurey upon hearing of the accident. Plans are already afoot for a major tour of Iceland.

building sites, and decided after visiting Nuremberg to head on up to Berlin by bus, where my pal Alan Sinfield had friends, and we could sleep in beds for a change. Nuremberg is the beautiful medieval city of Albrecht Dürer, now largely reconstructed after Allied bombing flattened it. It houses the infamous rally site where the Führer experienced his fatal ecstasies. This is a huge area, as big as six football fields, and we stood on the Leni Riefenstahl spot and spouted German nonsense and goose-stepped about in the traditional British way.

▽

Berlin in those days was an island surrounded by the Russian satellite Communist country of East Germany. To get to it by road you had to pass through various East German checkpoints and two suspicious-looking English boys were swiftly pulled off the bus by the far-from-gentle border Polizei and our rucksacks thoroughly searched. On the return journey, we got the same treatment, only this time all the pictures of the Wall (die Mauer) were confiscated. Wouldn't want that news to leak out. . . .

▽

We hadn't seen a newspaper in weeks and didn't know it but there was a strong reason for the heightened tension. Our timing was impeccable. John F. Kennedy was about to visit Berlin. We entered a city feverish with excitement. We were staying in a nice, clean, German apartment with friendly people, in a typical wooded suburb, except suddenly and terrifyingly at the end of the street was the huge, electrified, barbed-wire Wall, with guard towers and a cleared killing field beyond. Shocking. I had no idea Berlin was such a wide open city, with parks and hills and lakes with sailboats. East Berlin, through Checkpoint Charlie, was by contrast bleak and depressing, with huge gray workers' blocks. We passed the flattened site of Hitler's bunker and listened to the compulsory "guide" spouting about the triumph of communism, but one glance at the architecture was enough. We were happy to get back through the Wall, images of John Le Carré in our heads.

West Berlin was *en fête*. Streamers and banners everywhere welcomed J.F.K. and the U.S.A. who had kept the city alive during the Berlin airlift. We were taken to see the parade. The streets were lined with thousands of people watching the cavalcade go by: it consisted of sixteen limos of Secret Service followed by seventeen limos of international press. But finally they appeared: Willy Brandt (the legendary mayor of Berlin) standing up in the back of an open vehicle and JFK himself next to him. The Germans went nuts. He passed right in front of us. I remember the shock of his hair and how surprised I was by his ruddy appearance. A florid-faced JFK flashed that radiant grin and waved at us and was gone in a scurry of Secret Service vehicles, leaving nothing behind but the memory of that big, broad smile. Like the Cheshire cat. We returned to the apartment to watch his famous speech on television, where he proclaimed, "Ich bin ein Berliner." Which, as Eddie Izzard points out, means "I am a doughnut."[22]

Tania and I were once walking down a deserted street in Chicago when a back door to the Roosevelt Hotel opened

---

[22] In other circumstances he might have said "I am a Hamburger" or "I am a Frankfurter."

ERIC IDLE

and President Reagan emerged with a couple of Secret Service agents. He looked startled to see only us, waved, and then was whisked away in a black car. There was no one else around. We pinched ourselves. *Did that just happen?*

Robin Williams was due to host a Clinton fund-raiser in L.A., but his movie director, Ivan Reitman, wouldn't let him go. The president wanted him at his table, but his director would not release him! So Robin and Marsha asked Tania and me if we'd like to use their tickets. We weren't doing anything that evening so we thought, well, why not? Having faced the traffic snarl and passed through the security we entered the Harold Lloyd mansion, and when I say mansion I mean hotel. In England some towns are smaller than this.

We wandered around the cocktail party picking up a few friendly faces, who all asked us what the hell we were doing there, and finally we were called into another garden where a huge stage was erected before an outside auditorium. The audience was laid out in rows on the grass on those little golden event chairs that appear at weddings. We were walked toward the front. Great seats, we thought, no problem about hearing the Eagles from here. We kept being led farther and farther forward, until there we were on the second row being led into the center. Suddenly my wife gave a little gasp and clutched me. She was staring wide-eyed at the seats directly in front of ours. Two labels read THE PRESIDENT and MRS. CLINTON! People who had shelled out thousands of dollars stared at us in envy at our extraordinary position, wondering why the hell *we* were there, but we could only smile nicely and bask in the knowledge that sometimes life (like God) moves in a mysterious way.

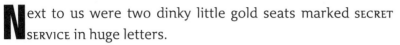

Next to us were two dinky little gold seats marked SECRET SERVICE in huge letters.

"Not much of a secret," I said to Harvey Weinstein, who was looking at me with new respect, wondering what he'd missed. But we were interrupted by "Hail to the Chief," and everyone rose and applauded as the First Couple came in and sat down right in front of us! My wife and I felt like Cinderella for a night. We had to pinch ourselves we were really there, decked out in fancy clothes, sitting for two hours within arm's reach of Hillary and William Jefferson Clinton. I could have reached out and touched both of them. But I didn't; the muscles of the men next to me were powerfully intimidating. It was an extraordinary thing for a nonvoting, tax-paying, part-time ex-transvestite English comic to be sitting behind the most powerful man in the world, watching him hug Hillary while the Eagles played, seeing him laugh at Tom Hanks, and watching him wipe away a tear as Barbra Streisand sang with thirty young kids.

Sometimes, as Barry Cryer observed, life is very well written.

MY DEAR SWEET FRIEND MICHAEL KAMEN

THESE LAST FEW DAYS I HAVE FELT DEATH STALKING, HOVERING IN THE WINGS. IN DAVENPORT WE WERE SHOWN THE DRESSING ROOM WHERE CARY GRANT DIED. THE ANNIVERSARY OF MY MOTHER'S DEATH HAS BEEN MUCH ON my mind, and then an NPR interviewer asked me all about death for a program this weekend on that subject. And now it strikes with the devastating news that my good friend Michael Kamen has died suddenly of a heart attack at the ridiculously early age of fifty-five. Michael had been bravely fighting M.S. for a number of years but seemed to be overcoming its invidious clutches, so that this was unexpected and totally heartrending news.

Michael was my friend since the early seventies, a classically trained American musician with two lovely daughters whom he adored and a lovely English wife called Sandra. He lived in great style in a splendid house in Notting Hill Gate, London. He was a total musician, equally at home in the symphony hall and the rock-and-roll recording studio. One minute he would be conducting Pink Floyd's *The Wall* in Berlin, the next waving a baton at Pavarotti and Sting at La Scala, Milan, then jetting off to Hollywood to compose film scores for Mel Gibson's *Lethal Weapon* movies, then zooming off to Canada to conduct the opening gala of the Winter Olympics, and back to Hyde Park, London, for the Queen's Jubilee. In short, a polymath. A man of great talent. A humane man, a wonderful, lovely, lovable, laughing big bear of a man. I hugged him recently at the opening of the movie *The Concert for George* in L.A., and he had his usual big wide smile and an elegant cane. You can see him in that movie, thin from the M.S., conducting the strings for that concert, with his usual beaming smile.

▽

I was shocked when Tania told me the dreadful news but somehow managed to contain it until I spoke with Sandra in London, when she said "there are no words," and I lost it. She was bravely planning an L.A. tribute to Michael. She said friends had been calling from all over the world weeping, and I lost it again. I know exactly how they feel. I spoke briefly with his longtime partner and friend Bob Ezrin, but what can you say? There *are* no words. I met them both in the late seventies in New York, when I was attempting to make a film version of *The Pirates of Penzance* and Jim Beach (the Queen manager) recommended Michael to score and Bob to record. We became great friends and spent happy holiday times in Barbados, where Michael would rent the same rickety old house perched precariously over a cove just south of Bridgetown. We hung out for hours drinking margaritas and laughing, always laughing. He always found me funny, and made no secret of it. He would collect things I said and remember them and quote them back to me with glee. Sometimes he would make me laugh by telling me a funny line, and when I laughed out loud and said, "Now *that's* funny," he would say, "It should be, you said it." For instance margaritas in his house were always known as Mrs. Lots because I once spat out one he had mixed, complaining it was far too salty, saying, "It was like going down on Mrs. Lot." Now I have no one to remember my jokes.

▽

Last year in St. Petersburg, we were returning from a sumptuous Summer Palace of the Czars to that most elegant of cities by hydrofoil. A very sweet, elegantly dressed, elderly lady came slowly on board and then asked me very politely if she could sit next to me.

"Well okay," I said, "but you keep your hands to yourself."

Michael nearly fell overboard.

▽

Michael always made me feel good. He always made me feel he loved me and wanted to be near me, and I can't bear the thought that he has gone. One memorable weekend in a hotel room in Rome we wrote and recorded an entire pseudo-Handel miniopera for *The Adventures of Baron Munchausen*, called *The Torturers' Apprentice*. A chorus of eunuchs sang lustily

> *A eunuch's life is hard,*
> *A eunuch's life is hard,*
> *A eunuch's life is hard,*
> *But* nothing *else is. . . .*

I was looking on my computer and found I had written a speech for him as recently as September, which I was going to record on film, as I couldn't make a dinner honoring him and presenting him with an award. Sadly no one came to film it, but this is what I had written:

Hello Michael.

Unfortunately my parole officer wouldn't let me be here this evening.

He says there are too many film producers present.

As you know this is the charity season, when film producers and studios give to charity all the money they've stolen from people like us over the past year, thus gaining an undeserved reputation for humanity while grabbing a large tax credit.

And I wouldn't honestly be seen in the same room as some of these shits.

Indeed, as you know I have been fucked by more film producers than Joan Collins.

So my advice to you, Michael, is to get out quick.

Don't wait for the rubber chicken.

Don't even count your fingers.

Just leave now.

[Cell phone rings.]

Excuse me. Hello. Oh hello, Harvey. Yes, lovely to hear from you. I'm making a film, well it's a charity film. A tribute to Michael Kamen. No, it's not important. Oh. I'd love to be in a movie. Five thousand dollars? For eighteen weeks in Poland in the winter? Playing a sympathetic Nazi? With some nudity? Sure. That sounds good money for Miramax. Yes, that sounds lovely. Looking forward to it. Bye.

Sorry, Michael. Where were we? Oh dear, we've run out of time.

I was going to talk about your humanity. What a decent chap you are.

How I have known and loved you since 1976 when we tried without success to make a movie version of The Pirates of Penzance, *and have watched with*

ERIC IDLE

pride as your career flourished and you became THE Michael Kamen—the celebrated composer of Mr. Holland's Anus. *The man who wrote "Have You Ever Really Really Really Really REALLY Ever Loved a Woman?"*

But I think we can take that as read, blah de blah de blah. Fabulous blah de blah de blah great musician blah de blah. I think that'll do it.

[Off camera.]

Hey, I've got a movie from Miralax . . .

Good-bye, my friend. I really miss you.

THE VIC THEATRE, CHICAGO

I LOVE CHICAGO. WE DRIVE INTO TOWN BEFORE DAWN AND I NAP FOR A WHILE, BUT IT'S A LOVELY, WARM SUNNY DAY AND TOO FINE TO WASTE INDOORS. I WANDER DOWN MICHIGAN AVENUE, DOING SOME EARLY CHRISTMAS SHOP-ping. I can't think what to buy Nicole Kidman. Or for that matter Halle Berry. And what do I get Cameron Diaz? Panties again? I always get Hugh Grant panties, he's easy to please, and I'm getting Russell Crowe a tool kit with his name on it. Mel Gibson, well, a copy of *The Life of Brian*, natch. *Can you believe he's made the same story and missed all the jokes?* And whatever will I get Kate Hudson? Will she want me to make her cookies like last year? It's so difficult with these big stars. [*Dream on.*—Ed.]

It is wonderful to be here. Chicago girls are *so* beautiful. I have to catch my breath sometimes. I like the way they look you boldly in the eye. I do hope we do the *Spamalot* tryouts here. I know it gets cold but this is a fine city to spend a few months, and I have lots of relatives here. Lily loves it and can't wait to come. I can't wait to see her. She flies in tomorrow: one can at a pinch live without a wife, but to live without a daughter as well, that's too much.

ERIC IDLE

We arrived at five in the morning after a sell-out show in Minneapolis. That's right, folks, a full house at last. It was a screaming, packed-out auditorium at the recently refurbished Pantages Theater. Our street teams seem to be working. During the show a lovely blonde came up, waving a pair of red panties provocatively, which she dropped in the encore bucket to cheers and applause from the audience. Peter grabbed them. (Say no more.) Later I asked her if she had come prepared, with her panties already in her pocket, and she obligingly bent over to show me that she hadn't. NVP! [*No visible panty line.*—Ed.] Another girl offered me ten bucks if I will let her touch my butt. Now there's a dilemma for a gentleman. Am I the sort of man who will let strange women touch his ass for cash? All her friends say please, oh please, she has an important wager. Finally, I decide to let her so that she can win her bet, but decline to take any money for it: that way I feel like a slut, but at least I avoid behaving like a whore. Miss Manners would be proud of me. In Madison a girl climbed *into* the encore bucket! Now there's a commitment. We gave her back. I don't think charities accept young women. Except perhaps for the Clinton Library. . . .

I awake this morning to see the sun rising magnificently out of the lake. A wind is picking up, and there are big waves. I'm in a hurry to get ready for breakfast TV. The toilet overflows. It's a sitcom moment. I'm standing in puddles of water around my ankles trying to stop a Niagara. I use my rudimentary plumbing skills, acquired from years of living in Provence, to prevent its flooding the bedroom and drowning the hotel from inside. Then I have to dash.

Scott Sampson is downstairs to take me and Scott Keeton, my ever reliable guitar tech, to WGN for *Good Morning Chicago,* where I sing "Always Look on the Bright Side" and "The Lumberjack Song." People crowd into the studio and join in the singing and whistling, and they all have a great time. Then we hustle across town to catch the end of Mancow's radio show.

Mancow is very sweet and genuinely apologetic about Tony Clifton attacking me last time I was on. I reassure him I really don't mind. In fact I'm quite proud of how I dealt with Bob Zamuda, when he accused me of "profiting from dead guys." I said that was rich coming from a man who pretended to be an Andy Kaufman character, when *he* has been dead for years. The studio erupted with laughter and applause.

"Touché," said Mancow.

On *Chicago Tonight* the interviewer asked me about Michael Jackson. I said, "It's funny, his career was going so bad; last year he couldn't get arrested. . . ."[23]

We dash over to CNN at the Herald Tribune building for a nationwide TV interview which Jam are particularly keen I do. Tiarra has set this up for 8:40 Central time. We are there early. Except, oops, we are an hour too late. We have missed the slot.

The doorman says, "They've all gone. They were waiting for you, but you never showed."

Scott Sampson is furious and calls Steve Traxler of Jam. Neither of them can believe it. I have grown accustomed to it so

---

[23]   A Peter Crabbe gag.

ERIC IDLE

it's no real surprise, it's about the eighth time this has happened, and I'm getting a bad reputation for no-shows, which I hate. Just then Tiarra calls. I tell her as calmly as I can that we missed the interview, because she got the time wrong.

"That's not possible," she says. "I can't have done that."

That's what makes me snap. An apology, some kind of "I'll look into it," or "I'm *so* sorry," *might* have made a difference, but total denial . . . fuck off.

"Tiarra," I said, "you're fired." It felt good. I don't want to unload on her now that she is history, but I have never in my life . . . etc., etc.

So au revoir, Tiarra. I have never fired anybody before. It feels surprisingly good. I feel like Donald Trump. I'm in touch with my inner monster.

DAY 54

THE VIC THEATRE, CHICAGO

THE VIC IS IN THE LAKESHORE WRIGLEYVILLE DISTRICT OF CHICAGO, WITH THE EL THUNDERING BY OVERHEAD EVERY FEW MINUTES. DURING THE SHOW THE HOUSE SHAKES AS THE TRAINS PASS. IT FEELS LIKE A MOMENT FROM AN EALING comedy. I am really enjoying doing the show now. After thirty-five performances and a couple of months on the road it all comes perfectly naturally. I feel very comfortable onstage, no panic, no alarm, no fears; indeed at one point, when there is a massive explosion from our sound equipment and we all completely lose our place in "The Money Song" and each pick up at a different spot so the audience sees four people each confidently belting out different lyrics and different tunes, it makes me laugh out loud with joy. The audience doesn't mind at all. They laugh right along with us. Jen wins; she has such a strong and powerful voice.

▽

Mancow is in the house, which is kind, because he said he would, and my very sweet and beautiful niece Sasha comes to the show, with her friends Joelle and Katy. She has grown into a fine and adorable woman. I have known her all her life. I am a fortunate greedy bastard to have a large Chicago family of in-laws and they are all coming tonight. Then we have almost a week off. We have come almost ten thousand miles since we set out from Boston. Now I'm going to take a break and spend Thanksgiving with my family. Some of the company are flying home to see their spouses, while the buses and the rest of the tour party make their way up to Edmonton via Fargo. I know Jen and Gilli are looking forward to finally getting into my bed. I hope they clean up afterward. While on tour I keep the door locked at night just in case. You never know with young women. Obviously I have powerful hormones which young females are unable to resist and— [*Oh, shut up.*—Ed.]

▽

I'll be rejoining everyone in Edmonton, Canada, on Thursday night. Meanwhile I shall miss my roommates. Skip has become invaluable. Jen is a delightful companion on the road and getting better and better in the show, while Gilli is a total amazement. As well as stage manager and lighting director and wardrobe whipper-in and general pooh-bah on the tour she is a gifted singer-songwriter in her own right. Now she works on my back! I am in pain after the sound check and she puts me on my face and cracks my back and massages my shoulder and, voilà, I am fine. Is there no end to her talents?

▽

A finely built young lady leaves her lacy red bra in the encore bucket and afterward kindly shows me where it came from. No, not Victoria's Secret, her *chest*. I have been asked to sign one or two breasts on this tour. It always seems a little weird. But you know I do it. Somebody has to. Our Greedy Bastard promoters are in the house. Arnie Granat is beaming after the signing. I give him a big hug. I like all the Jam people. Apart from Arnie, Steve Traxler, and Scott Sampson, their company seems to consist of very attractive young women. They throw us a party after the show and buy us dinner at Leona's, which is more than decent of them. Afterward I am sniffed appreciatively by their women. I told you about these Chicago gals, didn't I?

Arnie drives me home. We agree Chicago is a great city. "If the weather were better," says Arnie, "everyone would live here."

THE VIC THEATRE

PACKED HOUSE. SATURDAY NIGHT AT THE VIC. WE GO GANG-BUSTERS. I'M REALLY LOOSE AND THE MATERIAL GOES VERY WELL. WE SLIP IN AND OUT OF SKETCHES AND THE AUDIENCE JOIN IN LUSTILY ON THE SING-ALONGS. I OUGHT TO DO MORE writing for my stand-up bit, but most of my writing time is taken up with my diary. Writing comedy one-liners is what I started out doing way back in the sixties for the legendary David Frost, a great *appreciator* of comedy and someone who made a career from using other people's jokes. Usually he paid very well for them, but apparently at the beginning of his career he didn't, so that Peter Cook called him "the bubonic plagiarist" and "the thief of bad gags," and said that his only regret in life was saving David Frost from drowning. But David is still going strong, while Peter is sadly in the great Footlights Club in the sky. I used to impersonate David on TV. This was sheer ingratitude on my part, since he gave me my first TV writing job, and I ought to feel bad, except that soon after I played him interviewing Dan Aykroyd as Richard Nixon on *Saturday Night Live* he came up and said to me, "I loved your Frost." I think when people can refer to themselves in the third person you don't really have to worry about their feelings. Last year on his radio show I thanked him for giving me my start in TV and he was very sweet. He embraced me, and he almost wept.

Last night was great for me because Tania and Lily arrived from L.A. I was sitting in the hotel contemplating the view when in walked my girls. My heart lifted.

"Group hug," said Lil. "Come on, parentals."

I hugged them both and held them close.

Later, Lily rode with me to the show and we *both* did our makeup backstage, an unusual father-daughter thing. More of my in-laws came to the show, including my father-in-law, Alex, who is ninety-one, and my ma-in-law, Algea. Joyce, my sister-in-law, brought her two grown-up daughters, Kris and Kim (with their husbands, Victor and Bob), and my brother-in-law Mark, who is a cop in Hillside, was sitting right down front with his wife, Lori, beaming away at me. In act two I introduced all my folks to the audience. Afterward we popped out for pizza.

Near the end of the show during "Bright Side" I turned around, and there to my surprise and delight was Lily on-stage singing away. Peter brought her on again for the "Lum-berjack" encore. She's an old pro by now. Her debut was three years ago at the Chicago Theater on my last tour, at the tender age of nine. She also did the Toronto shows, singing backup with the girls, before capping that with two nights live at Carnegie Hall! Not a bad career start for a fourth-grader.

OFF TO THE BURBS, CHICAGO

AM STAYING AT A FOUR SEASONS HOTEL; I KEEP PLAYING VIVALDI'S *THE FOUR SEASONS*, AND IN THE LAST FEW DAYS WE HAVE *HAD* ALL FOUR SEASONS HERE IN CHICAGO. IT WAS SUMMER THE DAY WE ARRIVED, AND THE GIRLS WERE OUT shopping on the Miracle Mile in their revealing dresses. The next day it was spring, still warm but cooler; yesterday it poured, and there was a mighty fall wind; and today it's the freezing dead of winter. Overnight the temperature has halved to thirty degrees. From my room I can see a baseball field white with frost, and there is ice on the puddles where the rain lingered. Dotted flecks of frozen ground appear on the patchy holes of the building site below and there are soft, billowy clouds full of snow to the east over Michigan. A low-angled sun is lighting the lake with steel glints, shafting through the clouds like a holy card but then, suddenly, here it comes, horizontal snow dotted like scribble on a blackboard, blown sideways at tremendous pace past my seventeenth-floor window. It looks like poor TV reception. Then, improbably, the snow comes rising up from below, big cotton wool chunks, so that it feels like we're upside down in a snow-toy world. This morning Lily is very excited to wake up and see the snow, L.A. child that she is. But oh my God it's freezing out there. There's a wind chill of fifteen giving a total of minus fifteen degrees. I think of the poor bastards on the bus heading for Fargo. They pulled out at midnight, and they'll probably still be trucking through the snow. Just to stay spiritually in touch with my touring companions I head downstairs for a full body massage.

Last night I went to see Gilli perform at Jilly's, a small piano bar in the Wells Street district. She was clearly excited to be performing at this famous Frank Sinatra joint, and the owners were very friendly and welcoming. It has a horse-track-shaped central bar with two barmen working the patrons at stools, and down at the far end there is a piano that extends elegantly into a low cocktail bar. Jen was perched here nursing a large mysterious cocktail, doing Margo from *Fargo* impersonations, while Gilli was behind the keyboard. Before her was a glass jar, which, she explained to the audience, is a tips jar. Now where did she get that idea?

"Show us your tips," I yell.

"For those of you who just came in my name is Gilli Moon."

"What's your name for those of us who have been here ages?" I bellow rowdily.

▽

You've been watching Fart Nerdle Piddlecrap with Tim Wimbleton-Stoat Bathtub and his guest The Reverend Sump-Mangling-Gut Basket Spiggot Patcher, Vicar of the Holy Impossible Batman.

Jen is getting quite lit up and rambles on about the delightful cocktail she is downing, while Gilli does a series of songs about men who have dumped her and why they have all done her wrong. She is a wonderfully confident performer and clearly enjoys herself. There is a small group of Gilli Moon fans (Moonies?) who have come from the Ukraine. They tell me that Python is very funny in Russian.

The Greedaye Baftard

or Have it Yore Way
or fay no more

Dramatis Personae

Eric Idle . . . .*A greedaye baftard*

Sir John Du Prez . . . .*A piano tunerf friend*

Sir Peeter Crabbe . . . .*A crabbye olde baftard*

Miftress Jennifer Julian . . . .*A harlot*

Miftress Gilli Moon . . . .*A lunatic and ftrumpet*

M. Skip Rickert . . . .*A touring mafter & holder upper*
of ye figns

Signor Scott Keeton . . . .*A tuner of guitarf*

Signor Darren Mora . . . .*An amplificator of found*

Mifter Thomas Hussman . . . .*A feller of fouvenirs*

Mafter Morris and Mafter Carey . . . . . .*Coachmen*

The Story So Far

Eric, one of the seventeen original ex–Monty Python boys, is attempting to revive revue by taking a party of weirdos on the road to see if it is possible to go all the way from Boston to L.A. via covered wagon while performing a comedy show. So far they have traveled more than two months for almost ten thousand miles in ever widening circles and have reached Chicago. Harsh weather and bitter cold awaits them in the frozen land of Canada, but for the moment the circle has been interrupted. The fellowship of the ring is broken. The ten have been scattered: John to the west of L.A., Scott to Oklahoma, Skip to Arizona, Eric to the suburbs of Chicago, while the rest have struggled on through bitter cold via bus to Fargo, 690 miles from Chicago. Today they check out of their hotel to drive the 1,225 miles to Edmonton, where they will arrive sometime between 6:00 and 9:00 in the early morning of Wednesday. The remainder of the party will attempt to join them via plane in Edmonton Thursday night, so that they can continue their quest.

THANKSGIVING IN CHICAGO

IT IS VERY SAD BEING PULLED OUT OF A FAMILY THANKSGIVING DINNER IN CHICAGO TO CATCH A PLANE FOR CANADA. MY DAUGHTER IS IN TEARS, MY WIFE HUGS ME. IT'S LIKE GOING OFF TO ACTIVE DUTY. [*NO IT'S NOT, YOU TWAT. NO ONE will be shooting at you.*—Ed.]

I love being part of an American family. Tania's extended family of Russian, Italian, Mexican Americans have always accepted and embraced me. They are about as far from showbiz as it is possible to be. We are twenty-six at dinner. I sit among all ages from nine months to ninety. Kids are running around shrieking, everyone is talking at once, helping cook food, or watching football. I feel all the joy it is possible for a non-meat-eating limey to feel on Turkey Day.

I like the fact that this holiday is not about shopping. It's a thank-you festival. Before the dinner we sit at the table and hold hands in a big circle and everyone says what they are grateful for in the past year. I always find this very moving. I admire the way Americans feel at ease in saying what is in their hearts, without embarrassment or British reserve. I say how grateful I am for Tania and Lily and how proud I am to be part of this family.

▽

Unfortunately the car comes for me in the middle of our White Elephant game. I have just drawn a very tacky table mat of the Queen and the Duke of Edinburgh and was determined to hold on to it at all costs. Now I have to go. Lily is heartbroken that I am leaving again and dissolves into tears. I feel heartsick. I hate this parting. I have been away from her too long as it is. I have the familiar leaden feeling of heading back to boarding school. I try and reassure her it won't be for long, but who am I fooling? I sound like my mother.

▽

When I call her from Minneapolis airport a few hours later she has cheered up a bit. We were here on the tour on a warm sunny day only a week ago. Now Minneapolis is freezing and covered in snow. The airport is deserted as I await my connection to Canada. I wrap myself in my cashmere ring stole, woven from hair follicles hand plucked by a Pashmini serving wench from around the testicles of a mountain goat, and brood on the unfairness of life.

▽

Only fifteen shows left in twenty-two days, but there's still a lot of traveling: four and a half thousand miles to be precise, and I'm glad I had a few days off. I needed that break. Thanksgiving Day is a good day to travel. No one is around. The security people look happy to see a face and help me pass swiftly through the process, giving little hints.

"Watch that belt buckle, sir, there's nothing I can do if this alarm goes off."

In thirty seconds I am inside. Good job I left an hour and a half for this security process. I tentatively approach the empty Northwestern First Class lounge. Once again Python works its magic.

"Am I entitled to come in here?" I ask a pleasant young lady.

"*You* are," she says, "because you are Monty Python."

A couple of returning passengers grab my hand and thank me fervently. I'm too early even for the previous flight. So I catch up on e-mail. Turns out I was right about the Python reunion picture. I thought there was zero chance we'd all get together again just for a photo op, even for *Vanity Fair*. John is still sick and has canceled his Vancouver trip, so we are to be photographed in different parts of the world and stuck together by computer. Some kind of collage. A *virtual* reunion. I'm sorry, Graydon dear, but I did warn you.

DAY 58

FRANCIS WINSPEAR CENTRE FOR MUSIC, EDMONTON, ALBERTA

OU CAN TELL YOU ARE FAR NORTH WHEN THE SUN COMES UP AND IT'S STILL DARK.

YOU CAN TELL YOU ARE FAR NORTH WHEN ALASKA IS WEST OF YOU.

You can tell you are far north when bison appears on the menu. There is an ancient English joke:

Question: What's the difference between a bison and a water buffalo?

Answer: You can't wash your hands in a water buffalo.

[Warning this joke has to be said aloud in a cockney accent or it is incomprehensible.—Ed.]

Everyone has made it up to Edmonton, though not without some delays. The bus party changed Skip's plan and left Fargo early and consequently had to sit at a border crossing for five hours. They were not very happy but hello . . . that's why Skip spends so long making these plans. I am not at all looking forward to life without Skip. Okay, so the sex isn't as good, but he's always smiling and glad to see me. He was there waiting at the airport after having left Tucson at the crack of dawn. A wife is just no substitute for a chap like this. My prolonged absence on the road has given me a whole new perspective on marriage. I always suspected that being white, male, and married sucked. Now I'm sure of it. A married man has all the freedom of a mollusk. They are essentially bivalves with credit cards. For a woman the point about having a husband is the same as having a fashion accessory. Or a diamond. You don't need one but you have to show other women that you can get one. I have been married since I was ten. Well, since 1969 anyway, except for a few short years of freedom in between. I'm not sure I can entirely recommend it. It seems a very inefficient way of getting laid. No wonder the French ignore the rules. I am thinking of writing a very brilliant piece on the current state of matrimony. It will be so good that the *New Yorker* will call up and beg me to reprint it, Graydon Carter will ask me philosophical questions about it, future generations will quote it, and it will become a famous statement about married life in the twenty-first century on a par with Lord Chesterfield and his cigarettes. [*He's rambling.*—Ed.] It will go something like this [*Kiss your female demographic good-bye.*—Ed.]:

Meditations on the State of Marriage
by a frequently grumpy married man

New rules for the wary.

1: Never travel with your wife.
For many women the real point about marriage is to have someone to carry their bags. When I see men at airports laden with luggage and screaming kids, pushing trolleys or standing patiently in line while their women go off to the bathroom or make that extra pur-

chase of makeup and magazines, I am tempted to perform an intervention. I notice black men are more successful at avoiding the married state. You don't see African American men at airports covered in baggage in tow to a smartly dressed female busy working a cell phone call to her sister-in-law. If you're going to stay married, for God's sake travel separately. Then she'll pay some poor schmuck to hump all the bags that she has to bring because she cannot make up her mind what she might need to wear once she gets there.

2: Do not complain.
Remember that as a married man you rank somewhere below the dog. Get used to being invisible. Where the dogs and children get a tremendous greeting on the wife's return, it can often be up to half an hour before a married male is noticed. It's not that you are ignored, you are unseen. You are the thing that is not there. Practice being grateful for any attention.

3: Get used to being overweight.
The single male is sexier, thinner, better paid, and more active intellectually. This fattening-up process is deliberate. An overweight mate is less of a temptation to other women.

4: Sex after marriage: Don't count on it.
The longest a married man has had to wait for sex in my knowledge was five years. Admittedly this is an extreme case, but sex and marriage go together like a horse and cabbage. If it's sex you want, stay single.

4: Sexy underwear: Forget about it.
Women change after marriage, but not into Victoria's Secret underwear. Victoria's Secret underwear is strictly for the unmarried woman. This is her secret

weaponry in the sex war. Her weapons of mass seduction. Looking longingly at the Victoria's Secret catalogue is the closest a married male will get to enjoying that skimpy red underwear. It makes her feel too fat, or it's uncomfortable, or it's demeaning, or she simply doesn't have time to put all that stuff on. None of this she said when she was crawling around the carpet making goo-goo eyes at you trussed up like a turkey. But you proposed, fella, so take a good look, brother, because from now on it's all winceyette pajamas and woolen body wraps.

5: Pregnancy: Kiss your nuts good-bye.
Once they get pregnant, oh boy, are you screwed. Or not screwed, actually. The Estrogen Nazis come in and take away your sweetheart and replace her with a snarling replacement in a slightly larger body size.

6: Who is to blame?
Get used to this: You are. For everything. The married state is that of a docile donkey standing around nodding waiting to be thrown a straw. The most common refrain of the married male is, "Yes, dear."

7: The change of life.
Women go through menopause but men go through womenopause. You'll notice the signs. You'll start yearning to make your own decisions. You'll consider taking up golf just to get out of the house. You'll plan and take long business trips, in the vain hope that in the hotel bar you'll meet the perfect woman: someone who wants to fuck you and then leave without asking your name.

This is not a good idea for two reasons: the woman who wants to fuck you without asking your name is a

ERIC IDLE

professional called Dolores, who will charge you and may leave you with more than you bargained for. Secondly, when married for a long time it is unpleasant to discover that the single state is not only tolerable but preferable. It's tantamount to being guillotined and finding out life was better with a head. So make up your mind to forget the joy of being able to go somewhere when you said you would, or leave when you feel like it or live without waiting for someone to finish their makeup or make just one more call or feed the dog or change their mind about the restaurant or get out of the bath or feel insecure about their hair or go online to get their e-mail or set a tape. . . . A married male should not experience shore leave and liberty. It will only make him unhappy. There are no weekend passes in marriage.

8: Get used to waiting.
Time has no meaning in marriage. "Whenever" is a precise definer. "Whenever" means "Whenever I am ready." All married men are on whenever *time. Seven means whenever. Eight means whenever. Eight thirty means whenever. Remember, women have a whim of iron. Learn to accept. Be like the Buddha. Do not sit in the car with the engine running, the music turned up excessively loud, screeching in frustration at the top of your lungs. You know you aren't going anywhere until she's ready* and so does she. *Just wait.*

9: Do not consult a divorce lawyer. Ever.
The only serious reason for men to remain married is that if there is one thing worse than marriage, it's divorce. Divorce is like marriage without the money. You get even less sex, and you pay even more for it. For women divorce is so attractive it's amazing they

228

stay married for even a short time. "You mean you get the same money without the snoring old bastard?" What's not to like? There are some exceptions to this rule. Sometimes alimony is worth it. Some women are worth paying not to have to live with. But you'd better be extremely wealthy.

10: The simple fact is this: Women should be married; men shouldn't.

Of course none of this applies to my wife, the beloved Tania, who is a saint among women. She is the woman I was waiting for my entire life. And I have certainly been waiting for her ever since. Actually I think I stay with her because she makes me laugh. It isn't just the fact she has a great ass. I'm not that superficial. Well, I am that superficial, but there is more to her than that. No, it's the ass. Still, she does make me laugh.

DAY 59

JUBILEE AUDITORIUM, CALGARY, ALBERTA

DMONTON WAS PACKED, 1,350 PEOPLE CRAMMED INTO THE FRANCIS WINSPEAR, A VERY MODERN THEATER. THEY CHEERED US TO THE RAFTERS. WE PLAYED TO HUGE EXPLOSIONS OF LAUGHTER. AFTERWARD THE SIGNING LINE was immense. This morning we set off early to cover the two hundred miles of snowy plain to Calgary. We crossed the freezing white width of the Saskatoon River, its deeply wrinkled surface looking like boiling water fast frozen. Edmonton is perched magnificently on one bank of this river and on the other there is a tremendous escarpment, which I remember from all those years ago when we toured here on Monty Python's First Farewell Tour. Now we head for Calgary. The bus plows steadily along the dark, salted highway between flat plains of snow, the wipers beating time. We pass occasional moose, farms slumped under snow, agricultural machinery frozen in the fields.

▽

The Jubilee Auditorium is jumping. There are fifteen hundred people packed in tonight. I remember this auditorium well: it is monstrously wide. There is a huge expanse of thrust stage before you reach the audience. It is so big and deep it takes twice the energy and you have to wait for the laughs to come bouncing back from the three tiers of audience. This is the only theater I have visited on either of my two tours where I appeared with the Python chaps and it is an eerie feeling to think I stood on this same stage with Graham and John, and Mike and the Terrys thirty years ago. I tell the audience that the hook and I are the only two returnees from that time. They fall silent as I talk about George.

Today was a bad day for me. The anniversary of George's death two years ago is on my mind all day. I know I will have to write something about him and that's a painful thing to even think about. That man, so alive with those amazing eyes, lying so still as I scattered rose petals on him, my shoulders shaking, weeping. Sitting with him. Seeing him so thin, hearing that terrible merciless cough—no, it's too damn painful.

Even when we first met I felt like I'd known him forever. Not the Beatle George, he never seemed like that to me, nor the bearded garden gnome George, but the man, the real man with the deep, dark eyes and the crooked grin and the loud laugh. I felt I knew him already. I felt I'd met him as a child. In fact, I was convinced we'd met in Wallasey when I was about seven, in New Brighton playing in the sand hills at the Red Noses. There's no way to prove this, of course, but it was a very strong feeling I had, and still have. I would

When I met George it was love at first sight. He was absolutely irresistible. We'd stay up all night playing and laughing. He made me do all the Python sketches and I made him do all the Beatle songs.

ERIC IDLE

meet kids and play, as kids do, and have no idea who they were. So who knows sometime in the summer of 1950, might we really have met on the other side of the Mersey?

⚲

I never knew a man like him. It was as if we fell in love. His attention, his concern, his loving friendship was so strong and powerful that it encompassed your entire life. You felt comfortable and secure. We would stay up all night and talk for hours about our lives, about the hurts and pain, about the groups we had been in and the trying emotional strains and problems that being in such groups entails. He was always full of spiritual comfort, counsel, and advice. He saw everything from the cosmic point of view. Our deaths were natural and unavoidable, and he viewed everything from that perspective, even then in the midseventies. He had come off a tour of America, where things had been unpleasant for him. The "Dark Hoarse Tour," he called it. His pseudonym—for hotels, security (and guitar picks)—had been Jack Lumber. (He was always a raving certified Python fanatic as, of course, I was always a raving certified Beatle fan.) Drugs and brandy had ruined his voice on that tour, and I think he had set out to challenge and defy the expectations of his North American audiences, presenting Ravi Shankar and the Indian music first and then doing jokey versions of various of his songs. The good news was that he met Olivia, the love of his life, and retired to Friar Park, where he felt safe and from where he would only rarely emerge. Here he would discover the other great love of his life, gardening, which became a living example of his concern to create beauty on the planet wherever he could.

⚲

Like all the other important loves in my life (my wife, my daughter, my son, and my dog), it was love at first sight.

Terry Gilliam (another and inexplicable love at first sight) was with me the night in May 1975 when we attended the first screening of *Monty Python and the Holy Grail* at the old Directors Guild building on Sunset. I think I knew George was supposed to be coming, and was slightly anxious and even unsure about meeting him, as I had heard what a raving fan he was, but I was blown away when he appeared at the end in the darkened cinema, and hugged me and launched straight into the first of many intense conversations, which began as monologues and then, as I grew confident and emboldened to interrupt and share my thoughts, became long and deep conversations about everything in our universe: life, death, love, the nature of religion; hours of sharing and "catching up" as he called it, as if he too felt he'd known me before, and his apothegms and memories and jives and rants enlivened my life for almost thirty years. We had retired to the projection room to smoke a jay and were finally kicked out of there and went off to A&M Studios, where Tom Scott was working on George's album *Extra Texture.* He introduced me to Joni Mitchell in the studio next door. We then went on to the Beverly Wilshire Hotel, where I was staying, and talked and talked and talked, oh my God how he could talk. This was the quiet one! He never shut up. Thank God. Somehow it was immediately decided that I was to do a voice on his album—a pepperpot[24]—on "This Song," and then the minute I was back in the U.K. I was co-opted to work on the "Ohnothimagen" radio campaign for his album, for which I wrote and recorded several spots.

▽

Recently someone laid three CD bootlegs on me of George's work from the early seventies. It was the most remarkable gift. Suddenly George was in my car. The moment I began to

---

[24] Little old ladies on Monty Python were known as "pepperpots."

ERIC IDLE

play them I yelled with happiness, then I burst into tears. Tears streaming down my face, I drove with his presence all around me as his music revived all those hours we had spent in the studio at Friar Park, those long nights of his playing endless tapes, pulling out old songs, many of which I was now hearing for the first time since those great evenings. Oh those nights in the studio, when fueled by the visits of the Frenchman, we would talk and laugh all night, while he constantly moved between the machines, seeking tapes at will, loading the big one-inch reels of black magnetic tape and playing them through the huge studio speakers and lighting endless Marlboros. In the little kitchen filled with color Polaroids pasted to the wall there were snapshots of George and the many musicians who had been through the Park. There were beers and endless cigarettes, and next door a room with walls lined with guitars, hundreds of them, from the Beatle days, some tie-dyed, many familiar. Double doors led into the stained-glass Victorian studio itself, jam-packed with all manner of instruments, weird harmoniums and shiny metal xylophones and vast kettledrums. Downstairs our stunning women, Tania and Liv, both dark and beautiful and American, would hang out together or prepare sumptuous vegetarian curry dinners.

▽

The first time I visited Friar Park I was with my first wife, Lynne. The marriage was already over, and she didn't stay very long, driving back to London after dinner, leaving me behind for the first of many all-nighters of talk and music and beer and cigarettes. We greeted the dawn playing Frisbee on the lawn. I think I got home next afternoon by train. Perhaps I stayed two days. Nothing was nicer than collapsing into the four-poster beds in the sumptuously attired bedrooms.

▽

It was raining hard that first time when we came off the motorway and found Henley. We followed the directions out of the town up the hill and right toward the massive gates. Behind these monumental iron gates was the most beautiful little stone house with splendid gothic trimmings.

"What a beautiful house," I said, very impressed.

"Thank you," they said. "This is the gatehouse. The main house is up there!"

And up there it was. It was bigger than my boarding school.

▽

Nothing could prepare me for the first glimpse of that gothic palace as we rounded a bend and saw ahead that most extraordinary building. My first thought was it was exactly like my school. It was certainly on that scale, and of around the same period, but unlike the grim forbidding Victorianism of the Ophny,[25] this Victorian castle floated and twinkled magically. With its carved oak doors and windows in their lead frames, its fantasies and grinning gargoyles, its carefully stoneworked slogans enjoining thought and wisdom and the inevitability of death: nothing could ever prepare you for that. It was an overwhelming experience. I parked beneath the massive cedar outside the front door and stared at the house totally amazed. Its unique twisted chimneys and fantasy gothic gables and steeply pitched roofs and battlements; a riot of different styles that challenged the eye. I had never seen anything like it. A Hindu palace in Henley. An architectural work of inspired madness, the size of a small hotel, built as a private residence in 1890 by an eccentric and wealthy London lawyer called Sir Frank Crisp. Inside, the first sensation as I entered the oak-paneled hall with golden lettering offering philosophical

---

[25] The Orphanage. What we called the Royal Wolverhampton School.

advice, pre-Raphaelite decoration, and William Morris wallpaper was *that smell*. It's a special incense from Madras, and I can still smell it. All Beatle houses have it. I once visited Ringo's ex-wife, Maureen, in Bel Air to be greeted by that familiar, rich, pungent odor.

▽

Later my son, age three, would run around inside this richly oriental-carpeted home (the rugs supplied by my cousin Haig if you can believe that—one of hundreds of carefully prepared coincidences that awaited me).

"Wibena Ewic," George would cry in imitation of Carey's then childish way with words.[26]

▽

I would grow very familiar with the house: its soft silences at night, its twenty-four-hour warmth, with massive steel radiators drawing up heat from the cavernous depths below, its dark, echoey passages with the bright Victorian tile, its woody interiors, its oak paneling. And always the Indian presence, the floating scent of incense, the throb of tabla, sudden wild flutterings of rhythm, like a trapped bird beating its wings, the smoky chants, the thrilling runs of brilliant argument from the sitar, and George, always lighting another cigarette as he paused intently over one of the two jukeboxes filled with favorites, carefully and deliberately choosing what to play next: a version of "The Lumberjack Song," Ravi Shankar, endless Dylan, "Oh you must hear this, Eric." Early Elvis. "Spam." EC's "Layla." And yet more Dylan.

▽

---

[26] My son was very fond of Ribena, a sweetened dark grape juice drink.

His enthusiasm was contagious. He played the jukebox to inform and instruct. He reveled in sharing his delight in all kinds of music. He would go through periods of furious passions, often lasting for months or even years at a time, when he would insist you shared his joy of Smokey Robinson or the songs of Hoagy Carmichael or the Hawaiian music of Gaby Pahinui or even the ukulele nonsenses of George Formby. During this latter stage everyone had to learn the uke; even Liv he taught to strum away. His taste was, like himself, catholic. He embraced all forms of life. It was to be savored and enjoyed. But music was at the heart of it. It could speak more truly to the soul. And the soul was what George was about. The clear-eyed gurus gazed down in the hall from their photographs, looking straight at us. As we talked and grew to know each other I opened my heart to him as I have to no other man before or since. Indeed only my wife and my shrink have heard me speak so nearly (and at such length) of my existence and my experiences. It was, and I can only say this simply, like the beginning of a love affair, and I suppose in a way it was exactly that, because he won my heart and I fell in love with him and am filled with that love to this day. When he died, I could not believe it. I knelt at his feet and put my hand on him, and my whole body was wracked and shaken with sorrow. They had given us rose petals and finally my shoulders could stop shaking long enough for me to sprinkle them on him, and I could back away to the sympathetic embraces of the living. He now lay deathly still in his saffron and purple robes, his face painted white with the red dot on his forehead. We sat shivah, a small group of his friends and family in the room, now weeping, now laughing. Some reminiscence would start, something inappropriate he would want to share and then the realization that he would not be sharing it, that he was indeed gone, and sorrow would flood over us.

ERIC IDLE

George loved Python. He paid for the entire budget of The Life of Brian because he said he wanted to see it. It's still the most anyone has ever paid for a movie ticket.

"Come on, everybody, Dad wouldn't want this," Dahni would remind us, and we would play music, the chants he loved, recorded in Friar Park, or a few of the last tracks that would constitute the basis of his final album. And, oh, the pangs as I remembered our last phone conversation, me in France, he in Switzerland, sometime in August. His voice seemed weak as we chatted for about twenty minutes.

"What are you working on?" I asked him

"I'm doing the sleeve notes for my album. If I can ever finish them in time. And if not, then you will."

My heart felt like it was stabbed as he told me clearly he was dying. Even then I refused to believe it. Not him. Not George. George couldn't die. I needed him too much. He was my cornerstone. A Friar Park visit always an option. George didn't die. It wasn't possible.

On this day last year I was in the Royal Albert Hall at the amazing memorial concert for George organized by Liv and Dahni and Eric Clapton, one minute laughing with Mike Palin and the Terrys and the next losing it as Joe Brown played "Here Comes the Sun" and having to hide in the bathroom backstage, sobbing. I wasn't the only one with red eyes that night. Was ever a man so loved? So many friends. So many strong men in tears. I almost lost it again onstage at the finale when Joe played the ukulele so beautifully and sang "I'll See You in My Dreams" as thousands of rose petals fell from the ceiling. Everyone left the stage quietly, avoiding one another's eyes, here a friendly arm, there a hand on a shoulder. Too sad for words.

DAY 60

CALGARY TO VANCOUVER, BRITISH COLUMBIA

 WAKE UP IN THE ROCKIES. THE RISING SUN IS LIGHTING THE TIPS OF THE MOUNTAINS AS WE ENTER THE BANFF NATIONAL PARK. LAST TIME I WAS HERE, IN THE SUMMER OF 1973, TERRY GILLIAM AND I CAME FOR A DAY TRIP.

It's only a couple of hours' drive and we were taken by a publisher's rep to a book festival at the Banff Hotel. Unfortunately we got rather drunk at lunch and misbehaved ourselves, and having somehow procured two water pistols we ran through the sedate exhibition halls shooting at pretty girls. This inexcusably boorish behavior was somehow forgiven on the grounds that we were from Monty Python, at which everyone relaxed and smiled and enjoyed the "joke." Shameless days. The Canadians have always taken to Python. The screams for "Lumberjack" here are deafening.

The bright yellow morning light shines crisply on the pure white snow. Above us great gray granite peaks tower against the clear blue sky. We are traveling along a flat glacier bed, on a two-lane highway that we share with an oyster-colored river and a single-lane railway. Hanging valleys on either side drop into V-shaped, tree-lined funnels of snow. Frozen waterfalls hang

ERIC IDLE

suspended like icicles. Beside the road, snow-speckled Christmas trees are blasted with white. Black crows sit in the treetops or rise reluctantly from roadkill as we pass. We are traveling due west, with the sun low and golden behind us, intensifying as it rises, lighting the road ahead. The far mountains gleam like dentures in the sunlight, monstrous peaks and huge tubular piles of rock awesome in the yellow of the morning. Occasional plumes of snow like smoke are blown off their icy tops. In the chasm of the glacial valley we travel through the deep blue of the morning, staring up at awesome pillars of mountain piled high into mighty citadels. We pass beside great swirls of rock, folded and scooped and twisted by the earth. Everywhere the freckled fir trees flecked with icing sugar stand knee-deep in soft scoops of pure white sparkling snow. It is awesome to be here. Monumental. Inspiring. Like wandering through an Alpine travel brochure. The sky is Krishna blue, though it's arctic cold outside our snug, warm bus. The girls are curled up under a blanket on the front seat next to 'Lish. We swallow hot chocolate as we ride through this winter wonderland. A river with frozen banks keeps us company. It is covered in wisps of icy breath, tiny mist clouds steaming in the morning light. The horizontal rays of the sun cast long shadows of the trees on the dazzling white landscape as we pass every possible shape of rock formation covered in thick, creamy blobs of snow.

We cross the Yoho valley into British Columbia, and are finally back on Pacific time. We pass an endless Canadian Pacific freight train to enter a town called Golden, with the Kicking Horse Hotel, where we are suddenly shrouded in white mist. These frozen clouds looked pretty till we entered them; now visibility is down to thirty feet and we are descending very slowly on the brakes. We are in a steep gorge and crawl to a standstill. The road has been closed here. Snow plows covered in snow sit by the roadside. An unfinished bridge is waiting for the spring. A single lane is open and as we pass through, the mountain peaks suddenly emerge from the mist and the sun comes out again revealing little cottages with smoking chimneys.

The hours pass. It's very comfortable riding through this constantly changing snowscape. I flick on the TV to watch Arsenal playing Fulham on the satellite. It seems very decadent to lie in bed watching Sunday-afternoon soccer as this extraordinary landscape slides past. It's certainly a long way from Highbury. There's only an intermittent signal, so the game keeps freezing or breaking into surreal pixels or disappearing completely as we crawl under the lee of a great mountain.

We cross the mighty Columbia River and now we are traveling through a land of lakes; deep, wide waters, some completely frozen, others big, broad expanses of choppy blue fjord. They look like lochs and have odd names like Blind Bay and Salmon Arms. We stop for lunch in Kamloops at a very acceptable Grecian Italian restaurant, where the waitress asks me if I'm John Cleese. I tell her I'm Michael Palin.

We are so far north the sun never clears the mountaintops, it only staggers up so far and then sinks back, exhausted. The Rockies are behind us now but we still have four hours and two big climbs over the Sierras. Here the trees seem wider spaced, the mountains somehow less tortuous, but they are steep all right and packed with thicker snow, and we pass through some mighty deep chasms as the sun sets arctic green in the west. Lights in the valleys pop on, twinkling, and soon we are crawling into Sunday-night traffic, with Vancouver just a few klicks away. A towering high-rise with hot water and warm beds awaits us, and it's a full twenty degrees warmer. But what a day. What an unforgettable journey.

DAY 61

DAY OFF IN VANCOUVER

'M ALL BATHED AND READY TO POSE NAKED FOR *VANITY FAIR* [*BOLLOCKS.*—ED.] WHEN I GET THE MESSAGE AT THE LAST MINUTE IT'S BEEN CANCELED. THIS IS REALLY RIDICULOUS. BUT I LAUGH AND PUT MY CLOTHES BACK ON. I WAS KINDA hoping to be the new Ashton Kutcher, but I guess the old one is still doing fine. This Python picture saga continues. When we were in New York to promote *Monty Python and the Holy Grail* we went to have our picture taken by Richard Avedon. In the limo on the way to his studio we discussed Avedon's awesome reputation and what a great job he had asking young women to remove their clothes and pose naked for him. What sort of photo should he take of us? we wondered.

"Well, we won't take our clothes off, that's for sure," I said.

We all roared with laughter. It was clear that was *exactly* what we would do.

That was how a rather puzzled but amused Richard Avedon got to pose four Brits and one American stark naked for a memorable photo. John of

ERIC IDLE

course wasn't there. Later we stuck a picture of him on location in his underpants on the Avedon photo.

▽

My wife is not pleased with my tirade on modern marriage. In fact she is mighty pissed off. I explain that it is ironic and that she has missed the disclaimer about how adorable she is, and that I utterly worship her.

"I don't expect you to say 'Yes, dear,'" she says.

"No, dear," I say.

"Fuck you," she says.

▽

The married men have enjoyed the piece and sit around discussing it in the bar. I think we're all a bit lonely for our wives.

"The Marital State is like Poland," I say. "It is constantly in danger of disappearing overnight."

> I'm very much in favor of gay marriage. I think it's about time they suffered, too.

244

DAY 62

ORPHEUM THEATRE, VANCOUVER

PERCHED IN MY AERIE ON THE TWENTY-EIGHTH FLOOR OF THE WESTIN GRAND HOTEL ON A RAINY VANCOUVER DAY, TAPPING AWAY ON A LAPTOP, I AM INEVITABLY REMINDED OF THE DAYS WHEN I WROTE HALF MY *ROAD TO MARS* NOVEL here while filming *Dudley Do-Right*. I loved the rain then as day after day of filming was canceled, and I could stay in my suite at the Sutton Place Hotel and just write. As I Look down on the rainy grid of a gray Vancouver day, the cars have their lights on, the mountains are shrouded in mist with just the thin white streaks of the ski runs showing against their whalelike hulks. Below me the large, white crane, which at night is lit up like a Christmas tree, is swinging what looks like a grand piano around. Surely not?

▽

The Vancouver show was a blast. I don't remember a noisier reaction from an audience ever. Not even in the old Python days. Two thousand one hundred people were jammed into the Orpheum Theatre, and boy, did they have a good time. Huge explosions of laughter greeted my opening

ERIC IDLE

gags, waves of sound like thunderclaps came bounding back from the depths of this old theater. They almost pushed me over onstage. It was gigantic. I don't recall anything like it. It was almost scary, and this old house, decorated in Moroccan bordello style, reverberated with their response. I can die a happy man, with "Remember Vancouver" on my lips as I expire backstage in some Birmingham shithole.

The Canadian Northwest has been triumphant for us. All our houses were sold out by the local House of Blues guys, who presented me with an engraved silver pen in gratitude. I am glad to say they used our original poster, and it was everywhere. We started out loud and full at Edmonton, built in Calgary, and last night in Vancouver capped it all. They screamed and bayed and stood and roared. At the end I said I'd like to try out a new piece John and I had just written, and craved their patience for the world premiere of this new song. Well I could hardly get past the first line. John played a soft Christmassy "Jingle Bells" intro. It was Bing Crosby time.

"Fuck Christmas," I began.

Well, I had to stop. The gales of laughter that greeted that line were overwhelming. We began again, more huge laughs. They laughed and cheered at every single line. At the end of verse one I had to stop them, they were applauding and yelling so hard. We managed to get through verse two to hysteria but the capper last two lines had them screaming. I have never witnessed anything like it. It was beyond gratifying. John stood up behind his piano, beaming, and we shook hands. We have been working together for many, many years and have got used to being ignored, unpaid, and rejected, and yet we soldier on because we like each other and we like what we do, but neither of us will ever forget the reception for that song. It was like the end of a movie. As we shook hands with tears in our eyes you could feel the credits rolling. A remarkable moment in life, and one I feel very proud to have experienced. I sometimes look at John onstage and feel so grateful he is in my life. He follows me about on these insane trips with never a complaint or a murmur. He is constantly working unpaid twelve-hour days in unpaid studios turning my sketches into fully orchestrated music. He is a total joy to be around, and is the wisest and most patient and most professional of men. How did I ever do without him?

Peter had been against this song from the beginning. Something about it really upset him, though Jen and Gilli both said, "No, it's funny." But at the rehearsal he finally came up and said nicely, "I've changed my mind." Perhaps it was the two street teamers, Tracy and Amanda screaming with laughter from the back of the hall; perhaps he had realized that it really isn't an attack on Christianity, but on shopping. Still, I took the precaution of trying it out in the encore slot after the main body of the show with just John and me onstage and with "Lumberjack" to follow as an escape route. I needn't have worried. "Fuck Christmas" is going to become a legendary song, a perennial, played and sung wherever disgruntled shoppers gather in superheated malls.

> *Fuck Christmas!*
> *It's a waste of fucking time*
> *Fuck Santa*
> *He's just out to get your dime,*
> *Fuck Holly and Fuck Ivy*
> *And fuck all that mistletoe*
> *White-bearded big fat bastards*
> *Ringing bells where e'er you go*
> *And bloated men in shopping malls*
> *All going Ho-Ho-Ho*
> *It's Christmas fucking time again!*

THE
GREEDY
BASTARD
DIARY

ERIC IDLE

Fuck Christmas
It's a fucking Disney show
Fuck carols
And all that fucking snow
Fuck reindeer
And fuck Rudolph
And his stupid fucking nose
And fucking sleigh bells tinkling
Everywhere you fucking goes
Fuck stockings and fuck shopping
It just drives us all insane.
Go tell the elves
To fuck themselves
It's Christmas time again!

DAY 63

VANCOUVER TO SEATTLE, WASHINGTON

BACK IN THE GOOD OLD U.S.A. AFTER A 1:15 A.M. STOP AT THE BORDER. THEY MADE US GET OUT OF THE BUS AND PRESENT OUR GREEN CARDS AND PASSPORTS. ONLY ONE GUY WAS ON DUTY AND THERE WAS A HUGE TAILBACK OF TRUCKS waiting to cross. 'Lish cleverly drove past this big line of waiting vehicles and then cut in at the last minute, saving us about an hour and a half of waiting. Very rock-and-roll. It was another two hours to Seattle but I couldn't sleep, I was so exhausted. We have moved south to some softer markets. San Francisco is looking very thin. I wish we could have brought the House of Blues guys with us. There is an audience out there, and this show really rocks, it's just a question of letting them know we are in town. We have found that posters and street teams have really paid off, but each local promoter has his own ideas, and we are totally at their mercy.

▽

What a clever fellow is Skip. He knows all the best hotels. In Seattle we check into the Sorrento, a most admirable boutique hotel, decorated

ERIC IDLE

like an Italian palazzo, with white marble bathrooms and square-shaped sinks, and large warm beds with soft white comforters and three types of rectangular European pillows in the softest down. As we approach at 3:15 A.M. in a soft drizzle, the hotel shines out, welcoming with hundreds of white lights and decorated Christmas trees and hedge bears holding golden balls; kitsch, but warm, comforting, and friendly. The carpets are deep, and the interior is mahogany and leather with carved gilded wooden frames on mirrors and pictures and a quaint, ancient single-person elevator. It's like arriving for Christmas with friends in Italy. Fabulous. At the heart of the hotel is an octagonal wooden fireside room with capstan-like spokes of deep warm mahogany beams radiating out to all eight sides. It's lit up with tasteful Venetian Christmas decorations, tiny white fairy lights and ferns and Italian marionettes and scrolls of ancient music. There's a big backgammon set and a huge chessboard and a cheerful fireplace with large comfortable leather seats. They serve a great tea here in the afternoons, with scones and cakes and yummy sandwiches and at night there is a cool jazz trio while you linger over hot chocolate or a warm toddy. The beds have high-count cotton sheets and comforters and are warm and perfect for well . . . I guess reading. With a nice naked companion. John and I have tea downstairs and discuss what we have to do for *Spamalot.* In the evening I take hot chocolate with Jen and Gilli, who has a shiner. She whacked her head backstage in Vancouver, almost knocking herself out, and a huge egg rose on her brow. She was so badly concussed she didn't come out onstage for her bit with the hook and you know she's really badly hurt when that happens. Now she has a purple eye. Poor Gilli. Skip is sick from eating some frozen Mac thing. Looking at it made me want to throw up. I'd forgotten that junk food is an accurate description.

John gives me a cassette of the "Fuck Christmas" song recorded onstage in Vancouver. It's incredible the noise the audience makes. It is like an oven door opening. There is a blast of heat. It is massive instant approbation. They get it, and they love it, and they want more. We are both as proud as new parents. I have never had an experience like that. I once played Ko-Ko in *The Mikado* for the English National Opera and every night I would rewrite the lyrics of "The Little List Song," updating them with topical references, and occasionally when some of my new gags worked, it felt a bit like that, but not for an entire song.

DAY 64

THE MOORE THEATRE, SEATTLE

AT LEAST THREE OF THE SEVEN DWARVES ARE PRESENT TODAY: CRANKY, GRUMPY, AND HORNY. I NEED A GOOD SPANKING, A STIRRUP-PUMPED ENEMA, AND A THOROUGH WORKOUT BY A BUTT-NAKED, HEAVILY OILED SEXUAL ATHLETE. I HAVE TO settle for doing my show in Seattle.

▽

Our hotel sits on a hill of hospitals. Swab Hill would be a good name for it. I eye one or two passing nurses in a purely professional way, but they sensibly scurry on. Gone are the days when five dollars would get you whatever you want from anyone in scrubs in a medical building. Now they are all *Health Carers*. What the hell are rubber gloves for, anyway?

▽

I'm testy because Jen inveigled me into getting up early and going to a radio station where a friend of hers works, and three interviews in a row before breakfast put me in a very bad mood. I'm cranky and angry and somewhat depressed all day. I want to stay in and write my diary and be grumpy.

▽

Everyone votes the Hotel Sorrento the finest on the tour and nobody wants to leave, but sadly we have to embark this afternoon on a five-day run of gigs, sleeping on the bus, with no nice, warm festive hotels. As an incentive I propose we stay an extra night in Vegas instead of leaving directly after Sunday's show and we won't even have to leave until midnight Monday. This goes down very well with the scurvy crew. It's a clever ruse so that they'll spend all their per diems gambling and on titty shows and then they'll be in the palm of my hand. This trip feels more and more like *Master and Commander*. If only the Royal Navy had sailed about doing revue instead of bombarding people with cannon, the world would be a far better place. Think of the time we Brits spent blasting away at the French. What a waste of good chefs! We should have been teaching them silly walks.

▽

The Moore Theatre was more like a mine than a theater. Backstage the entrance slid steeply down a long concrete goods slide to some dodgy stairs, and then you crouched—there was no standing up—and proceeded along a series of narrow passageways before stumbling up a staircase with a four-foot overhead speed bump onto the stage level. It was so low even Gilli had to bend. Another series of bewildering turns led me to a tiny dressing room. A steep narrow staircase led up to the others. To say the theater has seen better days is flattering. It is utterly dilapidated, and the floor uneven, and the house badly needs a paint job. Tall and narrow, with two high balconies, one a nosebleed balcony, it is also very deep, but amazingly, once the houselights dim, and the bright stage

Here's a little number I wrote the other day while out duck hunting with a judge....

lights go on, it does its job. It's only a small stage so we can see and hear one another perfectly, and the audience yelps and laughs and falls about and shouts and applauds and stands up and demands more. As with all our shows after a night off, we are looser and yet tighter and have tons of energy. Jennifer, who said the immortal words "a c**nt as big as Canada" onstage the other night, tones down her wild words for the coffee-swallowers of Seattle. I however don't tone down mine and give the first American performance of "Fuck Christmas." It is greeted with rapture. So Vancouver was no accident. Afterward Seattle people ask me when it will be released!

The Greedy Bastard agent is on the phone trying to sell me further tours. I reasonably point out we haven't finished this one yet. Before planning another I have to find out the MAE factor. That's the Margin of Agent Error, the difference between what he *says* I will get and what I *really* get my hands on. In my experience with William Morris agents this MAE factor can be at least 75 percent, and as high as 90 percent. *Then* we will see just how ironic the Greedy Bastard Tour title was. The Greedy Bastard promoters have already clawed back all the Canadian profits from their Canadian partners.

I'm further depressed by finding no mention of *The Rutland Isles* in the Grammys list. John and I spent six months on this CD recording all the sounds and songs of these fictitious islands with Larry Mah, in a tiny garage studio, a recording triumph, and surely worth some mention, but not a nod of recognition. That's it. I'm giving up. I'm nasty to the wife on the phone, and I feel rotten all day. So it's a surprise when Hairdresser Marc leaves me a message congratulating me on my Grammy nomination. I have been nominated for reading *Charlie and the Chocolate Factory,* my second solo Grammy nod in this category. I got one for reading my kids' novel *The Quite Remarkable Adventures of the Owl and the Pussycat,* though I lost out to a dead guy, Charles Kuralt. I thought that was very unfair. I think you should at least be alive to compete. Otherwise Mozart would win every year. Now I'm up against Clinton and Gorbachev. Fat chance there.[27]

---

[27] Gorbachev won.

DAY 65

HULT CENTER FOR THE PERFORMING ARTS, EUGENE, OREGON

 WAKE UP IN OREGON. AMAZINGLY, IT'S STILL FALL HERE. I HAVEN'T SEEN LEAVES IN A MONTH. WE HAVE COME A LONG WAY SOUTH FROM THE FROZEN SNOWS OF EDMONTON. A MAPLE TREE ON WILLAMETTE STREET IS FLAMING RED AND beyond it I can see a delightfully green poplar hanging on to its leaves, which are bright green against the darker forest of pines behind. It's raining, and cars hiss past us along the busy street on which we are parked. Bizarrely my name is in lights outside my window. HULT CENTER, it says, DECEMBER 5TH, ERIC IDLE 7:30. It's a mild day, threatening rain; but it doesn't actually arrive till after the show, when it buckets it down.

I saw "Fuck Freud" chalked on the sidewalk in Seattle, proving that even the homeless in Seattle are intellectuals, but here in Eugene they are nicely dressed and very polite. Eugene is an altogether nice place. There are pedestrian-friendly shopping streets lined with art galleries, advertising an art walk. I find a Tibetan gift shop and splurge on Christmas presents. Since all the profits go to the Dalai Lama I feel morally okay. Nearby there is a very pleasant, well-ordered secondhand bookshop, where I find a fine copy of *Liberace,* by Liberace. This is too good to resist as a Christ-mas present. But for whom? On the phone my friend Jim asks me particularly not to give it to him. But what *is* the perfect present for a Crystal Palace supporter? Can I find a suitable book on masochism in time?

The incredible Hult Center is a breathtakingly beautiful the-ater with a basket-weave ceiling, scalloped tiers, and a deep, comfortable interior. It seats two thousand six hundred but I don't think there are that many people in Eugene. We get a pretty good turnout. From the way some of our crowd are dressed I get the idea that there are teepees and tie-dye com-munities just outside the city. Even though they may be ex-hippies they are not tightfisted, because surprisingly Eugene beats the all-time record for the encore bucket with $162 do-nated. This is amazing when you think that the audience are not told it will be going to charity until afterward. They *think* they are donating this to me. So far we have collected more than $2,000 in the encore bucket as well as several pairs of panties, some bras, and a few cans of Spam. The money will go to a good cause, the Spam will be given to the homeless, and the panties? Well, perhaps I can find some suitable lap-dancing charity.

My wife was very forgiving of my appalling grumpiness yes-terday. A good wife learns when not to listen. I call her to tell her about the Grammy, but Lily, who is sick and off school, tells me she has gone to an allergist. She has more doctors than a hospital. But she still looks great in a swimsuit.

DAY 66

EGYPTIAN THEATRE, BOISE, IDAHO

ALONG AND OCCASIONALLY BUMPY DRIVE OVERNIGHT AS WE CAME BACK OVER THE ROCKIES AGAIN. I WOKE UP AT EIGHT THIRTY AS WE PULLED INTO BOISE. MIKE AND 'LISH LOOK TIRED AND THEY ARE TAKEN OFF TO A HOTEL TO RECOVER.

It's an intermittently rainy day and we hang out on the warm bus watching soccer and making porridge. There isn't anywhere else to go. Jen parades around in her pajamas and silk dressing gown, becoming increasingly frustrated by requests for her family arrangements tomorrow. Her people are coming out in force in Spokane.

▽

This is a tough stage of the tour for us. Five dates in a row, each separated by a long drive, but today in Boise is the real challenge. The good news is we are sold out. The bad news is that we are playing a cinema. They are building a temporary stage but there are no wings, no dressing rooms, and no depth to the stage so we can't bring out the twelve-foot-high lyrics for the "Bruces' Philosophers Song." Still, we are a well-oiled machine by now and our gang are in there solving the problems. We plump for handing out lyric sheets rather than cutting the Bruces' sing-along, and tonight we will be using the buses for dressing rooms.

The temporary stage worked great and made a very intimate space to play. I like the audience that close; it's great for comedy. You can get a laugh from just raising an eyebrow. It's far less exhausting than the huge two-thousand-seaters where you have to really work hard. The Egyptian, as you might expect, had a Nile-themed interior, decorated with brightly colored birds and sideways-facing ladies in three dimensions. It had large painted columns flowering at the top into palm trees, and between these columns squatted a larger-than-life-size Pharaoh with pert golden breasts. I don't recall ever seeing a Pharaoh with breasts before.

"*Tit*ankhamen," said Jen wittily.

The color scheme was thoroughly authentic, as I can verify from Major Cleese's expedition up the Nile. In the spring of 1991 a most generous John and Alyce-Faye Cleese invited a party of forty friends to celebrate their joint one hundredth birthday by going up the Nile by boat. It was the most amazing trip, with some very funny people along, including Peter Cook, Stephen Fry, and Bill Goldman, the screenwriter. We slid quietly up the ancient river at twelve miles an hour on a luxurious, flat-bottomed boat with comfortable air-conditioned bedrooms below. On the top deck was a Jacuzzi. Can you imagine sitting in warm water surrounded by bare-breasted American ladies watching the ancient and unchanging Nile slide by? Now *that* is the way to travel. Forget bouncing about on the back of a grouchy camel. Egypt *is* the Nile and we floated gently through it, between the most amazing rocks and hills, past

ERIC IDLE

people in brightly colored robes winnowing, an entire village flailing corn, looking like pictures from the pages of an illustrated Bible.

▽

At sunset I would sit on deck playing guitar while the banks of the Nile slid slowly past. Each afternoon we would gather in the shade of the deck while Stephen Fry read a chapter of the British schoolboy classic *Bunter on the Nile.* In the evenings the great Peter Cook would hold forth in the bar, spinning fantasies of comedy out of his own brilliance. From time to time we would stop at an ancient city and go ashore with two guides who would tell us two different stories about what we were looking at. One was an authentic Egyptian guide from the Cairo Museum and the other was a New Ager and revisionist who wore authentic Hollywood Egyptologist costume complete with mustache and pith helmet. He held alternative theories of the age and significance of everything, increasingly frustrating our Egyptian guide with his wild theories—he was even banned from one or two archeological sites, where he would hide behind pillars and tell us not to listen, that they had got it all wrong. He gave lectures every evening on the boat and I felt vindicated in my choice to avoid them in order to play a selection of Beatle songs to the sunset when Stephen Fry burst out of the lecture room with a great snort of derision, cursing out loud about his latest "theory." He had just revealed that the pyramids had been made by spaceships. I still see this man on the Discovery Channel breathlessly revealing more "discoveries." By the end of the tour he had tried even John's patience when he escorted them to the center of the Great Pyramid, told the local guide to leave and turn off the lights so that they might experience the silence and the darkness and then after about twenty minutes announced he had come without a flashlight. John sent him back for one, and said with glee he could hear him crawling up the tunnel, banging his head and cursing all the way.

▽

The temples and palaces on the Nile are the most extraordinary remains on the planet. Perhaps fortuitously they have been covered in sand for centuries so that their recent excavation has left the paint as bright as when the craftsmen first applied it. You feel that the decorators have only just left although several thousand years have elapsed. But we've all felt that way about contractors, haven't we?

▽

Before leaving England, John and Alyce-Faye had organized a private after-hours trip to the British Museum, so that we could visit the antiquities, and at the end of our fantastic journey they arranged to open the Cairo Museum early, so that we could see Tutankhamen and his treasures. When I got back from Egypt, my mother, who was given to creative malapropisms, asked me if I'd seen the tomb of Carmen Tutu?

THE MET, SPOKANE, WASHINGTON

T HE MET, SPOKANE, IS A GEM. IT'S AN OLD VAUDEVILLE HOUSE BUILT IN 1915, AND HAS BEEN LOVINGLY RESTORED. INSIDE THE AUDITORIUM THE FRONT HALF OF THE HOUSE IS AN ENORMOUS STUDDED SHELL, WHICH STOPS ABRUPTLY WHERE the second tier of seating begins, and is gently angled, so that you are looking down into a brightly lit bowl. It's a most unusual shape but highly effective for comedy; with the arc of the thrust stage you are almost in their laps. Once again I am struck by the variety and splendor and loving restoration of the theaters of America.

I go for Sunday lunch to a beautiful old hotel that is entirely filled with little girls dressed in blue and red velvet dresses with lace, off to see a matinee of *The Nutcracker*. I feel very nostalgic for my little girl, though Avril Lavigne is now more her style. We can all sense the tour winding down now. Only seven cities left. With the Christmas lights everywhere and the malls full of shoppers, we all feel we will be home soon. It feels good, though Peter proposes we spend it in Iraq, entertaining the servicemen. I'm not sure the State Department would be keen to send a Brit with a bunch of Bush jokes. Today we follow the Air National Guard into the theater. They are still packing up their drums and flags as we unload. This is the outfit in which Bush defended Texas from the North Vietnamese. He now posts them overseas to Iraq so that they can enjoy the active service he was denied. Perhaps there should be a special Bush medal: the Iron(y) Cross.

People have driven five hours from Canada to see tonight's show, some have even come seven hours from distant Montana, and there are several Jennifer Jay deejay fans, including a rather attractive lady in a pith helmet who looks like Meryl Streep and who clings warmly to me for about five minutes while her son's camera constantly malfunctions. While she embraces me and the minutes pass, I breathe a silent thank-you to the god of technology.

Bush has the Alabama Air National Guard Service medal—for bravely attending a dental appointment while officially AWOL.

During the gig a sweet young thing comes up and slips her panties in the encore bucket. She has written her phone number on the outside with an invitation to join her after the show. On the crotch she has written "Scratch and sniff!" She is very cheery afterward, and I warn her to be careful, as the entire crew may take her up on it.

"No problem," she says, and her aunt says proudly, *"That's* my niece!"

A young lady with a very fine bosom requests I sign her breasts and I reluctantly consent. She has delightful skin and although I rush the job, after fifteen minutes I am done.

ERIC IDLE

▽

I continue to be the recipient of breathless innuendo from older women in the signing line. One approaches me on her knees. Several told me they loved me. In Eugene teenage girls wore handpainted shirts with sexually flattering references to the Greedy Bastard and a couple of hippie ladies revealed they had sexual fantasies featuring me, while in Boise an attractive teenage girl called Alison climbed into the encore bucket. It was a pity to have to give her to charity.

▽

Is it possible I might become swollen-headed and egotistical with all this aftershow adulation? Surely not. How could being flattered and flirted with by sexually attractive women possibly influence my character? I am a strong-willed man. Girls sinking to their knees in front of me hardly turns my head at all anymore, though I am thinking of rereading very closely through my marriage vows. Did that Clinton definition of sex thing stand? [No.—Ed.] I am slightly piqued by my ever-loved-one's refusal to come join me overland on a bus stage to Vegas. She says she'll meet me there. What could possibly be objectionable about traveling overnight in a queen-sized bed in a tiny cabin with me? I admire her restraint. Of course she doesn't leave me the option of getting a substitute in. Women can be so selfish. The closest I have come to sex on this tour is watching Thierry Henri score.[28]

---

[28] An obscure unnecessary soccer reference. Thierry Henri is an Arsenal footballer.

264

ALADDIN THEATRE, PORTLAND, OREGON

I FEEL NOW THAT I AM FINALLY A COMEDIAN. I DIDN'T BEFORE. THERE IS A WORLD OF DIFFERENCE BETWEEN BEING A COMEDIAN AND A COMIC ACTOR. YOU USE MANY OF THE SAME SKILLS: TIMING, MULTIPLE VOICES, LOOKS, TAKES, AND so on, but being alone onstage is the key. Talking to an audience in your own voice and making them laugh with no one else to help you, that's the difference. Of course I am lucky. I don't come on alone. I have the ghosts of the Pythons with me, and the audience is already alive and warm and welcoming and buzzing with expectation, and yes I do get a huge greeting, which I now shamelessly milk, but I still have to make them laugh. And that is something I have learned how to do on this tour. How to extend my monologue and edit it, and go with new thoughts. How to forget what's next and not panic. How to listen to the audience and pick up the pace. How to fly solo. How to perform five different nights in five different cities and still be *able* to stand up! All this has been a new experience for me. The bus has been my secret weapon. It has made all the difference on this tour, carrying your world on your back, it's like traveling in your own suitcase.

ERIC IDLE

It's a cozy, warm den, and I shall miss my little space, so carefully organized with tea and books and music. You can keep the curtains drawn and have some Beethoven on the stereo and a nice cup of tea and a laptop to tap away on and you might as well not be parked outside a former porno cinema in Portland, Oregon. The Aladdin Theater is famous for having screened the longest-running film in history: *Deep Throat*. It ran here for more than twenty years. There is still an old print of it somewhere on the premises. Frankly I think the movie sucks. [*Yes we get it.*—Ed.] But at least there is something appropriate about having the whole audience sing "Sit on My Face."

O ur magical stage crew transform this unlikely venue into a warm golden bowl ready to leech the last leavings of comedy. [*Pretentious bastard.*—Ed.] Because it is a cinema with no backstage we can only use one side for entrances, and I have to change in the bus, but the house is full and responsive and the show goes off like a rocket. They make so much noise by the end for the Christmas song that I think they will never stop bellowing. In all my four hundred years in comedy I have never known anything that generates more of a response than this song. It's fantastic. It's like touching the comedy G-spot. Very appropriate for this venue. . . .

Of course, it really should be Day Sixty-nine.

DAY 69

PORTLAND TO SAN FRANCISCO

WAKE UP TO FIND WE ARE PASSING THROUGH OLIVE GROVES. THOUSANDS OF BUSHY GREEN OLIVE TREES LINING THE ROADSIDE INTERRUPTED BY OCCASIONAL PATCHES OF BARE-BRANCHED FRUIT TREES. WE COULD BE TRAVELING southward down the Rhône Valley. I love olive trees. There is something magical about them. I own a few hectares in Provence and they are as tough as any life-form on the planet. You can't kill them. Twice our property has been burned in fierce forest fires, both times missing the house, but once destroying a little woodland writing shack. Before the fires I had a lovely pine forest, now I have great views; but both times the olive trees survived. Even though they continued to burn and we were pouring water down into their smoking roots as much as three weeks later, they still grew back. In the cold Provençal winters olive wood is the finest to burn. Forget the spitting pine, the pure strong flame of a twisted black olive root will keep you warm for hours.

ERIC IDLE

We are passing through land as flat as the ocean floor. This is estuarine country, with flooded meadows like Balinese paddy fields. Ah, the Paddy fields where the little Irishmen grow. . . . Flocks of birds thick as clouds of midges rise from the flooded nesting grounds, heading off for the day. Tubular grain elevators, like gigantic batteries, loom out of the mist. We pass our first stand of palm trees. We must be in California. We have left the mountains behind and are heading due south. The plains extend on either side. Still tractors stand in the freshly plowed fields. Stands of skinny almond trees and regiments of walnuts are lined up for inspection. Tall roadside poplars give way to our first vineyards with their arms spread wide over iron supports.

We pull into a truck stop and hit the store amid the bleary-eyed truckers. We are being met by a TV film crew and 'Lish decides the bus needs a wash. I think that's a good idea, too, so while the bus is inside the truck wash I take a shower. There is something surreal about standing under a shower while the bus is also having a shower. We are finally one.

We pull into San Francisco where we are met by a local morning TV host who films me getting off my tour bus and onto a trolley, where I incite a couple of middle-aged ladies dressed as Santa's helpers to come visit my show. Nudge nudge, plug plug. Then off to the much-postponed *Vanity Fair* shoot for the Python "reunion" montage. Apparently *VF* are a bit pissed off that I mentioned this in my diary. Perhaps it's the montage bit that gets them. Gosh, if it leaks out that all those air-brushed divas are not actually in the same room together, Western civilization will collapse.

▽

The trouble and strife[29] arrived at the hotel just as I was leaving and we almost had a classic comedy moment. Tania was

---

[29] Wife. Cockney rhyming slang. Trouble and strife = wife.

about to step into the "up" elevator as I stepped out of the "down" elevator. Another two seconds and we'd have missed each other completely. Sometimes I think that about our lives. It's amazing we ever met. I persuade her to come with me to the shoot so I can be the target of her dry comments as they groom me.

"Stay here another night," I say.

"I can't," she says. "I have workmen in."

Call Sheet

Project: Monty Python
            Shoot Date: Tuesday, December 9

Location: Blue Sky Studio, 2325 3rd Street, Suite
            434, San Francisco, CA 94107

Call Time: Talent @4:00 P.M.

After all my kvetching the *Vanity Fair* shoot was a lot of fun. I thought the curse of Python was going to strike again when the limo company called up and said the car they were sending had crashed en route, but they soon found a replacement. The "costume" turned out to be a coffin. It should be a funny spread when it's done but it was shocking to see the pictures of John Cleese in his coffin. I was very moved. I really must like him, then. Good to find that out before it's too late to tell him.

It was very sad watching Tania look down at me in my coffin. There is something deeply poignant about seeing your wife looking at you lying there. It's one of those experiences, like being crucified, that you won't ever forget. You think, "So this is what it is like. The moment of death will be something like this. This time I'll get up and walk away but *that* time. . . ."

ERIC IDLE

I liked your President Clinton's attempt to introduce a slightly gayer army. I like the idea of a much better dressed army that marches to Barbra Streisand records. An Armani army. You could have Queer Eye for the Straight GI.

"Just remember that the last laugh is on you. . . ."[30]

Disturbing and prescient. I saw Tania for the first time as a widow, like so many of our friends.

▽

They stuck me in a nightshirt and a dressing gown designed by an incredibly famous and expensive Japanese designer whose name I have already forgotten. I know, I know, I'd make a terrible gay man. I'd *like* to join their team. They seem to have far more fun. And they dress very nicely . . . but I think I'm just too old to swap sides. Who wants to read a personal ad: "Sixty-year-old British virgin, no previous experience, one ex-wife, one current, ready to change teams, seeks similar in the Bristol area." It just doesn't have the appeal, does it?

The amazingly swift and efficient photographer Art Streiber had been reading my tour diary and opined I must write it at night, since I sound so grumpy, but no, I replied, "I can be very sweet at night. I am *naturally* grumpy in the mornings." He decides I should have a guitar with me in my bier, and so a swift call to the unflappable Skip and they fetch my Baby Taylor off the bus. I'm happy to lie there playing "Bright Side": "Always look on the bright side of death . . ."[31]

My tiny baby guitar was given to me by Clint Black to celebrate the birth of his daughter Lily Pearl. He gave me another great Taylor guitar when I wrote a new opening for "The Galaxy Song" and sang it with him on his album *D'Electrified*.

---

[30] "Always Look on the Bright Side of Life." Lyrics quoted by permission of the author. Er, me.

[31] *Always Look on the Bright Side*. Lyrics quoted again by permission of the author. [*Enough already.*—Ed.]

No matter how much I beg her, Tania won't stay for the show tomorrow night. She is coming to Vegas this weekend. She was a bit bummed that I mentioned her reluctance to come with me on the bus. The reason is she has been having horrendous migraines. I feel chastened. But fortunately not chaste. . . .

My wife came to visit me here in San Francisco. I had to run out to Victoria's Secret and buy lots of sexy lingerie: a thong, a black teddy, and some long black stockings.

It's amazing what I have to put on these days to attract her. . . .

DAY 70

THE FILLMORE, SAN FRANCISCO

THE FILLMORE IS A TOUGH GIG TO PLAY. IT'S A HUGE CUBE, WHICH IS IDEAL FOR ABSORBING THE NOISE OF ROCK-AND-ROLL, BUT NOT SO EASY FOR THROWAWAY LINES. THEY HAVE FILLED THE ROOM WITH ROUND TABLES SO IT'S MORE LIKE A bar mitzvah or a Hollywood Ratfuck[32] than the nicely laid-out theaters we are used to. It's also beastly cold. Ancient psychedelic posters look down on us everywhere. There is even one in my dressing room for the Bonzo Dog Band. I think joyfully of the young Neil Innes playing here in the days when he had hair. . . .

▽

I don't have a lot of voice and worry about the next two nights as I pour lemon and honey down my throat. But we get them. They are standing and applauding and demanding encores at the end . . . and the *San Francisco Chronicle* gives me one of the best reviews of my life. "It's an evening of

---

[32] A rubber-chicken charity dinner.

eye-opening hilarity with a master comic at the top of his game. . . ."

Today has gone pear-shaped, as they say in England. It's 3:25 and I'm waiting for a car that hasn't shown up to take me to a live radio show that begins in five minutes at a radio station I know not which in a location I know not where. And my feeling? Anxiety? Panic? Anger? Mounting frustration? Nah. *Relief.* Thank God I don't have to answer any more questions. I can sit and have a cup of tea in peace. After many phone calls betwixt Wendy, our new PR person, Skip, the concierge, and the radio station, they finally figure out what went wrong. The car was waiting downstairs all the time but they were waiting for *Mr. X*, my super-secret pseudonym. This is the identity I am registered under at the hotel so that I am safe from the legion of panty-throwing women who would otherwise be unable to resist the impulse to call me up in the middle of the night and offer me sex. *Mr. X* is not, of course, my real pseudonym but a phony pseudonym for the purposes of this diary, intended to conceal my *real* pseudonym, which is *Mr. Y*. Oh shit. Dammit. Anyway, when the bellman asked the driver if they were waiting for Mr. Idle, the man naturally enough said "No." I always thought these pseudonym things were daft. They mainly prevent my family getting through to me.

When I check into a hotel I always go under the name Mick Jagger. I find I get a better class of wrong number.

At the Fillmore I get a note from Sheila Buhr, who was with me in *My Girl Herbert* at Cambridge University in 1965. We perform the madrigal from that show every night, so when it comes time I introduce her to the audience. I can see her unexpected delight, and she and her husband beam throughout the show. She was one of the first women to be admitted to the Footlights Club, in 1965. The Footlights is a famous old re-

273

ERIC IDLE

vue society founded at Cambridge in 1883, and it's where I first saw John Cleese perform and where I met Graham Chapman, a recently departed alumnus. I became a member by auditioning in 1963, and in my final year they made me president. This meant you had to wear a ratty old pink dinner jacket. At the end of the year when everyone else was doing finals the Footlights would mount a two-hour professional stage revue at the Arts Theatre Cambridge, which would then go on tour, ending up at the Edinburgh Festival. Since the club did not admit women it was always a difficult job finding funny girls with experience performing sketch comedy. I determined to alter all that and my first act as president was to change the ancient rules to admit female members. I was quite a radical chap in my little leather jacket. Gay dons wept and begged me not to alter the tradition, but it was clearly nuts not to have funny females on an equal footing in a comedy club. Oddly almost the first woman through the door was Germaine Greer, who was hilarious, and later bet me she could sleep with every male member of the cast of *My Girl Herbert*. I took the bet and won; she got stuck on the horn player.

The great and good PythOnline editor Hans Ten Cate was also at the show with Mrs. Hans. They are a couple of very nice chaps. His devotion and dedication to the Python religion is legendary. He is the Paul of Pythonism, with Kim Howard Johnson as Peter. I think it is high time Python was recognized as a religion. People say it changed their lives. It seems to give people hope. They gather together in groups to chant mass quotes. We have all spent three days on a cross. And it would give us a very decent tax break. For fuck sake, if Scientology can be rated a religion, then Pythology ought to qualify under any decent tax system.

DAY 71

THE FILLMORE, SAN FRANCISCO

IT'S A BEAUTIFUL SUNNY DAY IN SAN FRANCISCO WITH CLEAR BLUE SKIES AND FRESH AIR AND I AM ABSOLUTELY CREAM CRACKERED[33] AFTER LAST NIGHT'S SHOW. I CAN HARDLY STAGGER FROM MY BATH BACK INTO BED TO WRITE this. [*Doesn't sound that tough.*—Ed.] Cecilia Bartoli is singing Mozart arias on the excellent hotel sound system and I sip a warm tea from the finest porcelain. *Ah, the simple things in life.* Like luxury. The Four Seasons is totally fab, from their comfortable cottony beds to their deep-water baths. I have a high suite looking out over the Moscone Convention Center and across the bay. My wife has thoughtfully left her bathrobe behind so I can still smell her.

I lunch alone at the Yank Sing at Stevenson Place. The most fabulous dim sum in town. You see, I really *do* like Chinese. I am now totally committed to dining solo. The great thing about eating by yourself is you don't have to

---

[33] Cream crackered = Knackered = Exhausted. English cockney rhyming slang.

talk to anyone. The train of thought can go by without stopping at anyone else's station. I have now entirely adopted the John Cleese position about dining alone and I hope soon to embrace the Garry Shandling position, that it is better to have sex alone . . .

There was a heartrending moment at the signing last night when a lady called Wendy tells me her husband died on Wednesday, but she had to come to see me. She says she is very glad she did. I am touched and saddened by her loss, but I am also very glad she had the courage to come. The laughter has done her good. I am even more heart-struck when she tells me she has a daughter (Chelsea), age fourteen. That one really reaches home. I think it is very brave to come out with her recent loss. I'm not going to lecture you about laughter and tears, but when George lay dead and we were all sitting there very gloomy consuming Kleenex, his son, Dahni, said "Come on, Dad wouldn't have wanted this." And I said, "Yeah, he wasn't all he was cracked up to be," and we all laughed, because it was one of George's favorite lines from Python. Laughter can be such a wonderful release. Saying the unsayable at these moments can work really well.

When George was stabbed by an intruder in early 2000 the first I knew he was going to survive that terrible experience was the quote displayed on the BBC Web site. When the police asked him about the intent of the intruder he said, "Well, he wasn't auditioning for the Traveling Wilburys. . . ."

"Why doesn't this kind of thing happen to the Rolling Stones?" he asked me wryly on the phone with that brave Liverpuddlian humor.

"Would you like me to come?"

"Yes, please, Eric."

Tania and I immediately jumped on a plane and flew to stay with him and Olivia at their home in Oxfordshire. We were relieved to find them both home, battered and bruised, but alive. We could so easily have been flying for their funeral. George proudly showed me his seven stab wounds. Some were both entry and exit wounds where the kitchen knife had gone right through him. One had punctured and collapsed his lung, leaving George dangerously short of breath, with his lung filling up with blood as he lay on the floor, chanting.

"I thought I was dead, Eric," he said.

Carried out to the ambulance, covered in blood, he said to his appalled house managers, who had just started working for him, "So, what do you think of the job so far?"

If you can imagine the ultimate nightmare, an armed intruder in your home at three thirty in the morning, breaking windows and screaming at you to come downstairs, you pretty much have the picture.

"I wrestled hand to hand with the face of evil," said George, "for fifteen minutes."

Fifteen minutes is an awful long time to struggle for your life with a man with a seven-inch kitchen knife while receiving multiple stab wounds. Think of it, *fifteen minutes* of exhausting terror.

"He came racing up the stairs, screaming dementedly," George told me.

Having called the police, Olivia ran out with a poker to find her husband on the ground and a man attempting to kill him. She bashed the intruder on the head fifteen times with the poker, but amazingly he was able to get up and turn on her. He knocked her over, and she lost the poker and retreated to their bedroom, where he followed her. Although stabbed by then,

George was able to get up and go to her aid. At which point Olivia picked up a huge Tiffany lamp and began to bash the man about the head again.

"It was like a movie," she said. "He wouldn't stop. There was blood everywhere. I kept yelling at him to stop, but he would just get up again."

He grabbed the cord of the lamp and came at her with it.

"I thought he was going to strangle me," she said, and she ran downstairs. She knew there was another, heavier, poker by the fireplace. He meanwhile picked up the Tiffany lamp and began to beat George with it.

"I'd had it by then," said George. "I just tried to put my feet up to stop him."

But he took several more blows to the head. Then Olivia heard the man coming downstairs after her. She felt she could outrun him, but to her relief he suddenly collapsed on the stairs; his head wounds had finally caught up with him. He would receive twenty-two stitches in his head, a measure of the success of Olivia, and George, who to his great joy learned later he had managed to stab him in the ass. Right then, though, the battle was over. There were three totally exhausted combatants. George was lying upstairs desperately wounded, his lung filling with blood, chanting "Hare Krishna"; the intruder was collapsed on their balcony, and Olivia was sprawled at the foot of the stairs as the police entered. It was a scene from a horror movie. Blood was everywhere. Dahni, their son, was faced with this dreadful sight. He kept his father conscious during the long wait until the ambulance came. He will always be proud of this, but no son should have to face what he did.

▽

By the time we got there they were back home from the hospital, patched up, but angry like all victims of violent crime, and in need of good friendship. Luckily they have that, for from all around the world, flowers and faxes poured into their home. We played guitar and sang and hugged him and were fortunate enough to be present for a *puja*, where a Vedic priest performed a short ceremony to thank Shiva for their survival and to clear the lurking presence of evil from their home. *Om shantih*. We went upstairs and walked around the various sites where the violence occurred, which is where I lost it. Many of us were weeping. It was impossible to be with them at these places and hear them say "This was where it got really bad" without weeping. But after the ceremony even an old agnostic like myself felt cleansed. It is the power of ritual within us that is so important, and how wonderful to see George, Olivia, and Dahni receiving blessings. We felt very uplifted by their bravery, their honesty, and their grace in dealing with such an experience. And incredibly there were many laughs. Of course I don't suppose you'll laugh when you hear that the intruder was declared insane and unable to plead to counts of attempted murder. Nor will you smile when I tell you he was released from a mental institution after a couple of years because he was "cured."

THE
GREEDY
BASTARD
DIARY

DAY 72

FLINT CENTER, SAN JOSE, CALIFORNIA

T HERE'S AN END-OF-TERM FEELING TO THE TOUR NOW. LAND IS ALMOST IN SIGHT. SOME INDISCIPLINE IS BREAKING OUT. I FEEL SOME OF THE MEN MAY HAVE TO BE LASHED, IF ONLY TO ENCOURAGE THE OTHERS. A GOOD SPANKING SHOULD clear the air. Last night, for instance, I was bummed at Peter. For some unfathomable reason he never told me he was filming the show. He happened to mention it just as I was going onstage for act two. That's *eighty minutes* into the evening. I was shocked and then furious. He was chastened and surprised by my anger, said he was doing it for me, thought it was understood, etc., etc. I should have suspected something was up when his act-one monologue suddenly doubled in length! But I was blithely ignorant and felt really let down. It threw me for a bit onstage but then anger surfaced and burned like a fine blue flame inside and I became very focused and, interestingly, *much* funnier. I have noticed before that anger is a close part of the comedian's armory, but I had never observed it so clearly in myself. Peter is utterly penitent and of course I utterly forgive him. After the show I promise him lashes, but only eyelashes.

first noticed this use of anger in comedy when I was direct-ing Robin Williams in *The Frog Prince*.[34] Robin was swathed from head to toe in a frog costume with a large green frog's head and very funny flippers on his feet. One morning I saw him sitting quietly on the set reading in *Daily Variety* that ABC had just canceled *Mork and Mindy*. A nice way for him to learn, eh? That's the sensitive way of showbiz, no polite calls saying "Thank you very much and good-bye," just a story in the trades. I could see through the mask that he had tears in his eyes and he told me what was up and then gathered around him a group of technicians and props men and camera crew and just let loose. He ripped into the ABC top brass, excoriated them, withered them, dissected them, and cut them all new assholes. It was brilliant, it was hysterical, it was incredibly healthy. I could see him come back to life. At the end, when we were helpless with laughter, he said quietly, "Ready, Boss," and we went back to work. It was amazing.

---

[34] The premiere episode of Shelley Duvall's *Faerie Tale Theatre*.

DAY 73

SAN JOSE TO LAS VEGAS

I WAKE UP IN THE DESERT. THE SUN IS RISING YELLOW OVER A CANYON RIM. GREEN SPIKY CACTI STAND LIKE ALIENS BRIGHT IN THE DAWN LIGHT. THERE ARE WEIRD SHAPES EVERYWHERE. I FALL ASLEEP AGAIN AND WAKE UP ONLY AS WE pull onto Frank Sinatra Boulevard. Vegas, baby. At eight o'clock in the morning we stumble into the deserted marble lobby of the Mandalay Bay Hotel and soon I am having breakfast in the luxury of the Verandah restaurant next door at the Four Seasons.

▽

I'm perched high in a huge suite. Spectacular soundproofed windows give me a 180-degree view along the Strip to my left and across the desert to my right. Directly outside my bedroom my name keeps popping up on the gigantic moving screen billboard, between the constant Shania Twain ads. It's funny to see the words "The Greedy Bastard Tour" over the Strip. Directly below me, so close I can almost touch it, is Las Vegas International Airport. Tiny toy planes are lined up. Between me and the airport are a few remnants of old-style two-story Vegas motels grouped around miniature pools, the last vestigial traces of the old Vegas, here where the Strip petered out into the desert, before they were dwarfed by these monstrous constructions.

I take a smoothly efficient tram past the gleaming pyramid of the Luxor to Excalibur. This is certainly the real site of *Spamalot*. The singing and dancing Knights of the Round Table belong here, no question. Too bad this tram doesn't continue any farther, it would be a great way to see the eccentric layout of the Strip, one fantasy world replacing another. I love the way you can walk from Paris to Venice in five minutes, but today limping down Las Vegas Boulevard in the fresh morning air is hard going on my foot, so I return to Mandalay Bay to the White Swan chocolate bar. Here I order chocolate, chocolate, Spam, chocolate, and chocolate and I am almost thrown out because my hotel room, registered under my pseudonym Mr. X, doesn't match my driver's license. They reluctantly accept my explanation that I need a pseudonym to protect me from my rabid fans. There is nothing more humiliating than professing a claim to fame to people who not only don't recognize you but haven't even heard of Monty Python. The fact that I am appearing at the House of Blues only twelve yards away is of no help whatsoever. I begin to doubt my own identity, but fortunately my wife arrives to clear up my doubts.

Tania, whom I think I shall have to rename Shania, so frequently is the nineteen-foot Twain woman outside my window, comes with me, Skip, Mrs. Skip, and Katy Skip to see Blue Man Group. We pile into a cab, and I begin reciting my sexual history out loud, to the amusement only of the cabdriver. The rest of our party looked totally bemused. Clearly they don't watch *Taxicab Confessions*. The Blue Man Group have a first for showbiz—a splash zone. Although I think we might need one for the Greedy Bastard Tour, the way we spit onstage. Elaborate precautions are taken to wrap the first seven rows in plastic rainwear, an unnecessary precaution in the event, since there is far less paint splashing than I remember from New York. The same blue aliens bang away on various things and cover the audience with paper, accompanied by loud music and heavy drumming. It's a cross between a sixties be-in and a play group. My feeling is that this is something mimes have discovered to reinvent themselves.

We join Jennifer and the rest of our Greedy Bastards at the Flamingo to see Steve Traxler's late show *Second City*: three very funny men and two alarmingly cute girls. Their impersonation of the dancing waters at the Bellagio is hilarious. They do a lot of fast blackout skits, which I haven't seen done for years. We used to call them "quickies," but my wife explains that means something different in America. I ask her to demonstrate.

▽

We walk over to Shark Reef just as it opens.

"Did you two have an enjoyable time last night?" a keen young attendant asks.

"No, we're married," I reply.

I like the stunned look on his face.

DAY 74

HOUSE OF BLUES, LAS VEGAS

A SMUDGY SUN STAGGERS OVER THE HAZE OF THE VEGAS MORNING. IN THE DISTANCE A POWER STATION SENDS UP A THICK WHITE COLUMN OF STEAM, A PILLAR OF CLOUD BY DAY, LIKE THE GOD OF THE ISRAELITES. THE TRIUMPHAL arch outside the Mandalay Bay today is advertising a gospel brunch. Surely two of the most scary words in the English language. Our suite is so enormous you need a taxi to cross it, but there are no minibars, no coffeemakers and certainly no kettle for tea. This is Vegas. Everything lures you downstairs into the casino. It's amazing you don't have to go to the bathroom through the casino.

The town seems a bit deserted at this time of year, though there are groups of men wandering around in black Stetsons. It's rodeo week. Cowboy time. Everywhere there are ads for men doing dangerous things to their balls on top of tortured steers. The Mandalay Bay sits virtually on the runway of Las Vegas Airport, which is also virtually deserted on this Sunday morning. Gilli wants me to go up for a joyride with her friends who have

ERIC IDLE

"She likes games, eh? Likes games? Knew she would, she's been around a bit, eh? She's been around?"

"Well, she has traveled, yes. She's from Purley."

"Say no more! Purley, squire? Say no more! Say no more! Say no more! Say no more!"

flown in from Burbank on a three-seater Piper. I tell her that with Tania in town I already have my joyride.

▽

Donald Trump is at breakfast. From where the Donald parks his plane you can practically walk across the street. Although what am I thinking, he probably takes a helicopter here. He looks in good form, the Trump, in excellent shape, with two very healthy-looking young ladies and a business companion. My wife pities the two young women having to be with these older guys, but I don't agree with her at all. It's not such a bad job, surely, giving the Donald a Donald.[35]

▽

It has always been a personal ambition of mine to play Vegas. Monty Python almost played here in the late nineties and it's a pity we didn't because *Monty Python Live in Las Vegas* is a great title, but in the end there were some cold feet and the whole thing fell apart. Over the years I have made several appearances here. Apart from my ass-whupping of Wayne Brady on *Celebrity Jeopardy*, which I'm happy to see still rankles with him, I sang "Always Look on the Bright Side" wrapped in chains and suspended upside down over a vat of boiling oil for Penn and Teller's TV show at the MGM Grand. Kevin Nealon and I appeared briefly with Clint Black at Caesars Palace, wearing identical black Stetsons, performing "The Galaxy Song," and last year for Dr. Pamela Connolly I sang "Sit on My Face" to a convention of sex therapists. I have always wanted to

---

[35] A Donald. English rhyming slang. Donald Duck = well, you work it out.

do a full gig here. We didn't include Vegas on my last tour, as I was reluctant to play clubs like the House of Blues or the Hard Rock, where they serve drinks during the show. Now that I have played these places I don't worry at all. They're not the same as theatrical venues, but they work just fine for comedy. In fact, the House of Blues is great. The waitresses make crouching runs throughout the show but nothing can faze us now. It's not an easy venue to play, as there are two audiences, one low below and one high in steeply tiered seats above, so you have to split your focus between them, but we grab them right from the off and make 'em laugh. Kevin Nealon makes a well-timed run at the encore bucket, returning moments later to get change. John McEuen and his wife, Marilyn, also made the trek from L.A.

"All of America must see this show," said John, beaming, afterward. He is a brilliant guitarist from the Nitty Gritty Dirt Band and plays everything stringed: mandolin, banjo, and even G-string fabulously. He wondered if the William Morris agents were selling us right and announced that I was now the "Willy Nelson of comedy!" I guess he means the tour bus. Tania was looking stunning in black leather. We both were wonderfully rubbed in the Four Seasons Spa. Heaven must be being massaged every day. Perhaps that's what the milk and honey is for. . . .

LEAVING
LAS VEGAS

AN INTENSE GOLDEN BLUSH OF DAWN IN A PALE GREEN SKY. THE SUN APPEARS AS A GOLDEN PINPRICK RAPIDLY SWELLING AS IT RISES, THROWING PIERCING RAYS ACROSS MY VISION. IT SWIFTLY PALES INTO YELLOW AND THEN TURNS BRILLIANT white. The green skyline segues into blue, the distant hills become outlines and another desert day has begun. It's a perfect day, too, as an intense wind has blown away all the smog and the hills appear clear and bright in every wrinkle and fold. To the west there is a slight brush of white on the rims of the red mountains. It's cold and the bellmen wear capes and earmuffs, and stamp their feet, laughing good-humoredly. Inside the Bellagio real snow is falling on thousands of red poinsettias from a real snow machine installed in the glass roof. I'm here to visit the treasures of Chatsworth, the improbable collection of an English stately home in a Las Vegas hotel.

▽

This morning Tania and I made a plan for me to go with her to a shopping mall. Over breakfast I asked her how she would feel if I didn't go.

"At first distraught and then relieved?" I suggest.

"At first distraught and then relieved," she says.

▽

Too often married people end up doing what neither of them wants to do because they think the other person wants, etc., etc., whereas in fact what the other person wants etc., etc., though they think what the other person wanted was etc., etc. So we cut to the chase. Tania goes off shopping, and I go to the Chatsworth Collection at the Bellagio, and we are both happy. The gallery at the Bellagio is just the right size for a decent hour's browsing and the sampling on offer here, from a huge collection at Chatsworth House in Derbyshire, England, is just perfect. Tiny jeweled objects, some paintings, and some letters, notably from Dickens, Thackeray, and Charlotte Brontë to the sixth Duke of Devonshire, known as "the bachelor duke." Hmm, funny he never married . . .

There are enough pictures of overdressed aristocrats to stimulate the taste buds of any revolutionary, but the art is fine, and I am amused by a miniature version of a splendid Renaissance painting by Domenichino, which shows God clearly giving the finger to Adam and Eve. It says "admonishing" in the title but with his large forefinger held firmly erect there is no doubting God's message.

While Tania shops, John and I take tea with Teller in the Verandah. What a nice, bright, intelligent man he is. John and I were consulting him on a technical matter [*How to make the tour go away perhaps?*—Ed.], and he couldn't have been more courteous or informative or helpful. His expertise clearly stems from a great love for and intense study of his art. He has an appealing modesty and a directness. There is no bullshit or hype, he just speaks the simple truth. My kind of guy. I visited Penn and Teller six months ago after their show at the Rio and sat with them in their dressing room for a couple of hours just

ERIC IDLE

talking. I had forgotten how pleasant it was to have intelligent conversation with witty and informed men on any subject that arose. I guess that's from living too long in L.A., where most conversations tend to descend fairly swiftly to movies and "the business." Eye-crossing. Penn and Teller delight in discussing unimportant subjects like the universe. A wonderful statuesque African-American woman with an amazing body comes across to say hello to him. We all stare helplessly at her.

▽

The first time I came to Vegas was with a bunch of Carrie Fisher's friends for the opening of her mum's hotel. Debbie Reynolds was opening a tiny boutique hotel, complete with minicasino, just off the Strip. I think she had been enticed by the success of the Liberace Museum. When we arrived from the airport we were taken by limo to the Debbie Reynolds Hotel, where we were greeted by the most extraordinary sight: there in the lobby at twelve in the morning was Debbie doing her act, in full glam, in sequins, in a red, glittering diamanté dress, singing "Tammy" on a tiny hand mike to a small party of bewildered Japanese tourists. Welcome to Vegas, baby.

Unfortunately we couldn't stay at the Debbie Reynolds Hotel because of a last-minute disaster with the fire department: when they tested the emergency sprinklers, water just trickled down the walls of the rooms, so they refused to grant a license and we were shoveled into a nearby hotel on the Strip: the Dunes or the Prunes, or the Sands or the Glands, I forget which because it has long since been pulled down to create Venice, or Paris, or Madrid, or is it Berlin? Long gone are the days of sand and sin. Nowadays Vegas succeeds because it creates everything *but* desert in the mind. It is built on illusions. A dream of naughty pleasure. Literally *titi*llation.

PERFORMING ARTS CENTER, SAN LUIS OBISPO, CALIFORNIA

T HE MANDALAY BAY IS A GREAT HOTEL BUT THERE IS ONE THING SERIOUSLY WRONG WITH IT: *THE FUCKING BIRDS.* THESE DAMN THINGS EMIT EAR-PIERCING SHRIEKS ALL DAY. THEY SHOULD BE IMMEDIATELY COOKED, STUFFED, AND eaten. They should be ex-parrots. A dead-parrot exhibit would be far more welcome in the lobby. How anyone can tolerate working at the front desk under these conditions beats me. We flee holding our ears each time we pass by. At least at night they are gone, and we, too, like Cinderella must leave at midnight.

Maestro John Du Prez can't wait to get out of Vegas. He rolls onto the bus slightly tipsy, presenting me with a peacock feather and a gift, thereby forestalling my own gift presentation. His is a small, carved, wooden Chinese scholar's traveling trunk. It acts as a pillow and has a double happiness sign on it. It is delightful. He also includes an ingenious brass lock. John always gives the most delightfully zen presents. I have an ancient highly polished piece of tree petrified millions of years ago and a large trilobite, both gifts from him.

ERIC IDLE

There is a great reaction from our Vegas House of Blues show. The HOB employees were all knocked out and said they had never seen anything like it and were surprised at the energy and variety of our show, and there was a very nice review in the paper. Just before I walk onstage at San Luis Obispo John very kindly tells me what a reviewer wrote about me. It makes me feel really good and I smile inside while I talk to the audience. What is that emotion? Ah yes, *happiness*. I don't read reviews on the road. I find they are dangerous. You can always find a nugget of criticism in even the most flattering review and this can rankle in your soul until you wake up at night sweating because someone found fault with your shoes. *They didn't like the shoes!* This interferes too much with your confidence, and since comedy is like tightrope walking, confidence is vital. So I postpone reading all reviews until later. And then I forget.

▽

I lunch on the Old Pier at Avila with Jane and Jon Anderson. We walk along the wooden planks past floating rafts packed with sleepy sea lions, who occasionally open a languid eye and flop into the water. Seagulls swoop, the sun sparkles off the water, and there is a fine salt tang of ocean. We sit and look at the gleaming beaches and swallow enormous amounts of fresh seafood. Ah, it's good to be alive and on a Greedy Bastard Tour.

▽

Jon Anderson is an old friend of mine who I met millions of years ago in the south of France and we would hang out together there and in Barbados. He is the lead singer of Yes, and today he is very excited.

"I am very excited," he says.

"Because you are coming to see my show?"

"That, too; but a wonderful thing happened last night," he said.

I look at his new young wife with a raised eyebrow. Surely too much information?

"No no," he persists. "My team just got through."

He is like a ten-year-old. Last night in a football cup eliminator between a team with the improbable name of Accrington Stanley, his little minnows beat a much bigger League side.

"I know. I saw it."

"But I was the mascot for Accrington Stanley when I was ten!" he says, absolutely thrilled.

After a very pleasant lunch we take a quick look at the legendary Madonna Inn. I was here for the Nash bash a couple of years back when Graham Nash turned sixty. (You haven't lived till you have seen David Crosby in a pink rabbit costume.) Each room is a riot of clash. The Christmas decorations take kitsch to a new level. Too bad we're not staying the night here.

Kim Howard Johnson appears after the show. He says he didn't know I did stand-up. Neither did I. Jon Anderson also had a good time. He is beaming and joyful. It's too bad we can't have dinner with these lovely people but once again we sail at midnight. There were one or two blue-rinse walkouts at the first sound of the word "fuck," an inevitability at a subscription theater. Good job they didn't stay till "Fuck Christmas!" We are after all in very rich country. People here still vote for Ronald Reagan.

Brian began life as a bad joke at the opening of Monty Python and the Holy Grail in New York. When asked what our next movie would be, I ad-libbed glibly, "Jesus Christ, Lust for Glory."

DAY 77

SAN LUIS OBISPO TO PHOENIX, ARIZONA

MY WIFE HAS MUTINIED. CONTRARY TO ALL MARITIME REGULA-TIONS SHE HAS MANAGED TO SMUGGLE SHOPPING ONTO OUR TIGHTLY STOCKED SHIPS. I TOLD YOU THAT WOMEN'S AIM IN LIFE IS TO BURDEN YOU WITH THEIR BAGGAGE. NOW SHE HAS ignored my strict instructions from Las Vegas that there would be no room on the bus to ship anything to L.A., and leaned on Skip and Scott to squeeze two occasional tables into our tightly packed hold. If she wasn't so god-damn attractive I'd have her flogged; except she'd kick the shit out of me. Now she blatantly taunts me on the phone telling me she wants "to *table* a discussion" about it.

"I'm sorry," she says, "if I have turned *the tables* on you!"

Mutiny and taunting!

Jen was getting sentimental last night on the bus after the show but all adventures have to come to an end, and this one is ending nicely with the high spots of Vegas, the beauty of the beach at San Luis Obispo, the morning desert here in Arizona and the roll up into L.A., for our final gig at the Henry Fonda Theater.

In two days I will be home. I spoke with my daughter and we are both happy about this. My wife tells me she "absolutely adores me." Actually to be honest she is really only winding me up again for her words are, "I think I should *put my cards on the table* and admit that I adore you!"

I received a letter one day from an elderly lady who wrote this: "I was listening to the radio and I heard one of the Monty Python boys, I don't know which one it was, confess that he was a homosexual. It says in the Bible—in Leviticus—that if a man lieth with another man he shall be taken out and stoned." So I wrote back to her and thanked her for her letter, and said we'd found out who it was, and we'd taken him out and stoned him!

Actually Graham was pretty stoned a lot of the time....

MARQUEE THEATRE, TEMPE, ARIZONA

A DESERT DAWN OVER AN ARIZONA SKY AS THE SUN RISES OVER PHOENIX. CANDY STRIPES OF CLOUD LIE LIKE THE AMERICAN FLAG BEHIND BIG GLASS OFFICE BLOCKS. WE SEEM TO BE IN A CRATER, AS DIRECTLY AHEAD OF ME ARE RED, bare, sharp-toothed hills with jagged peaks covered in scrub. The hills are treeless, though our hotel is surrounded by bushy olive trees. To my right an odd-shaped pair of mountains piled up like camel poop give the name to this region: Camelpoop. *Sorry*—Camelback. Now as I sit and write at my desk in the window of the Ritz-Carlton the sky turns fierce orange and fiery red and baby blue behind the neon signs of the AMC cinema. The low-angled sun lights up the Macy's sign with gold. I contemplate the meaning of life and decide to go shopping. Perhaps that's it? Maybe I should write *Zen and the Art of Shopping*. All those malls I have trolled; all those hotels; all those audiences; all coming to an end. Soon we, too, dear reader, must part. I think of you as my imaginary friend. It has been fun talking to myself publicly. I always loved that Roger Miller line "I may be schizophrenic but at least I've got each other."

There is a funny story about Michael in the press.

No matter where you look, even in some of the remotest parts of the planet, you can't avoid Monty Python. Just ask Michael Palin. The Monty Python member was recently in the Himalayas making the latest in his series of travel programs. As he climbed a peak in the Annapurna group, making a steep ascent of one of the highest mountains in the world, he stopped to catch his breath. At that moment a pair of mountain climbers came by. They saw Palin. "And one of them turned to me," recalls Palin, "and said, 'Oh my God! Eric Idle!'"

Oddly appropriate that our penultimate gig is in a tin shed near a flyover somewhere in the middle of nowhere. It won't be hard to give this up. After the show we pile into the buses for pizza and our final ride home.

You Yanks naturally assume that we Brits are all homosexual—which is very nice of you—but we are in fact like all boys, just sexuals. If there had been a goat farm next door to my school—my wife would be wearing fur.

Often forgotten at a show like this are all the backstage people who get paid so little and are so rarely thanked: and so tonight will be no exception.

DAY 79

HENRY FONDA THEATRE, HOLLYWOOD

COME SWINGING IN FROM PHOENIX, RIDING SHOTGUN ON THE BUS WITH 'LISH FOR THE LAST TWO HOURS OF A 15,750-MILE JOURNEY. WE FLOAT DOWN THE I-10, CROSS OVER TO THE 134, PAST THE SIGN FOR OCCIDENTAL College (Terry Gilliam's alma mater), coming on home from Pasadena. It all begins to feel familiar. Odd that this should now feel like home, but it does. It is a wonderful sight to see my tour bus outside my own front gate at last. Tania and Wee (our Thai wonder woman) come to the door bleary-eyed. The Greedy Bastard is home.

▽

'Lish and I drop lines of baggage in my driveway. The girls are still asleep on the bus and Skip gives a quick mumbled hello before popping back exhausted into his bunk. So with a wave and a handshake 'Lish rolls them off to sit in the parking lot at the final gig for a few hours. The dogs go nuts and I am swamped with canine affection as I crouch in the drive surrounded by a suitcase and about seven shopping bags. It's an hour earlier than I thought, a time change from Phoenix, and it's still too soon to wake Lil for school, so Tania and the dogs curl up with me on my bed. It feels so good to be part of the pack again. Bagel snores gently, Shadow lies against me, Tania smiles and holds me. Welcome home.

▽

T he first thing I notice is that the house has changed. My unbelievably fine wife has redecorated most of the entrance floor of our home. She has been very busy. It looks amazing. Our white dining room has suddenly become a warm plum red, with a reupholstered sofa in a pale toile. The lamps have been replaced and Tania's favorite painting hangs over the freshly polished sideboard. The dining chairs, all in danger of falling apart when I left, have been rejuvenated and the pink silk upholstery replaced by an elegant Regency stripe. There are curtains at the windows and she has created a feeling of an entranceway by the use of double curtains tied back and separated by a pale blue paint trim against the maroon. It's fabulous.

"Darling," I say, "you've become gay."

The entrance hall has been tarted up with silk curtaining and a new wheat color and she has curtained the living room and warmed up the white walls to a discreet ivory, with pale silk green curtains and new credenzas and finely chosen matching table lamps and shades. With our fine old John Smith furniture and some Bennison fabrics and the occasional new rust and green rug among the Christmas decorations it's like being in a wonderful warm country house in England. I'm thrilled. I feel like I'm on some BBC reality show. I beam and smile and say, "It's fantastic," with that silly grin on my face that they always seem to have.

▽

ERIC IDLE

I crawl onto Lily's bed and give her a hug. She doesn't open her eyes, just lets herself be held. Then she suddenly opens her eyes wide. She has smelled me. "Daddy!" she says with glee. It's one of the finest words in the English language. I never had a dad I can remember, so to become one is the best thing in the world. Lily is thrilled I'm home. She holds me tight. We have breakfast together. I spend the day being spoiled and napping. I am a very lucky chap and a proud father of a loving son and a lovely daughter. But I still have a final show to do.

DAY 80

HOME, SWEET HOME

'M HOME. I WAKE UP PROFOUNDLY GRATEFUL. THE THOUGHT CROSSES MY MIND THAT I DON'T HAVE TO DO A SHOW TONIGHT AND I SMILE OUT LOUD [*WHAT?*—ED.] I PUT *AVALON* ON THE CD. BRIAN FERRY LOUD IN THE MORNING?

I must be joyful. What no Haydn, no Bach, no Pondicherry? The clear bell tones of the classic opening and the drumbeat kick in.

"More than this there is nothing . . ."

It's still early and I resolve to finish my diary before the live football (soccer!) match beams in from England. Shadow, Tania's big German shepherd, comes in to lick my face.[36] He is very happy to see me. It's mutual, though I don't lick his face. Bagel, our beagle, follows. I let him out for a poop. Back to my job of dog-poop attendant. Yesterday Bagel smiled all day. I made him the happiest dog in the world when I arrived off the bus out of

---

[36] That's a dog, not an Alsatian farmer.

the blue at six in the morning. He went nuts. Three months gone, he must have given me up for dead. He beamed all day. Nice to be a dog's Christmas present.

▽

Last night we returned to L.A. in triumph. We had to hold the curtain for twenty minutes as the walk-up line was so long. It must have been because of the very nice piece in the *L.A. Times*. The house was packed and warm; the dressing rooms placed conveniently close so we can hear one another as we make up.

"I'm going to really miss you all," yells Jen in a blatant attempt to solicit emotion.

"Shut up, you stupid old bag," I yell, to cheap laughter from the boys. There is a fine joyful spirit abroad that cannot be denied. The traditional gifts are exchanged. Larry Mah turns up beaming and presents me with a fantastic book of his eight-by-ten photographs from the tour.

▽

The show goes even better than we could have expected. We are tight and trim, and they are very responsive. Hell, it's our forty-nineth gig! We could set this show down in a Starbucks parking lot and still get laughs. But it's really nice to be appreciated in your hometown. Skip has determined there will be no signing after the show.

"This is L.A.," he says.

Instead they have set aside an upstairs bar area for the hundreds of people who simply *have* to go backstage at any L.A. concert. There are complicated degrees of wristband which ensure that some people are denied entry. This is very important to those with the *correct* wristband. Everyone looks like they have just escaped from hospital. After I successfully pass through the lines of happy yelling Python fans and listen to a heartbreaking story of bereavement from a recent widow and her son, Olivia Harrison is the first person I see. She opens up like a flower and gives me a huge smile and hugs me. It's so great to see her looking happy. I know she had a good time before she even tells me. She is with her sister Linda and they have been remembering with glee the George story that I tell onstage. Olivia clearly remembers George preparing to set me up for the great Indian gag that he pulled on me. (*Shag a sheila for me!*)

B y the way, this is yours," I say, handing her a package of $3,000 in cash that we have collected from the encore bucket. We decided unanimously that the money should go to George's charity, the Material World Foundation. It feels appropriate. George has been present in my thoughts onstage every night, and these are clearly his royalties from "The Pirate Song." Tonight I almost choke up as I speak of him, while mentioning that Liv is with us, but I manage to hold it together. Of course I'm not ashamed to lose it in public anymore, but a blubbing comic just ain't entertaining. So I keep it all positive.

T he L.A. audience broke the encore bucket record with $208 in cash in our big gleaming bucket. The most generous cities were L.A., Spokane, and Boise, and there was a surprisingly generous crowd in Davenport, Iowa. The least generous was San Luis Obispo. The wealthy are always the tightest. And of course the Canadians, who hold on to their loonies with a very tight grip while freely donating a fortune in tire dollars.

A t the party Garry Shandling is beaming. Positively glowing. He looks me in the eye and says very nice things indeed, but I can tell from his eyes I've done well. Alan Zweibel is impressed by the writing and the shape of the show. Dave Mirkin hugs me and says he loved it. Jeff Lynne compliments me. Ian La Frenais gives me a big kiss. He, too, has had a great time. He acts proud of me. These are the compliments that count, from the boys who know. Doris, Ian's wife, is totally over the top.

"I had no idea you were this good," she says! "I never saw you live before."

The Greedy Bastard is in ego heaven. The admiration of strangers is one thing, but the admiration of friends is what it is all about. We, after all, do it for our peers. Geena Davis is beaming and bearing twins. She is with her very cute husband. They came to see us last time in San Fran and they say they had a good time again. Peter Asher is looking fit and well and thin and he enthusiastically tells me how much fun he had. He was very encouraging to me on this tour. Maybe he doesn't even know it, but his advice was really useful to me. He advised me to move away from the Python sketches format and exploit my own speechmaking skills. This was excellent advice at just the right moment, so no wonder he has been the manager of so many great people.[37] I'd ask him to manage me in a heartbeat if it wasn't for the fact that I really value his friendship. Plus as a friend he can't charge me for the advice. . . . I know it's a heresy in this town but friendship is far more important than business and hopefully ours will survive to our memorial concerts. I hope he has to sing "Always Look on the Bright Side" before I have to sing "World Without Love." I am tired of saying good-bye to pals. Though of course I promised Lily I will live long enough to dance at her wedding. It's going to be an interpretive dance . . . a cross between Martha Graham and Twyla Tharp.

---

[37] Linda Ronstadt, James Taylor, Randy Newman, Joni Mitchell, Morrissey . . .

It's really great to be back home. From the simple joy of luxuriating in a bath to just sitting down and staring at the curtains. I am looking forward to becoming a bit of a slob and kicking back in my private pig heaven while being spoiled rotten by my womenfolk. They are all very proud of me, and that should last at least two days.

After our show there are tearful good-byes in the parking lot of the Henry Fonda Theatre. Final hugs from Jen and Gilli. Manly farewells to John Du Prez, off home to England. Cheerful good-byes from our drivers, 'Lish and Mike, immediately heading off to Florida. Marc the hairdresser-agent turns up and is catching shit from his goy wife for not being home to light the first candle on the menorah. I tell him it doesn't matter, he's an agent, he's surely going straight to hell anyway.

There is a fond farewell from a sad Peter, who is outside the stage door with all his baggage, waiting for a ride.

"I'm just off on a three-month tour with Terry Jones," he says, smiling bravely, but I know he is really going to miss all this.

If you have enjoyed ourselves half as much as we have— then we have enjoyed ourselves twice as much as you! Good night.[38]

---

[38] Old Footlights gag stolen from Graham Garden.

ERIC IDLE

Saying good-bye to Skip isn't easy, either, but I guess Mrs. Skip deserves a crack at his patience and abilities for a while. Everyone is muttering about other dates, other places; there is a genuine reluctance to say farewell. Half a dozen dedicated fans linger in the parking lot. A few scribbled autographs, a couple of flashes, and it's all over.

AFTERWORD

 DIDN'T INTEND TO WRITE A DIARY, MUCH LESS A BOOK OF MEMOIRS. IN TRUTH IT BEGAN TO WRITE ITSELF ON THE DAY I LEFT HOME. IT BEGAN WITH TOO MUCH TEA AND TOO MUCH TIME ON AN AIR CANADA FLIGHT AND IT SIMPLY didn't stop until I returned home eighty days later, after fifteen thousand miles by bus. It was posted daily on PythOnline for an uncertain audience that grew as the tour progressed.

I have never been a diarist. I began one at boarding school in 1957 for two weeks and it was so stultifyingly dull that I forever eschewed the practice. However, on my journey it became the part of the day that I most treasured, the time when I could be most truly myself. Like letter writing and e-mail, the diary is a form of improv. I like not knowing what I am going to say next; writing the sentences down as they form in my head and seeing where they lead. Life itself is a form of improv and this diary is a lap dance across America via laptop.

For this book version I have shortened and rewritten the more clumsy

ERIC IDLE

passages and included some fresh bits where I thought I had become prolix or dull. My thanks must go to Hans Ten Cate, my trusty PythOnline editor, and to Mauro DiPreta, my trusty off-line book editor. To Matt Bialer, my trusty agent, whom I searched for and found because I knew he would understand. To John and Peter and Jen and Skip and all the folks on the road (Gilli, Larry, Scott, Darren, Tom, 'Lish, and Mike), thank you for sharing the journey and your lives with me. To Tania, my beloved, and my two dear children, Carey and Lily, I leave all my worldly goods . . . sorry, I thank you from the heart of my bottom. For my nanny Wee, and all my good friends all around the world who have made my life really a joy to live, thank you for all the food and all the laughs.

My "gout" was no such thing. An MRI reveals I had snapped a tendon in my ankle. I limped across America with a snapped tendon! As I write this I am about to undergo surgery to see if I will ever do ballet again. [*He never will, thank God.*—Ed.]

In any event the Greedy Bastard Tour proved to be an ironic title. I reconcile myself with the thought that it was never really about the money. However, I never expected the return to be quite so ironic. The MAE (Margin of Agent Exaggeration) turned out to be so high that the greedy bastard agent was sent packing and returned to hairdressing at William Morris. There is only so much exaggeration a gentleman can take. . . . It is an expensive business taking people on the road. To be truly greedy one should voyage alone, but then, where's the pleasure in that? The expensive bastards I took were worth every penny. I had hoped to buy myself some time until *Spamalot* hits whatever future lies in store for it. Ah, well, I keep telling myself, it's not about the money. It truly isn't. If, as the Footlights motto says,[39] the art lies in conceal-

---

[39] Ars Est Celare Artem.

ing the art, then the art is also for art's sake. I really believe that. It was an honor and a privilege to go out there and make 'em laugh. My life, if not my family, is the richer for it. Thank you all.

POSTSCRIPT

SPAMALOT!

MY GREEDY BASTARD PUBLISHER, SENSING COMMERCIAL POSSIBILITIES, HAS SUGGESTED I PROVIDE SOME ADDITIONAL MATERIAL ABOUT *MONTY Python's Spamalot*. I'm at the moment sitting in a wheelchair with a huge pink cast covering my leg up to my knee, my dancing days may be over and, sadly, England will have to turn to someone else for soccer this season. An MRI revealed that the irritating foot injury from my Tour was a snapped tendon, and so now I've had major foot surgery, a weekend in the Valley on morphine, several days of Vicodin which have left me as solid as Elvis (*All Things Must Pass*), and I have had to sit around for a couple of months awaiting the painful process of physiotherapy to begin. What a summer. No walks. No swimming. No

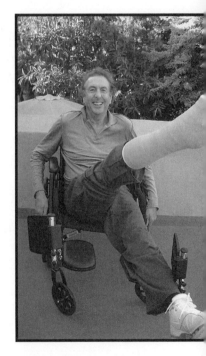

I fart in your general direction...

ERIC IDLE

trips to Europe. Just writing and rewriting *Spamalot*. So perhaps it is a good time to provide you with a fairly excursive, exclusive, incomplete and far from utter history of *Spamalot*. I am, of course, very aware that writing anything about *Spamalot* at this point is a hostage to fortune. ("*Little did he know that it would close after only three minutes on Broadway . . .*") None of us can foresee the future and even the Psychic Network is, I believe, unreliable, so these lines are written in a spirit of fatalistic optimism. I know we can screw up, believe me . . .

You've Got Grail!

It's April 2004 in Shubert Alley and hard by Broadway I'm stopped by a rough and ready street person.

"Are you *really* doing an adaptation of *The Holy Grail* for the stage?" he asks.

"Yes."

"Will there be a Killer Rabbit?"

"Yes."

"Then I'm coming," he said, and went off gleefully shouting, "*Ni!*"

Mike Nichols looked shocked. And impressed.

Another ticket sold.

Almost three years of my life so far on *Spamalot* and it still seems like a good idea to transform *Monty Python and the Holy Grail* into a musical. For several years I thought about it; after all, there are three songs in the movie and there are several points which seem almost to demand a song:

"I'm not dead yet!"
"Run away!"
"I fart in your general direction!"

Well, a *Python* song anyway. It's practically a musical already.

So now with only a week to go before the start of rehearsals we have Mike Nichols to direct Tim Curry as King Arthur, David Hyde Pierce as Sir Robin, Hank Azaria as Sir Lancelot (and an hysterical French Taunter), Chris Sieber as a very funny Sir Galahad, Michael McGrath as Patsy, Christian Borle as a very funny Prince Herbert, Steve Rosen as Sir Bedevere and Galahad's mum, and Sara Ramirez as a supersexy siren who pops up out of a lake. We begin public previews at the Shubert Theater, Chicago, on December 21, 2004, and then move to the Shubert Theater in New York, for an opening night of March 17, 2005. Exciting? Yes. Terrifying? You bet. Tickets available? Actually not in Chicago. We sold right out in a week! Even more terrifying. But yes for Broadway.

So how did it all come to be? Flashback to London in 1986, where I am playing Ko-Ko, the Lord High Executioner, for Jonathan Miller in Gilbert and Sullivan's *The Mikado* at the English National Opera. Each night I rewrote the lyrics of "The Little List Song" reflecting what was currently in the news. I was getting big laughs. I became convinced that the musical comedy theater is not only the most fun in a theater but that it was certain to return to popularity after the long desert years of Andrew Lloyd-Webber, when there was little to laugh at but the acting . . . . I wanted to be ready and write one. John Du Prez and I spent the next fifteen years trying to create and sell a comedy musical. It was to be a long and frustrating period.

We first tried adapting an old screenplay of mine called *The Road to Mars*. This was a bit of nonsense about the future of show business known for a while nauseatingly enough as *Outta Space!* (Ouch.) It was about a couple of comedians on the road in space but the best moments featured a chorus of quite possibly gay Welsh robots singing to a diva they adored:

ERIC IDLE

Do we love Irena Kent?
Yes we do. Yes we do.
Is she down from heaven sent?
Yes she be. You can bet your sweet arse she be.

It's still the first gay white Negro spiritual. Nobody bought it.

Our next venture was a musical version of *The Owl and the Pussycat* that we wrote as an animated film. I spun a tale from the Edward Lear poem, and John and I wrote some songs in a tiny Cabanon in Provence.

Shopping! We're always happy when we're
    shopping!
We're always happy when we shop until we drop
In search of bargains we will never stop!

When God created the Universe
He pulled out all the stops
First He created all mankind
*And then **She** created shops.*

Shopping we're always happy when we're shopping
We're always happy when we shop until we drop
In search of bargains we will never stop stop stop
We'll shop and shop and shop, shop, shop!

In Hollywood, working on *Casper*, I pitched this project to Steven Spielberg, but no one on this side of the pond had ever heard of Edward Lear and everyone kept mentioning Barbra Streisand. Ultimately I turned *The Quite Remarkable Adventures of the Owl and the Pussycat* into a book for my daughter, and John and I recorded it, with ten songs, for Dove books, for which I later received a Grammy nomination. (Of course I didn't win. Charles Kuralt won it posthumously. I *do* think you should be alive to win an award. It simply isn't fair competing with dead guys.)

In all these years of hopeful collaboration JDP and I did manage to make a musical, albeit only on the radio. We began writing *Behind the Crease* at first called *Sticky Wicket* in March 1986, originally for the stage. It was eventually recorded in front of a live audience for BBC Radio Four in April 1990. An original story, based on a real life experience of mine in the West Indies, this was a satire about the three things the British care most about: sex, royalty, and cricket.

"Couldn't get a dog in it, could you, Des?"

I played Desmond Boyle, a seedy tabloid journalist on the trail of the sex life of a famous cricketer. We recorded it live in front of a BBC audience, with a small eight-piece band conducted by John Du Prez. It got huge laughs and applause, and was eventually broadcast by the BBC. John and I were somewhat encouraged by this limited success, and there was talk of a TV version and options and even a couple of drafts for *London Weekend Television,* before this too slipped into the sand.

At some point over the long and frustrating years, I told John Du Prez about an idea I had to adapt *The Holy Grail,* and he loved it and was most encouraging, but *would the Pythons ever permit it?* The history of post-Python projects has been like middle-age courtship, fraught with frustration. Byzantine negotiations, hot flashes, disappointing flurries of enthusiasm usually ending in stalemate, and droopy disappointment. And would anybody ever back such a silly idea?

I became convinced that *The Grail* might really work on stage at the opening night of *The Producers* in New York. Sometime in the late 1980s I had visited Mel Brooks in his office in L.A. He utterly embarrassed me by entering on his knees, making obeisance to me and salaaming low to the ground, while uttering high and flattering praise, to the utter disbelief of his entire office staff. Mel Brooks was on his knees at my feet! I didn't know what to do. I was the first Python he'd ever met, so I copped the full force of his admiration for *Monty Python.* When I finally persuaded him to stand up, I revealed why I was there: to ask him if I might turn his movie *The Producers* into a stage musical. Jonathan Miller had just been given the Old Vic Theater to run for a year and we thought it would make a terrific stage show.

"Let me write the songs and adapt the book," I suggested to Mel, "then I could play Bloom and you could play Bialistock on the London stage, directed by Jonathan."

Mel was utterly unexcited by the thought of appearing on the boards again.

"I don't want to do that right now," he said. "I want to continue directing movies."

What, pass on the chance to appear nightly on stage in South London just to hang around and direct movies in Hollywood? Madness.

"It would make a great musical, Mel," I said. . . .

Now, fifteen years later, the Seig-Heiling pigeons were coming home to roost! From the very first number at the New York opening of *The Producers* in February 2001 it was clear to me that it was a huge hit. Wildly, wonderfully and wittily directed by Susan Stroehman, it was a sheer joy to witness. When Mel came onstage at the end, the house went wild. I had been right. At last—a musical *comedy*. What John Du Prez and I had been trying to create for fifteen years. And maybe, I thought, just maybe I was right about *The Holy Grail.* Perhaps now it would be possible to find people who would take it seriously. And maybe the Pythons wouldn't say no. We decided that the only way to find out was to take the bull by the horns and try it. We agreed that I would write a book and JDP and I would do some songs "on spec" and see what happened.

▽

Thank God for computers, because mine tells me I began writing the first draft of *Spamalot* on Monday December 31, 2001. I had filled a small red spiral notebook with notes and sketches and now I downloaded the text of *The Grail* from one of the many illicit websites, which thankfully saved me all the bother of typing out the script, and I could paste and cut and rewrite as necessary. I worked hard and fast and early, usually starting at dawn with a cup of tea, a pencil and a plain piece of paper. It went well and I printed out a first draft on January 24, 2002, at 6:37 A.M.

On that same January day I met John Du Prez for breakfast at a deli in Studio City where I presented him with the still warm first draft. That night, to celebrate, we went to see a very funny all-male version of *H.M.S. Pinafore* somewhere on Melrose. Inspired by this particularly silly production of Gilbert and Sullivan, we started work writing the songs the next day at 9 A.M. on January 25. John and I are fairly prolific. We write fast. We'll catch an idea and run with it, stopping to tape record snatches that we like. I'll be frantically scribbling down lyrics on a legal pad and John will be at the keyboard polishing chords and changes and melody. Sometimes I play guitar along with his keyboard, sometimes not. Later I go back and revise the lyrics for individual songs. Usually it takes me about a day to hammer out a lyric for each song and then when we come to record it I'll polish them again before we go into the studio. We like the studio. It helps us to focus our work. Songs come to life in there. We usually lay down a live track to get the feel of the song, John on keyboard, me on guitar, right there in the same room with Larry Mah, who plugs us directly into the

ERIC IDLE

board. Then I'll have a rough stab at singing the lyric in his tiny triangular glass closet. There is just room for John and I to squeeze in together and add chorus voices. I usually leave them to it after lunch and when I hear the songs again they have been totally transformed into magic: accordions, geese squawking, coconuts clacking, full orchestrations. It is truly amazing what you can do with John Du Prez, Larry Mah, and pro tools.

Looking back now at the first draft, I am struck by how little of the original lyrics we kept. In the text I had indicated areas where I felt we needed a song, but it was all still fairly loose. There were some completed lyrics, some snatches of dog- gerel, and some fairly sketchy rhyming gags to indicate song possibilities. Here and there we lifted a line for a song, or we picked up a theme from a suggestion, but there was a total sea change the minute John came on board. That's the great thing about a partner, they get you to places you would never even have imagined. We got so into writing that at one point we ad libbed a complete song directly onto the tape recorder, John at the piano and me screaming lyrics. We just opened a vein and out the song poured. It is still our favorite song in the show and it was the one that all the Pythons immediately responded to. ("The Song That Goes Like This.")

We wrote songs solidly for two and a half weeks and then went into Larry's tiny garage studio in Sylmar for some fairly intense recording. The resulting CD is largely John and me on everything, though we did drag in Shawana Kemp, Jennifer Ju- lian, and Samantha Harris, our girls from my 2000 tour, to add the essential glamor of female voices. Now it even sounded like Broadway. We finished the recording sessions at about 4 P.M. on February 27, when John drove straight to LAX to catch his flight back to the U.K., while I tinkered with a few last minute revisions. Five weeks in total since the time he touched down . . .

Of course, don't get me wrong, this was only a first draft. I have learned one thing about writing and that it is all about rewriting. I have just completed draft #11 and we have chosen what we feel are the best of more than thirty songs. As I said, the great thing about a partner is they get you to places you could never imagine, and when Mike Nichols came on board, boy did we travel! He sent me scrambling back into the original for suggestions, picking up hints of character, constantly honing, tightening and polishing. He is the finest taskmaster. But at this point in the process we had a First Draft book and a CD of demo songs, and the next thing to do was approach the Pythons. How would they react? I sent them each a package and waited, nervously.

A Hard Day's Knight

I have to confess that I think *Monty Python and the Holy Grail* is a very funny film. Even after three years working on the book, much of the original writing still makes me laugh out loud.

> *"You're using coconuts."*
>
> *"What?"*
>
> *"You're using two halves of coconuts and banging 'em together."*
>
> *"I don't want to talk to you no more, you empty headed animal food trough wiper! I fart in your general direction! Your mother was a hamster and your father smelt of elderberries!"*
>
> *"Is there someone else we could talk to?"*

It's endearingly silly. It has a freshness and a simplicity which is rare. I think it has some of the same charm as *A Hard*

ERIC IDLE

Day's Night: young men ignorant of what they are doing but supremely confident about doing it.

Arthur's attempts to round up his knights and stop them bickering and running away is perfectly mock heroic. Almost epic. While dealing with large themes like the Quest for the Holy Grail the movie is really quite small in scale. Since the budget was a mere $400,000 we couldn't afford armies or even horses (thank God for coconuts), and that means most of the scenes can be fairly easily reconstructed on stage. There are, of course, technical problems: *Just how do you lop off people's arms and legs on stage?* But these are *technical* problems, which means somebody else has to solve them. That's the great thing about being a writer . . . .

The movie itself is discursive; characters pop up for one scene only to disappear immediately. Unless I was careful we would end up with a cast of sixty-eight: not good theater, and appalling economics. So it was always clear to me that our actors would have to play multi-roles. I also felt that we were missing good female parts for a Broadway show. I don't know about you, but for me a show isn't a show without leggy girls in spangly tights putting their legs over their heads, and that's just backstage, but in the movie apart from the Witch and the memorable bathroom scene with Zoot and the Maidens who ask Galahad for a spanking, it's all guys. I felt we needed to create a new part for the Lady of the Lake, who is referred to but doesn't appear in the movie. All right, there is the Mother:

"Dennis, there's some lovely mud over here!"

But, *come on*, that has to be a guy, doesn't it? It's a classic Terry Jones ratbag. Pure panto. Perhaps for American readers I should attempt to explain panto, since all English people grow

up with it, and it's probably the most popular form of theater in Britain. Here goes: the pantomime is a Christmas entertainment in the U.K., where the leading man is the principal boy who is played by a girl, who romances the leading girl in tights, so that two girls kiss onstage, while the stepmother of the girl is a man in drag, and her two ugly sisters are both men playing women . . .

I've lost you, haven't I? You think we're weird, don't you? Let's face it, your eyes have glossed over and you're wondering how we ever managed to take an empire. It's hopeless. It's like trying to explain cricket to Americans. It's utterly impossible. Let's just say that panto is an odd hybrid of vaudeville, stand-up, drag show, variety, revue, Broadway musical and fairy tale. It's full of double entendres and cheap theatrical effects—well *Spamalot*, really.

So, just how did the Pythons respond? Terry Jones was the first to reply. He called to say he loved it and was filled with enthusiasm. He had played the songs to his friends and they were all overjoyed. Next came an e-mail from Michael Palin:

> *First, fresh impressions. I loved most of it. Lots of good lyrics and very silly new songs which made me chuckle to the point of open, gurgling laughter. I think there is a core of very strong, very funny, catchy and very well-produced material here. Love and congratulations to all, M*

Terry Gilliam too responded by e-mail:

> *El*
> *I loved Spamalot a lot. I laughed. I danced. I pranced.*
> *What is wrong?*
> *Tel*

Even the great John Cleese responded enthusiastically:

I really enjoyed almost all of the songs. My personal favorite is "The Song That Goes Like This." As I listened to it, I thought that the idea of parodying the kinds of songs you get in a certain type of annoying musical was wonderful. There were two other songs in the second act, both involving your female vocalist . . . which seem to be developing this theme. I've never come across it before, and it's very original . . .

The blessed and venerable Jonesy even organized a meeting, so keen was he on the project.

Re Spamalot!
Terry G., Mike P. and John C. (via the electric telephone) and I all met yesterday to see what everybody else thought about Spamalot! *There was an unnerving degree of agreement. First of all we all think it's a jolly good project and that the songs and book are generally pretty spiffing. And I think we all think it could be a big success.*

Terry G. and John were both (surprisingly) tempted to get more involved in the whole project because they thought it was so good, but were tempered by the feeling that it is really your project and that you wouldn't appreciate interference from superannuated, white-haired ex-Pythons. There was a general agreement that the thing would get done more efficiently and effectively as your project. There was, however, a hope expressed that the rest of us could be useful as sounding boards and coming up with some ideas and thoughts and criticisms.

Wow! Not only did they like it, they wanted to help! It doesn't get much better than that. Fired up by their enthusiasm and inspired by their encouragement, John Du Prez and I plunged into another writing session, using their criticisms and suggestions. The response to this new material was just as encouraging. This was Mike Palin:

I've listened to the new Spamalot *material and like it very much. Knights of Ni song is jolly and superbly silly and I love "Whatever Happened to My Part?" A rather beautiful song and very funny idea. I particularly like the way it becomes Whatever Happened to This Show? and wondered if there might not be scope for it to escalate even further into Whatever Happened to This World, ending, via a series of climactic key changes into a great universal anthem of nostalgic longing. A huge cathartic moan.*

Anyway, I think that generally the show is in an impressive state, full of life and good ideas . . . I think that the songs and jokes about Broadway are some of my favourite moments.

So, good work all round. Some great changes of mood and tempo, lovely melodies and, as I say, just a feeling of great, ebullient and redeeming silliness. Congratulations to all. Onwards and upwards,

Love M

Terry Gilliam wrote a very long and useful note clarifying his feelings about one of the songs, and added this . . .

I'm tempted to get involved with the design . . . however, my problem is that when I start thinking down those roads I start thinking of how it should be staged and then how the dance numbers ought to go and then . . . . . . You can't keep a bad director down, but I don't want to do that job. However, there are some excellent chances to do some outrageous stuff. For example, puppets could be a visually fantastic other element. I'm talking about big puppets . . . giant three-headed knights. . . . dancing. I think the sets should be based on the medieval illustrated manuscript artwork I used for the animations. Then I think . . . I miss the Beast of Arghhh and it could prove useful as an element of different scale and pace. When I get like this I have to remind myself that I'm supposed to be busy directing films. And probably will be when you are trying to stage the show.[40]

So if he wasn't going to do that job who was? And who was going to produce this show, which was now looking as though it could really happen. Tom Hoberman, my friend and lawyer, suggested Bill Haber.

"He'll get it completely," he said.

He did.

Bill is an extraordinary man. One of the four original partners who founded The Creative Artists Agency in Hollywood, he has now moved on to producing shows on Broadway. His real life, though, is devoted to running the Save the Children charity, for which he flies tirelessly around the world. He has just returned from the Sudan; in the spring he flew to Baghdad. I have never known a finer man. His priorities are totally right. As he said to me recently, "He who dies with the most toys, dies."

He came to visit me at my house. I had all the *Holy Grail* dolls out. I played him the CD and laid the script on him, but it

---

[40] He is.

didn't matter: *He was already in*! It was the easiest pitch of my life. At the doorway on his way out we discussed who we might get to direct it.

"Well, Mike would be great," I said.

"Mike Nichols?" He laughed. "Never in a hundred years," he said. "Mike's a friend of mine, but he is so busy you can hardly even get him to read something. It'll probably take him ages to even respond."

But what the hell, might as well give it a try, we thought.

Three days later Mike Nichols called. "Yes, yes, yes," he said.

Wow, my cup runneth over! In a few short months we had managed to achieve a project which everyone had said yes to. *You know how rare this is?* Now came the anticlimax. It was time to make a deal with everyone. Time to go to the Broadway lawyers. Almost nine months of frustration followed. I guess that's what lawyers are for. In fact, we spent more on the lawyers than the entire total budget of the original movie! But then again, that's what lawyers do . . . .

Now, under our great and good leader Mike Nichols we have had two hugely hilarious reads. The most recent, with David Hyde Pierce, Tim Curry, and Hank Azaria, was a hoot and now they, too, are on board. We have a great cast, a great choreographer, Casey Nicholaw, and amazing sets designed by Tim Hatley, a man who really understands panto! We begin rehearsals next week. It's very exciting, but it's Broadway. Millions of dollars can disappear overnight in a bunch of damp hankies. We can go off the rails at any stage, but we are dedicated to laughter, and if we fail to achieve at least that in Chicago I will be very surprised. Fingers crossed. Wish us well. And come and see us!

Eric Idle
L.A., July 2004